P9-AQM-434

MY JOURNEY IN MYSTIC CHINA

MY JOURNEY IN MYSTIC CHINA

OLD PU'S TRAVEL DIARY

JOHN BLOFELD

Translated from the Chinese by Daniel Reid

Inner Traditions
Rochester, Vermont

Inner Traditions
One Park Street
Rochester, Vermont 05767
www.InnerTraditions.com

Originally published in 1990 in Chinese under the title *Lao Pu Yo Ji: yi ge wai guo ren dui jung guo de hui yi* [Old Pu's Travel Diary: The Memoirs of an Englishman in China] by Ming Pao Publications, 651 Queens Road, Hong Kong
First U.S. edition published in 2008 by Inner Traditions

Library of Congress Cataloging-in-Publication Data
Blofeld, John Eaton Calthorpe, 1913–
[Lao Pu you ji. English]
My journey in mystic China : Old Pu's travel diary / John Blofeld ; translated from the Chinese by Daniel Reid. — 1st U.S. ed.
p. cm.
Summary: "The only English translation of John Blofeld's memoirs as a Westerner living in China prior to the Communist Revolution"—Provided by publisher.
ISBN: 978-1-59477-157-6
1. China—Description and travel. 2. Blofeld, John Eaton Calthorpe, 1913–. —Travel—China. I. Reid, Daniel P., 1948– II. Title. III. Title: Old Pu's travel diary.
DS710.B65413 2008
951.04'2092—dc22
[B]

2007047366

Printed and bound in the United States by Lake Book Manufacturing

10 9 8 7 6 5 4 3 2 1

Text design and layout by Priscilla Baker
This book was typeset in Garamond, with Runa Serif used as a a display typeface.

In memory of John Blofeld and the precious time he shared with me in the sunset of his life.

Daniel Reid

John Blofeld at work on this book late into the night at his desk in Thailand. (Photograph courtesy of the Blofeld family)

Contents

TRANSLATOR'S PREFACE

A Friend from Afar

I first met the English writer John Blofeld in April 1987, at the House of Wind and Cloud, his home for thirty-five years in Bangkok, Thailand. How we met and quickly became good friends—or "brothers," as the Chinese would say—and the remarkable events that occurred in the wake of his death later that year are all detailed in my introduction, The Wheel of Life.

When I met John he was dying of cancer, but that did not prevent him from receiving "a friend from afar" with the traditional good grace and old-fashioned Chinese hospitality for which he was so well known among his friends. While preparing Chinese tea for us one afternoon, he told me that he had always wanted to write a book entirely in Chinese, but had procrastinated year after year. When he discovered he had cancer, he decided it was now or never and finally sat down to start work on the book. However, the effort completely sapped his energy, and after only a few chapters he found it impossible to continue.

"I'm less than halfway through the manuscript," he lamented, "but I simply cannot write another word. I've run out of steam. My brain is a blank!"

I knew that John had recently done a course of chemotherapy, and I knew that chemotherapy severely depletes the blood's capacity to carry oxygen and deliver nutrients to the brain, which no doubt accounted for his exhaustion. So I suggested that he try a Swiss pharmaceutical called hydergine, which quickly increases delivery of oxygen and glucose to the brain and stimulates the repair of dendrites, the filaments that connect brain cells. He agreed to try it, and the next day I brought him a week's supply. When I returned to visit him a few days later, he was already bubbling with energy and had resumed work on his book.

"That stuff you gave me is wonderful!" he said. "I've sent my daughter out to buy more, and I'm writing again every day now. I'm going to finish this book for sure!"

And so he did.

My Journey in Mystic China is John's personal account of the eighteen cherished years he spent living and traveling in China, beginning with his arrival there in 1932 and ending with his abrupt and heartbreaking departure in 1949, just before Mao's army marched into Peking. "Old Pu" *(Lao Pu)* was the Chinese name by which his friends in China addressed him. *Lao* ("old") is an ancient Chinese honorific, and "Pu" was his formal Chinese surname. His full name in Chinese reflected his character and his interests—Pu Le-dao, Mr. Pu who "delights in the Tao."

In *City of Lingering Splendor* and other books John also reminisced about his life in China, but he was writing about China in English for a Western audience, which required all sorts of cross-cultural explanations and a certain degree of self-censorship. Here, in his Chinese memoirs, John is writing in Chinese as a true connoisseur of traditional Chinese culture, for a Chinese audience with whom he shares a sense of cultural complicity and common values. This reveals an entirely different, far more personal and private facet of John's life than the face he reflected in his English writings about China.

For those friends and fans who, like me, feel a profound respect and deep affection for John Blofeld and the books he left us, *My Journey in Mystic China* offers an intimate portrait of the man during his formative years in China, a period of his life that he fondly regarded as his "Golden Age" which provided much fodder for the books he wrote later in life. These memoirs provide a rare glimpse of his private Chinese side, a side of his mind that he usually shared only with his closest Chinese friends and fellow sinophiles.

Whether John ever anticipated that this book would appear in an English edition, and that I would be the translator, I do not know, for we never discussed such a prospect. I never even saw the completed manuscript until the Chinese edition of his memoirs was published in Hong Kong in 1990, three years after his death. Nevertheless, since I was the one who introduced him to the medicine that enabled him to finish writing the book, and since he shared so many of his fondest Chinese memories with me during our long talks together at his home in Bangkok, I feel quite certain that he would approve. I only hope that he likes the way I've portrayed his Chinese face to his Western readers.

My thanks to Bom Blofeld for inviting me to live at the "House of Wind and Cloud," John's home in Bangkok, where he wrote this book, and where I began working on this translation, writing in the same room at the same desk John used to write these memoirs.

To Rayson Huang (Huang Li-sung), for kindly arranging the English translation rights for me from Ming Pao Publications, who published the original Chinese edition under the title *Lao Pu Yo Ji: yi ge wai guo ren dui jung guo de hui yi* [Old Pu's Travel Diary: The Memoirs of an Englishman in China], and to Ming Pao Publications for granting me this opportunity.

To Red Pine (Bill Porter), for his brotherly encouragement, and his shining example as a translator of Chinese literature.

To Shi Jing (Allan Redman) of the British Taoist Association, and Chungliang Al Huang of the Living Tao Foundation, for their enthusiastic support and appreciation of my work.

And to Jon Graham, acquisitions editor at Inner Traditions, for his clarity of mind in recognizing the value of John's China memoirs when other editors saw nothing.

DANIEL REID
JANUARY 2007
BYRON BAY, AUSTRALIA

A Note on the Translation

John Blofeld spoke and wrote Chinese in an elegant, old-fashioned literary style that prevailed among the Chinese literati with whom he associated in Peking during the precommunist era. This style, which makes abundant use of classical allusions, poetic terms, and antiquated literary devices that are today regarded as rather quaint by contemporary Chinese readers, clearly reflects the spirit and the tone of John's experience in China as an aspiring young sinologist and spiritual seeker. I have therefore tried to preserve the traditional style and flavor of the original Chinese text by rendering it into a form of English that not only translates the meaning of his words but also expresses the personality of the author and his Chinese way of life. John liked to punctuate his Chinese writing with old-fashioned interjections such as "Alas!" and "My Heaven!" and *Ai Ya!* and I have retained most of these, either in English translation or romanization of the Chinese words.

Historical references and cultural terms whose meanings are not self-evident within the context of the translation are explained in footnotes.

For the convenience of Western readers with no previous background in Chinese studies, I do not use the so-called pinyin system of romanization for spelling Chinese words in the text. Although this system has come into common use today in the Western media, after it was arbitrarily imposed on the world by China two decades ago, it's so illogical and misleading that it not only confounds Western readers who wish to approach at least a semblance of proper Chinese pronunciation when they read romanized words in a text, but it also confuses Chinese readers who are trying to learn proper English. How on earth, for example, would an uninitiated Western reader know that the pinyin spelling "cai" is supposed to be pronounced "tsai," that "zhou" is pronounced "jou," that "xiao" is really "siao," and even more befuddling, "qin" is "chin" and "qi" is "chi?" So let's just call a "chin" a "chin" and be done with it!

Fortunately, there is no law that requires us to use this perplexing way of spelling Chinese in the English alphabet, and there is in fact a legitimate alternative way, known as the Yale System, developed by sinologists at Yale University during the early twentieth century. Though rarely used today, the Yale System remains the most accurate way to romanize Chinese syllables, and its spellings cleave closest to the way English is actually pronounced. Therefore, with the exception of a few prominent people, places, and terms that are spelled in the old Wade-Giles System (e.g., Hsu Yun, Hung Hsiou-chuan, Tao Teh Ching), all Chinese words that appear in the text are spelled in the relatively simple and phonetically accurate Yale System.

TRANSLATOR'S INTRODUCTION

The Wheel of Life

As a writer, I've always felt a strong interest in the personal lives of other writers whose work I admire. Among my favorite writers, especially during my younger years as a freelancer in Asia, was John Blofeld, whose books helped inspire my early interest in Buddhism and Taoism and fired my imagination with colorful visions of life in China before the communist revolution swept away traditional culture there.

I'd always imagined John as an eccentric old scholar long retired from his Asian travels and living a reclusive life in his native England. So in 1986 when I heard from a journalist friend on assignment in Taipei, where I was living at the time, that John Blofeld lived right nearby in neighboring Bangkok, I decided to go there to visit him. The journalist, who'd had dinner with John in Bangkok the previous week, gave me his address, and I immediately wrote him a letter expressing my long-standing admiration for his work and my sincere wish to meet him. He delighted me with a prompt reply, thanking me for my letter and inviting me to come visit him at the "House of Wind and Cloud," his home in Bangkok.

John Blofeld was born in England in 1913. One day when he was still a little boy, his favorite aunt took him out shopping. As they passed by an old curiosity shop, something that would ultimately mold his mind and steer the course of his life caught his eye: it was a small Chinese statue of the Buddha. He hadn't the slightest notion what it was, nor did his aunt, but it captured his heart and he knew with absolute certainty that he must have it. Tugging his indulgent aunt into the shop, he made such a fuss about it that she finally relented and bought it for him as a gift.

Treating it like a treasure, he took the little statue home and reverently placed it on his bureau. Soon he realized that simply gazing in silence at this image of the seated Buddha engendered extraordinary feelings of peace and tranquility in his heart. Later, when he learned from a book what the statue represented, his devotion grew even deeper, and he began placing offerings of incense and flowers before it, secretly becoming a "closet Buddhist."

After two years of studies at Cambridge, the call of the East beckoned him with such urgency that he ignored his family's pleas to stay and finish his university degree and instead boarded a ship bound for Hong Kong, where he landed in 1932 at the age of nineteen. There he taught English and studied Chinese, biding his time while he waited for a chance to enter the "Dragon Gate" of China, the fabled land of his dreams. After several false starts, his chance finally came when a Chinese friend arranged a teaching post for him in Peking. And so in 1934, at the age of twenty-two, John's childhood dream came true. Passing through the gigantic gates of Peking, he joined the privileged ranks of residents in the fabulous old capital of imperial China.

Later in life, long after the strife of war and revolution had spoiled his dream, John wrote a poignant memoir of his early days in Peking and called it *City of Lingering Splendor*. For me, as a sinophile who went to Taiwan with the same dreams of China at the same age as John was when he went to Peking, this book and its charming depictions of traditional Chinese ways that have vanished from the world reveal the magnitude of the loss that my generation of "China hands" suffered when China's colors shifted from imperial gold to revolutionary red.

In 1949, shortly before Mao's army stormed into Peking, John married a Chinese lady and escaped to Hong Kong. "Why Hong Kong rather than Taiwan?" I asked him during one of our long talks at the House of Wind and Cloud. "Because at the time," he explained wistfully, "we were all convinced that soon Taiwan would be swallowed by the same red tide that engulfed China." Flat broke with a wife and two infant children to support, and not yet a writer by profession, John accepted an administrative position with a United Nations organization in Bangkok, and in 1950 he moved to Thailand. "One thing led to another," he told me, "and I've been living here ever since."

By the mid-1950s, John's literary inklings began to stir, and he started writing books about his travels in China, focusing particularly on his lifelong spiritual quest, his pilgrimages to sacred mountains and remote monasteries, and his frequent encounters with Buddhist monks, Tibetan lamas, and Taoist hermits. When his wife took their two children and moved to England a few years later, John became a recluse and devoted most of his time and energy to the cultivation of his spiritual practices and cultural interests, and to the writing of his books on Buddhism and Taoism.

The Tantric Mysticism of Tibet, The Gateway to Wisdom, Taoist Mysteries and Magic, Beyond the Gods, The Zen Teachings of Huang Po, Bodhisattva of Compassion, and other inspirational books on the spiritual traditions of the East flowed from his pen, introducing a whole generation of Western readers to the wonder and wisdom of ancient Asian mysticism. Despite the esoteric nature of his material, John always wrote with lucid clarity and cogent sense, in a style both elegant and intimate, anecdotal yet authoritative. In his later years, he summed up his life and his spiritual discoveries in *The Wheel of Life: The Autobiography of a Western Buddhist.*

I'd never been to Bangkok before, so when I arrived there to visit John in March 1987, I had no idea what this smoldering city held in store for me. On the one hand, I'd come to pay my respects to a literary elder and fount of spiritual wisdom. On the other hand, the lyrics to the song "One Night in Bangkok" kept running through my mind as the plane glided in for a landing, because a few days before I left Taipei, by some strange twist of fate, an editor telephoned me from Hong Kong and offered to fly me to Bangkok to write a short guide to that city's notorious night life, all expenses paid. A young freelance writer living on a shoestring budget is in no position to refuse a well-paid assignment, so I accepted.

As I approached the House of Wind and Cloud for the first time, my immediate impression was, "It looks like a temple!" It sounded like one too, with Chinese chimes ringing in the breeze from the swooping eaves. Splendidly perched on stilts in a Chinese garden, with steeply peaked roofs etched gracefully against the blue sky, stood a traditional Thai house built entirely of polished hardwood and glazed tile, without a trace of metal or concrete. This was the first time I'd ever seen a real Thai-style house, yet somehow it all seemed so familiar to me, like the Buddha in the old curiosity shop had to John when he first set eyes on it. As I rang the bell at the gate, I said to myself, "Some day I must live in a house just like this."

The maid let me in and showed me upstairs to John's room. I'd called ahead to announce my visit, so I knew that he was expecting me, but when I entered the inner sanctum where he wrote and slept, I was surprised to find him lying flat on his back in bed. "Come in, come in, Dan, have a seat here beside me," he said, sitting up and greeting me like an old friend. "We have so much to talk about." He rang for the maid and told her to bring a kettle of hot water so he could prepare Chinese tea for us in the room, and mentioned briefly and unemotionally, as though noting the weather, that he was dying of cancer. Then, without any further formalities, we launched into a lively talk about China and things Chinese.

And talk we did! All afternoon and into the evening we ranged across the length and breadth of Chinese history and civilization, pausing here to examine a favorite period or poet, there to analyze an ancient anomaly or debate a simmering historical issue, discussing "everything under Heaven" like two old friends in China might have done a hundred years ago. I signed a copy of my book on traditional Chinese medicine for him, and he in turn autographed a few copies of his books for me, including my favorite, *Taoist Mystery and Magic.* Our taste in things Chinese ran in remarkably similar tracks, and sometimes we had to pause and laugh at the way we kept reflecting each other's views. His terminal illness never once intruded into our conversation, but its silent presence prompted us to speak all the more frankly and openly, and we exchanged some hilarious stories about our respective experiences as Westerners living among the Chinese—his in China, mine in Taiwan, each for eighteen years.

What I'd planned as a two-week visit stretched out to become a two-month sojourn. I would visit John three or four times a week, staying with him from early afternoon until sunset, then foray out into the sultry Bangkok night to do my field work on the city's sensational night life. It was a heady blend—spiritually uplifting deliberations by day, sensually seductive pursuits by night—the dualistic poles of life on earth that cause such contradiction and anguish in Western civilization but are smoothly integrated in Eastern life as complementary aspects of the human condition. This wise and compassionate compromise between the physical cravings and the spiritual yearnings, which all humans feel, without the compulsive need to sacrifice one for the other, is one of the greatest gifts that traditional Chinese civilization has to offer the world. It's a theme that appears often in John's books, and it arose repeatedly in our conversations.

Sometimes John's health would rally with a sudden surge of energy, and we'd go out for dinner with his family and friends. He always chose one of his favorite Chinese restaurants, where he knew the chefs and could go into the kitchen to tell them exactly how he wanted the food prepared. At the table, he and I kept up a running dialogue in Mandarin Chinese to which only we and the waiters were privy. His adopted Thai daughter Bom usually joined us for these culinary extravaganzas, as did Susan, his daughter by his Chinese wife, who was visiting from England. Somehow John always managed to arrange things so that almost all of the guests who joined us at these lavish Chinese banquets were both Asian and female, which allowed us to share another one of our favorite Chinese traditions—enjoying good food and wine in the company of charming women.

I got to know and like John well during those two months in Bangkok. In many ways, his life was a mirror that reflected key aspects of my own life, both past and future, and in me he found a friend who felt as enamored and nostalgic about the vanished splendors of old China as he did. We were both what I call "sinopaths." While a sinophile is simply a scholar with an intellectual interest in China, a sinopath has a visceral interest that runs far deeper than scholarship, pursuing an almost pathological obsession with all things Chinese and molding his life to the model. When I met John, he even looked Chinese, with his Fu Manchu mustache and goatee, his frog-buttoned Chinese chemise and baggy silk trousers, his straw sandals and old-fashioned Chinese mannerisms.

Finally, regrettably, it came time for me to leave. I'd spent my entire expense account and had two deadlines to meet the following week. On my last visit to the House of Wind and Cloud, John invited me to stay for dinner with him at home, just the two of us. He kept a special cook in his household whose sole job was to prepare authentic Chinese food for him, and that evening she outdid herself to impress John's newfound friend. As we ate, we mused over some lines of Chinese poetry brushed in elegant calligraphy on a tattered old scroll hanging by the dining table. Plumbing our minds for just the right words and images, by the time dessert came we'd deciphered the poem and rendered it into fairly good English verse. He seemed overjoyed by this accomplishment, and felt greatly relieved as well. "For years I've been pondering the meaning of those lines as I sat here alone having dinner," he said, "but with so many possible interpretations and no one else to discuss it with, I never felt that I got them quite right. Now I have, thanks to your help, and I can tell you that it's a load off my mind!"

We celebrated our achievement with a toast and drained a few more cups of the special Chinese wine he'd opened for dinner. The next morning I flew back home to Taipei. The only line I still remember from that poem is, "The pines sigh in the breeze."

Exactly one month later, in early June, I received a letter from his daughter Bom, informing me that John had died.

In July, en route back to Taipei from an assignment in Singapore, I stopped briefly in Bangkok and paid a visit to the House of Wind and Cloud. A somber pall hung over the house. Even the chimes were silent. "My father's still here," Bom whispered, nodding her head toward the shrine room upstairs. "We haven't been able to find a place to keep his ashes."

John's last wish had been to have his ashes interred in a Kuan Yin temple in Thailand. Kuan Yin, the beloved Chinese "Goddess of Mercy," had always been John's favorite Buddhist deity, and he devoted an entire book to her, *Bodhisattva of Compassion: The Mystical Tradition of Kuan Yin.* After John's cremation, Bom had gone to all the Kuan Yin temples in and around Bangkok, trying to find a final resting place for her father's remains, in order to fulfill his wishes. To her great surprise and frustration, not a single Buddhist temple in Bangkok, where John had made his home for thirty-five years, would accept his ashes, even though he'd been a devoted Buddhist all of his life and his books had been instrumental in introducing Buddhism to the Western world. So his ashes remained in an urn in his shrine room, unsettling the entire household of family and servants, who felt the restless presence of his lingering spirit. No one dared go upstairs except Bom's ten-year-old daughter June, who often went up to commune with her grandfather. "She goes up there all the time," Bom said with an involuntary shudder, "and talks to him."

I went up to the shrine room to pay my respects and returned to Taipei the next day.

Later that year, in December, I returned to Thailand on holiday, and the first place I went was the House of Wind and Cloud. Bom opened the gate beaming with a big smile. "We found his temple!" she exclaimed.

"His temple?"

"Yes, my father's Kuan Yin temple, his final resting place, just as he wished! We're taking him there next week. The ceremony is set for the 27th, and you absolutely must come. I'm so glad you're here!"

She invited me upstairs to the tea pavilion, and we prepared Chinese tea in the same old Chinese pot John had used during my visits with him. While the tea steeped, she started to explain what had happened. "A few months ago, I began having this vivid dream. It was always the same. I saw my father sitting in a temple surrounded by monks. He looked so happy there. I called out to him, and he waved at me. 'Bring me here,' he said, 'this is where I wish to be.' But I was so overwhelmed by my emotions that I burst into tears and woke up crying. This continued for several weeks."

She paused to gauge my reaction, wondering whether I thought she was crazy. But I've always believed in the significance of dreams, and I was already hooked by her story, so I urged her to continue.

"Well, after a few weeks of this, I finally managed to control myself and pay attention to the details in the dream. For example, I noticed that the monks there wore gray robes, as they do in Chinese temples, not the saffron robes worn by monks in Thai temples. I also remembered a big yellow wall in front of the temple and a huge bodhi tree outside the main gate. And there was also a river. I finally realized that my father was using this dream to communicate with me, and that he wanted me to bring his ashes to that particular temple. I spent nearly two months driving all over Bangkok looking for that temple, especially along the Chao Phya River, but I found no place that looked anything like the temple in my dream."

She paused to pour us some tea, then continued. "Finally, I got an idea. My father used to conduct temple tours of Thailand for foreign visitors on behalf of the Siam Society, so I went there and told them my problem. They were very nice about it, and they remembered my father well. I spent day after day there, looking through all the books and journals in their library, searching for a temple that matched the one in my dream, and finally I found it. It was in a monastery located in Kanchanaburi province, about a two-hour drive from Bangkok, so the very next day I drove out there to look."

I could hardly bear the suspense. "What happened?"

"The moment I saw the place, I recognized it as the one in my dream! It was facing the River Kwai and had a big bodhi tree out in front, and a high yellow wall. I ran inside and found the abbot and told him the whole story. When I mentioned my father's name, he smiled sweetly and said, "Of course you may bring your father to rest here. John was my good friend."

A tingling current rippled up my spine when I heard those words, raising the hairs on the back of my neck, and I felt an uplifting surge of energy as I realized that John's spirit had been patiently guiding his daughter to this remote monastery, where he wanted his ashes to be interred and where the abbot was an old friend of his.

"Well, the abbot took me into the main shrine hall of the temple," Bom continued, "and sure enough there was a big statue of Kuan Yin sitting on the central altar. The abbot smiled sweetly again and pointed up to a faded old photograph hanging above the side entrance to the shrine hall. I couldn't believe my eyes! It was my father! He was standing next to another Englishman behind a chair in which the abbot himself was sitting. They all looked so young! The abbot told me that the photo had been taken in 1951, only a year after my father arrived in Thailand and nine years before I was born." Tears welled up in her eyes and rolled down her cheeks, and for a while we sat there in silence. A breeze jingled the chimes.

Then she sighed and finished her story. "The abbot told me that my father had helped raise the money needed to finish building that monastery shortly after he came to Thailand, and that the picture had been taken on the day the main temple was formally consecrated. None of us ever knew anything about this, and my father never mentioned it. Not only is it a Chinese Kuan Yin temple, it also has a close connection with Tibetan Buddhism, which is extremely rare here in Thailand.

As you know, my father's main Buddhist teachers were Tibetan lamas. Anyway, the abbot invited me to stay for lunch, and after that he checked his calendar and told me that December 27 is the most auspicious day for the ceremony, so that's when we're taking my father's ashes there. I do hope you'll come."

"I wouldn't miss it for all the tea in China!" I replied, thanking my lucky stars that my trip to Thailand coincided with this event.

Bom and Susan and their husbands and children picked me up at the crack of dawn that morning, and we drove out to the monastery for the ceremony, which was scheduled for 8:00 a.m. As soon as we arrived there, I recognized the Chinese and Tibetan scripts painted on the pillars at the main entrance, the Chinese style robes worn by the monks, and the Chinese and Tibetan iconography on the altars. Although John had lived the last thirty-five years of his life in Thailand, where Theravada Buddhism prevails, he practiced the Mahayana Buddhism of China and Tibet taught by his Chinese and Tibetan teachers. Through the connection he'd established with this Chinese monastery in Thailand, he insured himself a final resting place in the spiritual embrace of Kuan Yin, his beloved Bodhisattva* of Compassion and the guiding light of Mahayana Buddhism.

We were now bringing John home to rest in a Chinese monastery that taught the Tibetan school of Buddhism he practiced, with a Kuan Yin temple that he helped found during his first year in Thailand. The wheel of life had come full circle for him.

The ceremony was enchanting. For over an hour we sat on the floor in the shrine hall, while a dozen monks chanted Tibetan mantras in deep, vibrant tones, the air redolent with the fragrance of sandalwood incense. Lost in reverie, my head rocked gently to the mesmerizing cadence of the chant. This is how John must have felt half a century

---

*A Bodhisattva is one who has attained enlightenment (Bodhi), but defers final entry into the state of nirvana until all other beings attain the same state. Thus a Bodhisattva chooses to continue to reincarnate in the world in order to help all beings gain the freedom of awakened awareness.

earlier when he visited those remote mountain monasteries in China, and the spiritual inspiration he found there glowed like a candle in his books.

The abbot clearly demonstrated his deep respect and affection for John by arranging for John's ashes to be interred in the corner slot of a sacred stupa located on the terrace behind the temple. This is a rare honor even for a resident senior monk, and even more so for a foreign layman living in Thailand. The crypt was sealed with a marble plaque inscribed in gold with John's name and dates of birth and death. After making offerings of incense, fruit, and prayer, we all joined the monks for a big vegetarian banquet in the courtyard.

After lunch I went to Kuan Yin's shrine hall and gazed up at the faded photograph above the door. Again I felt that tremor run up my spine. There stood John in a starched collar and white linen suit, tall and handsome, next to another Englishman, with the youthful abbot sitting in a chair before them, holding a rosary.

With John's last wish fulfilled and Bom's dream finally come true, we got in the car and drove back to Bangkok in silence.

Two years later I decided to move to Thailand. Taiwan had become too modern, too fast for my traditional Chinese tastes, and had lost its old-fashioned Chinese charm, just as postwar China had lost its appeal for John. And like him, I took refuge in Thailand.

For the first two months I shared a spacious house and garden with an old friend in Bangkok, but then a Taiwanese developer came along and bought the property to make room for a condominium, so we had to move out. Hearing of my predicament, Bom came over to visit me and said, "Why don't you come and live in my father's house? You were the last friend he made in this life, and he liked you so much. I know that he'd be happy to have you living there."

So my wish to live in a traditional Thai house just like John's was fulfilled. Almost three years to the day after first arriving at the House of Wind and Cloud to meet John, I became its resident writer and sinopath-in-exile, writing and sleeping in the very same room in which I'd spent so many memorable afternoons with John.

So turns the wheel of life.

DANIEL REID
JANUARY 2007
BYRON BAY, AUSTRALIA

Daniel Reid has a master's degree in Chinese language and civilization. He moved to Taiwan in 1973 where he studied Taoist practices for sixteen years, followed by ten years in Thailand. He currently resides in Australia. He is the author of *The Tao of Detox; The Tao of Health, Sex & Longevity;* and *The Complete Book of Chinese Health & Healing.* For more about Daniel Reid, please visit his website at www.DanReid.org.

FOREWORD

My Lifelong Friendship with John Blofeld

HUANG LI-SUNG, FORMER DEAN OF HONG KONG UNIVERSITY

(Originally printed in the June 13–15, 1987, editions of the Ming Pao newspaper in Hong Kong)

John Blofeld was one of my teachers during my middle-school years. He was also the most beloved teacher among all my fellow students at the Min Sheng Academy, which at the time was my main school.

Although Mr. Blofeld was not at the Min Sheng Academy for a very long period of time, he nevertheless left a very deep impression on us. In those days, the middle-school department of the Min Sheng Academy was located in a three-story building in the Chi Teh Pin district of Kowloon. The building faced onto Kowloon Bay, with Lion Mountain standing behind it. The ground and second floors served as classrooms and offices, while the third floor was the living quarters for the principal of the school (who was my father) and his family, and also for several teachers who worked there, and it was in one of these rooms that Mr. Blofeld lived.

So in addition to attending his classes, I encountered him outside of the classroom as well. The Min Sheng Academy also had boarding students staying there, and they all were required to attend daily classes in self-cultivation in the morning and evening. The students enjoyed a friendly relationship with the teachers who took turns teaching these classes, and I and my fellow students always felt very happy when it was Mr. Blofeld's turn to teach, not because he was a foreigner, but because he was a foreigner unlike any other.

At that time, three of China's eastern provinces had already been lost to foreign aggressors, the domestic situation within China was extremely unstable, and the spirit of the Chinese people had fallen into a state of decline. Under the pressure of relentless military aggression since the middle of the nineteenth century, China's fortunes had by then sunk to their lowest ebb. Most of the Chinese people living in Hong Kong had developed a deep sense of inferiority about their own country and culture, and flattery of foreigners had therefore become a prevailing trend, further fueled by the underlying assumption that only things from the Western world had any real value.

In those days, most middle schools in Hong Kong were either directly operated or sponsored by the government, which paid absolutely no attention to the teaching of Chinese language and civilization. In schools run by the government, only one class per day was taught in Chinese, and that class was always scheduled for the very last hour in the afternoon. Studying Chinese seemed to be of no practical use whatsoever.

Back then, one did not even need to understand Chinese in order to pass the entrance examinations for middle school or university, and students were allowed to substitute French for Chinese as a second language after English. What most distinguished the Min Sheng Academy from other schools was the importance it placed on Chinese studies, including both ancient and contemporary forms of the Chinese written language, as well as Chinese history and geography. In addition, all students were required to learn how to speak Mandarin, and if they were unable to pass the Chinese language proficiency tests, they could not advance to the next grade level. Among our teachers we had first-degree scholars* and

*A first-degree scholar was a scholar who scored in the highest rank in the imperial civil service exams, thus qualifying for the highest posts in the imperial bureaucracy. After the fall of the last dynasty in 1911, these scholars became highly valued teachers in China's new universities.

advanced academics who taught us Chinese, as well as university graduates from mainland China who taught us history, geography, and contemporary spoken Chinese. As a result, students at our school acquired a high degree of understanding regarding topics related to our native country, and we developed a close familiarity and deep respect for traditional Chinese culture.

However, the average foreigner (generally referred to as "Westerners") living in Hong Kong at that time had no respect whatsoever for China, nor the least bit of appreciation for Chinese culture, which they viewed with disdain as backward and decadent, even to the point that some of them refused to swallow a single bite of Chinese food. When it came to the subject of Chinese culture, the more polite foreigners simply avoided any mention of it, while the ruder elements openly expressed their complete contempt.

Into this situation there suddenly appeared a Westerner who came from England's most aristocratic university (Cambridge) and held our nation's culture in the highest esteem, and his appearance turned us young students completely upside down. We quickly realized that this Westerner was totally unlike all other Westerners. At the time, I was enrolled in my third year of middle school and was at an age that was neither old nor young. I still remember the first time that I walked past the door to his room. I smelled the fragrance of burning incense and heard the sound of chanting. Unable to resist, I peeked through the keyhole, and there I discovered him kneeling down reciting sutras* before an altar that he had set up himself in his room.

An Englishman reciting sutras while paying reverence to the Buddha—this was something that I could not have imagined even in my wildest dreams! Furthermore, we also discovered that Mr. Blofeld had acquired a deep understanding of the philosophy of Confucius and Mencius, that he truly loved all things Chinese, and that he

---

*Sutra means "thread" in Sanskrit, and refers to the collection of written teachings recorded by the Buddha's disciples after his death, based on the oral teachings he gave during his life.

wished to learn Cantonese from us as well. He liked to wear Chinese clothes, he loved to eat Chinese food, and he always enjoyed the rice gruel, fermented eggs, and pickled vegetables that my mother sent to his room each morning for breakfast. His attitude and utter sincerity really touched our hearts. Before long, however, he left Hong Kong and went to Tienjin to teach at the Hopei Academy of Engineering.

In 1939, he returned to the Min Sheng Academy for a while. By then I had already entered Hong Kong University, but whenever I came home on weekends I had a chance to see him. A few years later, when Hong Kong fell to the Japanese, I escaped to the interior of mainland China. While I was serving as an assistant instructor at Guangshi University in Guilin, he came to visit the school in his capacity as Cultural Attaché at the British Embassy in China. Meeting like that again at such a remote place in wartime China further amplified the intimacy of our feelings. In the winter of 1943, when I went to Chungjing to apply for a visa to study abroad, I again had the good fortune of meeting him, and he invited me to stay at his home for three months. Since then, we have met frequently in England, Hong Kong, and Thailand. Over the past half century, he has become my closest confidante, and this has become one of the greatest blessings in my life.

During the years that Mr. Blofeld lived in China, he spent the most time in Peking and Tienjin, and the rest in Chungjing and Kunming. During these years he traveled to every corner of China—north, south, east, and west. In this book, he now describes the experiences he had during his long residence in China.

The place he loved most of all was, of course, "The Abode of the Son of Heaven," Peking. He describes the ambience, appearance, and lifestyle of this ancient capital in vivid, fascinating detail. He roamed through all the fabled mountains and beautiful waterways of China, and stayed in famous monasteries and remote temples, where he often had the good fortune to receive spiritual teachings from renowned masters. He often ascended sacred mountains in search of spiritual inspiration, climbing by foot to the peaks of Mount Tai, Mount Hua, and Mount Heng and offering incense at the altars of Mount Putuo, Mount Omei, and Mount Wutai.

In fact, he visited all of the sacred mountains of China. His descriptions of the scenery on Mount Wutai and the pilgrims at Mount Tai are particularly enchanting, making the reader feel as though he had been to these places in person. In addition, he wandered through Guilin, Yulin, Chufu, Chusien, and other places, as well as through many remote villages where no foreigner had ever set foot before. He was a big tall man and always dressed in Chinese clothes, and he spoke Chinese. Whenever he appeared all by himself in these remote places, his presence startled the local villagers, for whom his arrival was by far the most interesting event of their entire lives.

In the more than fifty years that he lived in China and Southeast Asia, he taught in both middle schools and universities, served as a diplomat in the foreign service, and held the post of editor for UNESCO in the Far East for twelve years. His circle of friends extended far and wide, and most of his closest friends were Chinese. During his years in wartime Chungjing, he became friends with such literary luminaries as Yu Pei-hung, Yu Tso-jen, Tsao Yu, Lao She, and others. Many students and followers came to his door, most of them from China, Hong Kong, and Thailand.

This remarkable man, who firmly believed that he had a predestined connection with China, was a devout Buddhist who, under the dharma name* Chih Hai (Ocean of Wisdom), spent a period of time studying and practicing meditation at the Hua Ting monastery in Kunming. He had a deep understanding and appreciation for the three great philosophies of China—Confucianism, Taoism, and Buddhism. He has written no less than twenty books on these subjects, and in the field of Buddhist and Taoist religious studies he has become one of the

*When a person becomes a Buddhist, the teacher monk with whom he/she "takes refuge in the Buddha, Dharma, and Sangha" gives the initiate a "dharma name," which the teacher and fellow disciples use to address him/her.

world's most respected scholars. Over the years since his retirement from his post with the United Nations, he has been invited every year to lecture at major universities in America and Canada.

Mr. Blofeld, at seventy-four years old, is not in good health, and yet for the past few years he has been diligently practicing writing in Chinese. Recently he has been working very hard to get this book written, often writing until three or four o'clock in the morning, before finally going to sleep. This is the first book that he has written entirely in Chinese, and its purpose is to express his lifelong appreciation and deep cultivation of traditional Chinese culture. This book is a record of his story, and also the voice of his heart. His hope is that through this book the voice of his heart will reach and be heard by his many beloved Chinese friends in China and throughout the world. It is with great sincerity and enthusiasm that I introduce him and heartily recommend this book.

FOREWORD

Old Pu's Travel Diary

Chungliang Al Huang

Founder and president of Living Tao Foundation, author of *Embrace Tiger, Return to Mountain,* and coauthor, with Alan W. Watts, of *Tao: The Watercourse Way*

Alan Watts first introduced me to John Blofeld's writing while we were collaborating on *Tao: The Watercourse Way*, Alan's definitive book, also his last, on Taoism. We were corresponding and conferring with John from afar, and had planned to visit him in Bangkok soon. Alan died suddenly in 1973, so we never made the trip together.

Several years later, when Joseph Campbell invited me to join him on his Asian trip, which included a week in Thailand, I immediately wrote to John to make an appointment to finally meet him. On the long flight there, I reread his autobiography, *The Wheel of Life*, and felt a close spiritual connection with him. It was apparent at first sight when we met at my hotel in Bangkok that we were deeply related in heart and soul. We both agreed that we must have been close kinsmen through many previous incarnations. From the very start, I felt moved to address him as Uncle, and he accepted me wholeheartedly as his Chinese nephew.

All through that week, we managed to meet several times. I arranged a joint lecture with him and Joseph Campbell for our study group in Chiang Mai. Later, a formal ceremony took place at John's home, complete with candles and incense lit at the altar, confirming me as his officially adopted nephew. I clearly recall Uncle John sitting graciously on his chair, beaming beneficently as he received his Chinese nephew's grateful kowtows, witnessed by all his intimate friends and family.

Subsequently, Alan Watts' Society for Comparative Philosophies and our newly founded Living Tao Foundation jointly arranged and sponsored several U.S. lecture tours for Uncle John in the late 1970s and early 1980s. What blissful and blessed times those were for me to receive teaching from this learned and humble scholar, with his abundant knowledge of China and his simple wisdom and clarity. During all our times together in those years, Uncle John told me that his most fervent wish, yet to be accomplished in this life, was to write about his experiences in China, for Chinese readers, entirely in the Chinese language.

Although his skill in writing Chinese was remarkably good, especially for a Westerner, he still felt self-conscious about the mix of different styles in his Chinese writing, with its interesting juxtaposition of archaic, old-fashioned Beijing lingo mixed with modern vernacular usage. He vowed to improve the clarity of his written skills, and requested my assistance in this effort by insisting that I should correct all his Chinese letters to me. In the meantime, I had introduced him to my mother, Lee Chih-chang, whom Alan Watts had asked to provide elegant Chinese brush calligraphy for the Chinese texts included in his book *Tao: The Watercourse Way*. Uncle John also humbly requested my mother, whom he called Da Jie, "elder sister," to do the same with all the letters he wrote to her. For several years this process continued—although I now regret not having kept those letters, or requested their return to me for posterity.

I had heard that parts of his memoir were serialized in a Hong Kong Chinese newspaper under the title *Lao Pu Yo Ji: yi ge wai guo ren dui jung guo de hui yi* [Old Pu's Travel Diary: The Memoirs of an Englishman in China], but I had not read any of it. Uncle John passed away in 1987. With good fortune, through the dedication of one of his former students, the former president of Hong Kong University, Rayson Huang, I finally received a copy of the posthumous publication.

Since reading it, I have often lamented that so few of my international friends and students could fully appreciate the unique legacy that John Blofeld has left us in this gem of a book. And now, a faithful translation of Old Pu's travel diary, from the Chinese into English, has finally appeared in print, thanks to the equally loving admiration and dedication from another much younger nephew and admirer of Uncle John Blofeld and his books, Daniel Reid. It is with great honor and pleasure that I introduce this book to all readers who have admired John Blofeld's unique teaching and writings and have wished to feel closer in spirit with the man, and to share his passion for China and everything Chinese.

This is a wonderful book to be treasured and deeply appreciated. It is a generous gift, a true legacy, from a man who clearly managed to balance his life blissfully by blending the very best of Eastern and Western cultural heritages.

A map of China as it was in John Blofeld's day.

The Dynastic Periods of China

This timeline is derived from the work of Lin Yu-tang, one of the most respected Chinese scholars of the twentieth century.

Hsia	2205–1766 BCE
Shang	1766–1123 BCE
Chou	1122–249 BCE
Chin	221–207 BCE
Han	206 BCE–220 CE
Three Kingdoms Period	220–265 CE
Western Chin	265–317 CE
North and South Ten Kingdoms Period	317–581 CE
Sui	590–618 CE
Tang	618–906 CE
Five Dynasties Period	907–960 CE
Sung (Northern)	960–1126 CE
Sung (Southern)	1127–1279 CE
Yuan (Mongol)	1260–1368 CE*
Ming	1368–1644 CE
Ching (Manchu)	1644–1912 CE
Republic	1912–present

*The overlap of time at the Yuan (Mongol) dynasty beginning is due to the conflicting opinions of scholars on when the Sung (Southern) dynasty ended.

Old Pu's Travel Diary

THE MEMOIRS OF AN ENGLISHMAN IN CHINA

AUTHOR'S PREFACE

My Ideal Shangri-la

When I was young, I experienced many extraordinary events. Whenever I recollect the magic and mystery of those events, I reach the conclusion that the concept of reincarnation is not incorrect, and that the theory of previous causes from previous lives is not false. Assuming these ideas to be true, I can understand why those strange and unusual events had such a decisive influence on the direction I took in life, and why they determined the path I would follow for the rest of my days.

As a young man coming of age in the world, I should have taken an interest in cultivating the ways of my own native land, but these things had no appeal whatsoever to me. Instead, my heart was entranced by a faraway place that I had never even seen. Later, after focusing all of my attention on intensive studies of Chinese history, culture, and philosophy, I began to feel a strong wish to experience all of these things in their own natural environment.

One day (while I was still studying at Cambridge), my yearning suddenly overwhelmed me, and without pausing to consider my studies or my family, I abruptly abandoned school and came to the East, where I had the good fortune to live for many years in China, until I was forced to leave in 1948.

After arriving to live in China, I came to love every mountain and every waterway, every city and every town, like an addict loves his vice. I felt as though I were living in a magical realm. I had the further good fortune of cultivating lifelong friendships with two Chinese scholars, and I enjoyed the good destiny of finding a Chinese woman as my partner in marriage. The son and daughter I sired in this marriage look more Chinese than Western. Indeed, I myself have gradually become easternized, particularly in my older years, and almost everything about my personal lifestyle now is rich with the flavor of Chinese spirit.

During the nearly twenty years that I lived there, I never dreamed that anything might ever happen to make me leave China. However, as the ancient adage states, "Man plans, Heaven decides." Owing to unforeseen political developments in China, circumstances finally compelled me to leave, and I had no choice but to retreat from "my ideal shangri-la." Oh woe and alas!

Resigned to my fate, at the time of this writing I have already lived in exile from China for the past thirty-eight years, and now I have decided to record the events alluded to above and try my best to describe it all in truth and vivid detail, without adding any extra frills in order to make it sound more exotic, and without trying to conceal my own or my readers' flaws. I have strived to keep everything pure and simple.

As I am not Chinese, my style of writing in Chinese is not elegant, but I believe that the contents of this book shall not prove uninteresting to read. Although the things that I write about here have already become past history, I think that contemporary readers today will be pleased to read descriptions of how people used to live in the past, and how society functioned in those days. With these thoughts in mind, I have mustered the courage to pick up my pen and write.

John Blofeld,
An Old Man of Seventy-four Years,
1986

I

My Preordained Destiny to Tread the Land of the Dragon

A Marvelous Mystery

I was born in London in 1913. My family descended from the gentry class, with an ancestral lineage extending back five or six hundred generations. However, my grandfather chose to enter the world of commerce, and my late father made his living drawing fashion designs.

During my childhood, I attended a boarding school, and there at the age of twelve I made my first contact with literary studies. In order to instill in us a love for reading books, the principal of our school often read novels aloud to us. Once he happened to select a novel about China. The main characters in this novel were an English couple, and the book portrayed this man and woman as flawless people of impeccable character and proper behavior, without the slightest fault whatsoever, while all of the Chinese characters were depicted as absolute villains, without any virtues at all.

At such a tender age, we students had no way of understanding how severely this book slandered Chinese people. As a child in a child's world, where none of us had any connection with China, I had no way of knowing whether the average Chinese was good or bad. Nevertheless, I clearly felt that I had some sort of predestined relationship with China, and therefore I could not help feeling contempt for the author of that book for writing such an absurdly malevolent description of that foreign land. Whenever the principal read a passage in which the couple experienced trouble, while the Chinese gained the upper hand, I could not suppress the feelings of joy that rose up in my heart, and I thought to myself, "They jolly well deserve it!"

In any case, it was due to that book that I began to feel an unusually strong interest in China stirring within me. After hearing that story read to us, I tried my best to find other books about China, and before long I began to realize what a highly developed civilization China had. From the age of fifteen, whenever anyone asked me what I planned to do when I grew up, I always replied, "I want to go live in China." If someone then asked me exactly what I wished to do to make a living in China, I found it difficult to come up with an answer. I felt sufficiently satisfied just to think that I would live in China, without feeling the need to make any further preconceived "plans." It would be easy enough, I believed, to find a job there when the time and opportunity came.

In my youth, I experienced another extraordinary and mysterious event. During summer vacation one year, my aunt took me for a visit to the seashore. One day we went into town to do some shopping, and there in a shop I happened to see a small statue of the Buddha, about three inches in height. I had never seen an image of the Buddha before, nor had I ever heard anything said about the Buddha, and yet, for reasons that I could not explain, the very moment I saw that statue of the Buddha, I felt a love for it arise from the depth of my heart, and I knew with absolute certainty that I must take it back home with me. When I realized that my aunt had no intention of giving me that Buddha, my tears poured like rain, and even after we left the shop and stood outside, I wept on and on. Eventually my tears softened my aunt, until she had no choice but to buy the Buddha for me as a gift. I could hardly contain my joy.

A few days later I returned to my father's house. From that time on, every night before I went to sleep, I shut the door to my room, then offered flowers and prostrated myself to the Buddha. At that time, I still had no notion what the Buddha represented in the world, nor had anyone ever taught me how to perform that sort of ritual. Moreover, regardless of whether they were worshiping God or having an audience with the King, Western people were not accustomed to prostrating themselves in such a manner, so how on earth could a child like me know that this was the proper way to pay respects to the Buddha? Whenever I recall this memory, I still find it difficult to understand what it all means.

A long time after I came into possession of this Buddha image, an older friend of mine informed me that the little statue I had been revering was an image of Sakyamuni Buddha.*

Thereafter, I felt a powerful urge to seek more knowledge about Buddhist beliefs, and sometimes I even paid secret visits to a nearby Buddhist monastery in order to request teachings from two Ceylonese monks there. Later, I decided to take refuge in the Triple Gem,† thereby formally becoming a Buddhist, but in order not to cause grief to my father, who believed in the Christian God, I resolved not to let my family know anything about this at that time.

That a little boy born and raised in the environment and culture of the West would fall in love, without any apparent reason, with an Eastern country he had never seen—China—and furthermore would bow his head in reverence before a Buddha about whom he had never heard a single word—these were truly extraordinary mysteries. At the time, I did not realize just how unusual these two matters really were,

---

*The name Sakyamuni means "silent sage of the Sakyas" and was the name by which the historical Buddha was known during his years as a wandering ascetic. Sakya was the name of the royal clan of which he was the crown prince before he left home and became an ascetic.

†The Triple Gem refers to the "three jewels" of Buddhism: the Buddha (teacher), the dharma (teachings), and the sangha (community of monks and lay practitioners). In order to become a "Buddhist," one simply "takes refuge" in the triple gem with an ordained monk.

but looking back on them today, I believe it all arose from a marvelous chain of cause and effect. Looking at it in light of the Buddhist concept of reincarnation, perhaps I was a Chinese Buddhist disciple in a former life, and consequently in this life I was able to "partially recognize" certain things that I had held as precious in a previous life.

Whatever the case may be, the fact remains that in this life, when I first heard word of a distant land named China and when I first laid eyes on an image of the Buddha, I instantly felt an instinctive emotional response, just like a refugee in exile feels when suddenly he sees something that reminds him of his native land. If it were not for my belief in reincarnation, it would be extremely difficult for me to explain these two extraordinary events, and thus I feel absolutely convinced that reincarnation is not mere fantasy. Indeed, my own experience may well serve as concrete evidence that reincarnation is a basic fact of life.

In 1930, at the age of eighteen, I passed the entrance examinations to study at Cambridge University. It was only then that I began to have the opportunity to associate with Chinese people. At that time, there were only about twenty or so Chinese students at Cambridge, all of them several years older than me, and I really enjoyed becoming friends with them. Although I felt certain that they regarded me as a naive youngster, I nevertheless loved to talk with them about China.

In my encounters with them, I always felt that they were very kind to me. Most of them were modern youth, and therefore they usually valued the new and discounted the old. They were all so eager to save their country. They felt that over the past few decades China had been severely mistreated, and that during this period not only had China been unable to punish its aggressors, it had also been defeated by them time and time again. China had lost its territory, lost its wealth, and also lost its social fabric, and all of this was clearly a result of China's own insufficient military power. It seemed obvious to them that Western civilization and Western thought, further boosted by modern science, had hugely enhanced the power of foreign nations to lay waste to their own country. From their point of view, modern science was far superior to traditional Confucian studies. Some of these young Chinese also felt that traditional Chinese civilization invariably gave rise to misgovernment and corruption, and for this problem they despised and blamed the older generation.

Although the words above really reflect their firm beliefs, nevertheless, whenever they heard a Westerner express such profound respect for the traditional culture of their ancestors, they could not help but feel pleased. Furthermore, they very rarely engaged me in debate regarding the good and the bad, the gain and the loss, in regard to the old and the new in Chinese culture.

A Lifelong Friendship

Not only at Cambridge, but also in China, Southeast Asia, and other places, I have always enjoyed the good fortune of winning the hearts of Chinese friends. Even now in my old age I am still the recipient of frequent favors and kindnesses from Chinese friends. Whenever I meet someone who shows a sincere respect for traditional Chinese civilization, I naturally wish to become friends with that person. It's most unfortunate that so many Westerners believe that Western civilization and Western learning are peerless throughout the world, and that they therefore adopt an attitude of implicit superiority toward people from other parts of the world. This sort of haughty condescension can easily cause feelings of animosity, particularly among Chinese people, who have a strong intuitive sense that enables them to quickly perceive what others are thinking.

Even before completing my second year at Cambridge, I already felt an overwhelming wish to go to China. Driven by this yearning in my heart, I suddenly left school one day and boarded a ship bound for Shanghai. (Years later, I returned to Cambridge to complete my studies and graduate.) Unfortunately, I fell ill during the ocean voyage and got no further than Hong Kong, where I had to enter a hospital for treatment. This cost me my last bit of money, forcing me to remain in Hong

Kong and teach school there in order to earn a living, and I had to stay there until I could make enough money to cover my expenses for traveling onward. This setback proved to have beneficial consequences for me. Shortly after leaving the hospital, I made the acquaintance of an outstanding good friend, Dr. Tsai Yuan-ruo, whose nickname was Da Hai (Great Ocean). At the time, I had no way of knowing that he was destined to become my lifelong friend, but from the very first moment I met him I regarded Yuan-ruo as my ideal model for human behavior.

Although Mr. Tsai was only in his thirties, he had already established his reputation as one of the best Chinese doctors in Hong Kong. Of medium height, with fair complexion and rather slender physique, he was the very image of a typical studious Chinese scholar; but he had a sparkling bright spirit and he always spoke with a strong tone of righteous conviction, and he moved with great energy and animation. His whole presence reflected the easygoing self-confidence of a brilliantly cultivated gentleman. I especially recall his big bright eyes—one glance and you knew for certain that this was a good man. The first time we met, what drew my attention the most was the way he dressed: on his head he wore a skullcap; over his body he draped a long gown of blue silk, on top of which he wore a formal black jacket; and on his feet he wore white socks and soft shoes of black satin. He continued to dress like this throughout his entire life, in the traditional style of the Ching Dynasty, and he did this because of his own personal background.

Mr. Tsai, whose family came from the province of Fujien and were descendants of high-ranking government officials, was born in the Shiguan district of Canton. His father was a famous physician during the latter years of the Ching Dynasty, and in 1911, in order to escape the raging warfare sparked by the republican revolution, he took his family and moved to Hong Kong. Staunchly loyal to the imperial dynasty, he would have preferred death to westernization. Without exception, his every thought and word, his manners and his clothing, the furnishings in his home, and everything else all cleaved faithfully to the elegant style of the old literati of the late Ching Dynasty.

Chinese flavor. The famous restaurants, the many teahouses, and the countless shops had not yet been westernized. Of course, Hong Kong had its share of Western-style enclaves, but for the most part the lifestyle of the average resident of Hong Kong did not differ much from that of city dwellers in Canton, and it probably had not changed much at all since the late Ching Dynasty. Nevertheless, I still did not wish to remain in Hong Kong for very long. Hong Kong was not China: it was a colony of Britain.

Sometimes the attitude that English people expressed toward the Chinese made me very angry. For example, whenever I rode the ferryboat across to Kowloon, I could not help but overhear the conversations of other Westerners. Thus I discovered that even the least educated, lowest class Englishman looked down on all Chinese. The lowest ranking foot soldier believed that all white people, regardless of whether their own social status was high or low, were without exception superior to each and every person of Asian descent. Indignantly I thought to myself, "*Ai ya*! How dare these beasts presume themselves to be superior to my dear brother Yuan-ruo and his class of Chinese?" Because of my views, I naturally felt rather ill at ease in the colonial environment. Sometimes I could not wait to leave Hong Kong, while at other times I could not bear the thought of parting with Yuan-ruo and his friends. Fortunately, I had frequent opportunity to make short trips over to the mainland, where I visited many places of interest.

First Taste of Opium: Risking a Dead-end Road

Soon after arriving in Hong Kong, I was hired as an instructor at the Min Sheng Academy. This academy was located along the seashore, not far from the Old Walled City in Kowloon, near the wharf where the airport is now situated. The principal of the school, Mr. Huang Ying-ran, was very astute, and he believed that both Chinese and English language courses were of equal importance at school. In order to insure that the students there received the best possible Chinese education, he invited accomplished Chinese scholars to come teach those courses. There were also several gentlemen at the Min Sheng Academy who taught Mandarin Chinese. In those days, very few students in Hong Kong could speak the Mandarin dialect.* Most of the English teachers at the academy came from England, and therefore the students spoke English with a distinctively British accent.

I don't think there were any other schools in Hong Kong that could match this one. The Min Sheng Academy included both elementary and high school education for boys as well as girls, with separate facilities for male and female students. I lived at the academy and was assigned to the boys division. Although I also taught a few classes in the girls division, they were few and far between, so I developed a closer relationship with my male students. Realizing how much I loved traditional Chinese culture, they were very friendly and affectionate toward me, and I felt delighted by the friendships I established with them. I still count some of those students among my closest friends today.

In addition to the principal and his family, there were also some young teachers living at the school. Among them were two or three who had married country girls selected for them by their elders prior to taking up their jobs at the school. Because these girls were virtually illiterate, it was difficult for them to truly win their husbands' hearts. I became good friends with one of these teachers, but please pardon me for not mentioning his name here. Let's just call him "Ah Tsai." We often went out to have a good time together, and sometimes we took the boat over to Macao and spent the night there. Although neither of us was much inclined to gamble, we didn't mind playing a little fan-tan,† winning a few dollars here, losing a few there, it didn't really matter to us either way. Young people are always so eager to experience the

*"Mandarin" refers to the dialect of spoken Chinese that prevails in northern China, particularly Peking. Today it has become the national dialect and is referred to in mainland China as "common dialect" and in Taiwan as "national dialect," but during the 1930s, very few people in southern China understood Mandarin.

†Fan-tan is a popular Chinese gambling game, which is almost impossible to win.

world, tasting the bitter along with the sweet, and while we were not specifically searching for romance, we did wish to try all different sorts of entertainment.

One day, right after lunch in Macao, Ah Tsai suggested, "Now that we've had our fill of white rice, how about going out for some 'black rice?'" He smiled cryptically and said, "After you've tried it, you'll know what I mean." He beckoned me to follow him down a small lane, where we entered a house. At first sight, the place looked like a bordello, so I wondered to myself, "Could 'black rice' mean a prostitute from Africa?" Just then, an old crone appeared and led us upstairs into a private room, where she brought us some tea. The only place to sit was a large mahogany couch. Arranged on a brass tray between us lay an assortment of small utensils, which Ah Tsai informed me were none other than the tools required to prepare opium for smoking. I felt so alarmed by what he said that I immediately stood up to leave. Just at that precise moment, a very young girl entered the room, curtsied politely, and said, "Gentlemen, please loosen your clothing, lie down, and relax. No need to feel inhibited here."

With her back to Ah Tsai, she lay down on her side facing me and rested her head on a cushion, then signaled me to lie down in the same fashion, facing her. Although she appeared to be only a young girl not yet fourteen years of age, her charm bewitched my soul. She was dressed in a white silk jacket and blue pants and had her hair cut short, very clean and simple. Although her face was rather plain, her smile and the playful look in her eyes had a powerful impact on my heart. I had always regarded opium as an evil thing, but I did not wish to invite her ridicule, so I decided to simply allow nature to take its course. She seemed to intuit that she had won the Foreign Devil's heart, and she felt so pleased by her victory that she could not resist giggling.

She busied herself heating the opium paste in order to form pellets for smoking. Each time she finished preparing a pellet, she stuck it into a small hole in the bowl of the pipe and pressed the mouthpiece to my lips. One small pellet produced a lot of smoke, so it isn't easy for the smoker to draw it all in with a single puff. Soon I began to savor the opium's exotic flavor, and felt an extremely comfortable sensation spread throughout my entire body. Fortunately, Ah Tsai firmly stipulated that we smoke no more than five pipes each, and he further advised me that under no circumstances should I smoke opium again for at least one week, in order to avoid becoming addicted to it.*

After we'd both finished smoking our five pipes, we went back to the guest-house and lay down on our beds to rest. Every time I shut my eyes, a profusion of images in richly varied colors floated before me, and this continued for quite some time. The next day, as we prepared to return to Hong Kong, I asked Ah Tsai if we could go out for another round of black rice. This made him quite angry, and he said, "You must be crazy! If you want to go, then go by yourself. I can return to Hong Kong on my own, but I will never be your friend again. If you wish to become an opium addict, there's nothing I can do to stop you, but don't blame me for leading you down a dead-end road!"

His reprimand touched my heart. How foolish it would be to risk addiction. I apologized and meekly boarded the boat with him back to Hong Kong.

The Braveheart Who Quit Opium Sitting in a Buddhist Shrine Room

Between semesters, I often took the train to Canton to spend the weekend. Every time I went there, I stayed at the home of Yuan-ruo's relatives, an extended family of more than twenty men and women, old and young, whose surname was Pan. They treated me as though I too were part of the family. The district in which they lived was called Shiguan, and it was the most highly cultured place in the entire province. During the previous Ching Dynasty, government officials and their families were particularly fond of this district, and this is where they preferred to build their official residences and private homes.

*It takes exactly one week for the body to flush opium residues from the bloodstream.

The language spoken by those who lived in Shiguan had been somewhat influenced by the formal speech of government there. For example, the Cantonese way of saying the word *chiao* was "hao-dze," with the final "dze" syllable pronounced as "chi" (hao-chi), but the residents of the Shiguan district used the local Cantonese term *hao* combined with the official court pronunciation for "dze" (hao-dze).

At that time, the exteriors of the residences in Shiguan were not particularly impressive to the eye, but the interiors were extremely elegant. The furniture was all crafted from mahogany and marble, and the scrolls of painting and calligraphy on the walls reflected a highly refined and sophisticated style.

Among the famous restaurants of Canton were several that had been established hundreds of years ago. (Recently I have learned that some of them encountered great trouble during the turbulent times of the Red Guards but were nevertheless still in operation today). While traveling in the region as a young man, I rarely had the opportunity to enjoy the famous local cuisine, but not a single day went by that I did not go to the teahouses to eat simple snack foods. When Cantonese people speak of going out to "drink tea," their primary purpose is to eat snack foods, while the tea itself is only a secondary consideration.

Very early each morning, residents of the city flocked to these teahouses to enjoy themselves, and only after that did they go to work. The wealthy clientele sat upstairs on the upper floors, while those of more modest means sat downstairs on the ground floor. Although the teas and snacks served on the second, third, and fourth floors were exactly the same as those served on the ground floor, the prices were very different. The higher the floor on which one chose to eat and drink, the more expensive the fare and the more prestige the customer gained. In those days, most Cantonese took this *yum cha* (drinking tea) cuisine as their breakfast, but today people tend to regard it more as a form of lunch.

And in the past, unlike today, women seldom went to the teahouses.

In the old days, popular customs weighed heavily in favor of male convenience, while imposing excessively strict restraints on females. Because I was a male and therefore generally associated with other men, I rarely gave much thought to the social difficulties endured by women. In any case, within the homes of the Tsai and Pan families, it seemed to me that the women all enjoyed peace of mind.

At the home of the Pan family in Shiguan, there lived a much beloved and deeply respected man by the name of Rh-ru, a gentleman of fifty whom the younger generation simply addressed as "Fifth Uncle." He treated me just as he would his own nephew. Except for Yuan-ruo, I loved and respected Fifth Uncle most of all.

When I first met him, someone told me just how admirable Fifth Uncle really was. When he was still a young man, some of his friends unfortunately led him down the wrong path, and he therefore became addicted to opium. However, having recently become a devout Buddhist, he had resolved to break his addiction. The method he used to quit opium was truly remarkable. One day, he made a solemn vow before an image of the Buddha never to smoke opium again, and he did this without entering a hospital or taking any sort of medication. Instead he just stayed at home by himself, sitting in his shrine room and chanting mantras, and endured the unspeakable pain of withdrawal. Because he had been addicted for over thirty years and smoked more than half an ounce of opium every day,* such abrupt withdrawal was extremely dangerous. His relatives all pleaded with Fifth Uncle to accept medical treatment in order to avoid risking his life, but he simply replied, "Life and death are matters of destiny. I am willing to bear this pain in order to express my sincere repentance, and I prefer to rely upon the blessings and protection of the Buddha's mercy." He tolerated many months of the most intense, relentless suffering. Finally, contrary to the expectations of his entire family, he had paid his debt accord-

*Half an ounce is equivalent to about sixty pipes of opium a day, which is an extremely large dosage that causes severe addiction.

ing to his wishes, and his addiction to opium was completely uprooted. This was an accomplishment that most physicians would have regarded as utterly impossible to achieve.

Once, Fifth Uncle took me and two or three other nephews to spend three days at a remote Taoist hermitage, where the nights were so desolate and lonely that it was hard to bear. His nephews wanted to smoke a few pipes of opium to relieve the oppression in their hearts, and since Fifth Uncle was the only one who knew how to prepare the opium for smoking, they asked him to do it for them. Anyone who has recently withdrawn from opium addiction cannot help but feel very tempted by the aroma of opium fumes, and such a person would find it extremely difficult not to succumb to such a temptation. My companions should really not have asked him to risk this danger! However, Fifth Uncle remained completely calm as he prepared four or five pipes of opium for each of them to smoke, and his attitude was totally normal from start to finish, a clear indication that opium no longer held the power to seduce him. This sort of resolution is truly a noble trait, and in my own mind's eye, I shall always see Fifth Uncle as a brave hero.

Entertaining a Guest from Afar on a Flower Boat

In addition to my frequent sojourns in Canton, I occasionally also went to visit the famous sights throughout the two provinces of Guangtung and Guangshi, usually traveling all by myself. The first time I traveled there alone, I started out on a train, then took a bus, and finally arrived at Huijou three hours later. This town is located in a region inhabited by the Hakka people.* The atmosphere here was for the most part

*The word "Hakka" means "guests" or "strangers" in Chinese, and it refers to a group of people who were driven into the remote southern regions from their homeland in northern China many centuries ago, for reasons that remain unclear. They are known for their fierce clan loyalty and business acumen.

quite similar to that which prevailed at that time in Canton. While the major streets reflected a bit of recent Western influence, the back lanes still retained the plain and simple flavor of the old world. The scenery outside of town was extraordinarily beautiful, with a large lake bordered by a landscape of rice paddies and mountains, and set along the banks of the lake were some ancient temples that looked as though they came out of a painting.

As soon as I disembarked from the bus, I left my luggage at an inn and went straight to a teahouse to relax. It was midafternoon, so only a few other customers were there having tea and pastries. Whenever a customer prepared to leave, the waiter never bothered to write up a bill for him; instead, he reckoned at a glance how many plates and teapots were on the customer's table, then shouted a coded phrase to the cashier sitting by the entrance, such as, "Table fifteen, one week!" The cashier would then know that the customer from table fifteen should pay seven cents. As I recall, a pot of good tea with three or four dishes of snack food did not cost more than four or five cents.

While I was drinking tea there that afternoon, a gentleman wearing a long gown came in. When his eyes beheld me, an expression of mild surprise crossed his face, and after staring at me for a moment, he came over and sat down. As we exchanged courtesies, he informed me that his surname was Suo. We talked for a while, and before long he said, "This rustic town does not have much of interest to recommend itself, and so I'm afraid, sir, that you may feel rather lonesome here. By happy coincidence, this very evening an old friend has invited me to drink wine on a flower boat. The breeze on the lake is very cool and refreshing, and the song girls here really sing quite well, so if you, sir, have the time to spare, I wish to invite you to join us." I agreed enthusiastically, and we arranged to meet that evening at the inn.

After he took his leave, I began to feel doubtful and asked myself why a complete stranger should be so friendly. But then I thought, "Unless one enters the tiger's lair, how can one expect to catch the tiger's cub?" And after all, there was not much that a poor fellow like me could lose. This train of thought proved to be a complete misunderstanding of the man's good intentions. Only later did I learn that the Chinese always treat "guests from afar" with great affection.

That evening, Mr. Suo came to the inn and escorted me to the lakeside, where we boarded a small skiff that rowed us out to the flower boat. The boat was lavishly decorated, and it had an unusually broad and spacious deck in the center. Seven or eight tables of the sort found in teahouses stood on the floorboards. The party was already underway, but there still remained plenty of empty seats. When I thought of the term "flower boat," I had always imagined that it would be nothing more than a brothel floating on the water. But this flower boat appeared to be an entire restaurant on the lake. Certainly there were a few "flower girls," but no more than three or four. Their job was to sing songs and play music. Mr. Suo informed me that whoever hired the boat for the evening could arrange to order food directly from the proprietor. If one also wished to have flower girls in attendance, that had to be arranged separately.

That evening all of the guests were dressed in long gowns. In Guangtung, regardless of whether the weather was hot or cold, well-mannered townsfolk rarely went out in public wearing short jackets. In the course of conversation, I told several guests sitting beside me that in my own humble country one very seldom invited foreign travelers to join a private party, particularly when one was not even the party's host. After hearing my words, one of them explained with obvious satisfaction, "You are what we Chinese refer to as a 'guest from afar.' The Chinese sage Confucius once said, 'When there comes a guest from afar, is this not indeed a pleasure!' For the past two thousand years, each and every word in the Analects of Confucius has been deeply imprinted in the minds of the Chinese people. Following the advice of Confucius has become a custom for us, and over the ages this custom has become instinct."

Continuing to address me, the guest said, "Although people today are no longer familiar with the Four Books and Five Classics,* nevertheless within their hearts they still maintain an innate sense of propriety. Our dear brother Suo saw at a glance that you are a 'guest from afar,' and so naturally we feel delighted to meet you. Isn't that right, brother Suo?" Smiling, Mr. Suo replied, "Your thesis is far too exalted. How could I possibly keep all that in mind? It's simply that since we have so few foreign visitors here, when I saw Mr. Pu, I felt a bit surprised. From his appearance, I could see that he was neither a missionary nor a businessman. I could not imagine what his purpose might be in coming here, and so I began to feel extremely curious. Only after talking with him for a while did I discover his interest in our traditional Chinese customs, and that he had come here because he wished to visit a relatively old-fashioned town. Fearing that he might feel disappointed with this place, I decided to invite him here in order to introduce him to a group of our town's most distinguished characters."

The party itself was not particularly remarkable, but my conversations with the guests there that evening made me understand why Yuan-ruo, Fifth Uncle, and others so readily associated with me. From the very start, they had accorded me the special hospitality reserved for the "guest from afar." Later, when they realized how much I truly love Chinese civilization, they treated me with even greater kindness.

During the course of the party on the flower boat, there was one thing that really surprised me. Besides the young girls, I did not see any other females on board. Only later did I learn that among relatively old-fashioned people in China, male and female never attended the same party together, even if they were husband and wife or father and daughter. Whenever a host invited a male guest to a party, he never invited any other members of the guest's family to join him. Alternatively, the host might arrange a separate table in a separate room for them, in

*These books are referred to as Ssu Jing Wu Shu in Chinese, and they contain the complete teachings of Confucius, which formed the foundation of Chinese civilization for over two thousand years, and shows signs of enjoying a renaissance in China in the twenty-first century.

order to conform with the Confucian principle of decorum that states "men and women should never have contact in public."

I recall one time when I invited Yuan-ruo to have dinner at the residence of one of my colleagues. Our host was a Christian, and so he did not take traditional Chinese customs into consideration. Not only were men and women sitting together at the same table eating dinner, they were seated next to one another in an alternating male and female seating arrangement. Brother Yuan-ruo was sitting directly across from me, and I could see that he felt rather uncomfortable; in fact, he looked downright ill at ease. As we rode the bus back home together, I said, "The old woman and the young one sitting on either side of you appeared to be quite a lively pair. They did not seem the least bit shy, so what have you to fear, my brother?" He replied, "This was the first time in my entire life that I have ever eaten a meal sitting together with women other than my own relatives. This is the first time I've ever violated a rule that was formulated over two thousand years ago, and it makes me feel uneasy. I am not suggesting that the customs you foreigners follow in regard to women are not correct, it's just that I myself am not accustomed to that, so I could not help but feel embarrassed."

After more than twenty years as a republic, there are still many people in China who are not accustomed to associating in public with the opposite sex. Particularly in the three great cities of Shanghai, Canton, and Hong Kong, the differences between old-fashioned and new-style people are huge. Even though these two types of people may come from the same place and speak the same dialect, their ways of thinking and their customary habits are totally different, just as though they belonged to completely different worlds.

Ancestor Worship Is No Superstition

During the winter of 1934, I traveled alone by boat on the Shijiang River to Wujou in Guangshi province, and the following day I took a bus to Yulin. Arriving there after dark, I found a room at an inn. While I was sound asleep deep in the night, something strange happened. A small drop of water splashed onto my face from the mosquito net, giving me a most peculiar sensation. The next morning, I asked the clerk where that drop of water had come from, and he tersely informed me that it came from a urinating rat. *Ai ya!* I immediately decided to move into a more expensive hotel.

I was just in the midst of unpacking my bag when a policeman suddenly burst into my room and told me that the county clerk wished to see me. Surprised, I followed him. The county clerk spoke no English, so he had invited a high school teacher by the name of Li to translate for us. Mr. Li had grown up in Peking, and I have no idea what prompted him to move to Guangshi to teach English, but in any case his English was quite good. He informed me that in order to travel in this province, foreigners were required to first obtain a formal permit from the provincial government authorities. Since I had failed to arrange my trip in accordance with this regulation, I was therefore obliged to return to Canton that same day. I pleaded with the clerk to allow me to stay on for three or four days, but all to no avail. He told me that foreigners required a local guarantor in order to stay there, and that the guarantor must be someone who knows the visitor well. I of course had no close acquaintances in Yulin, but Mr. Li, noticing the disappointment on my face, suddenly suggested, "How about if Mr. Pu stays at my home?" The county clerk smiled and agreed.

Thanks to Mr. Li's kindness, I did not lose this fine opportunity to experience and enjoy the classical Chinese flavor of an old country town that had remained totally untouched by Western influence. The town's most noteworthy feature was an avenue along both sides of which stood rows of ancestral temples. There were many of these family shrines, and they were beautiful, all of them constructed in a strictly formal style. Some had been built during the early Ching Dynasty, and a few of them probably included some shrine halls and pavilions that had survived from the Ming Dynasty (1368–1644) to the present time. In prerevolutionary China, old buildings with an ancient history were to be seen everywhere, but I have no idea how many of them still remain standing today.

After seeing all those ancestral temples there that day, I naturally began to think about ancestor worship and related matters. This is something that is very difficult for most Westerners to understand, so I said to Mr. Li, "I have heard that in your worthy country there are special days each year on which people make ceremonial offerings to their ancestors. Please explain to me how someone who has already "crossed the river"* could possibly come back to enjoy the fine flavors of these offerings." Mr. Li laughed and replied, "Uneducated people may well believe that their ancestors can return to enjoy these offerings, but we educated people have never held this belief. As the ancient sages suggested, 'One should worship ancestors as though they were present,' which means that when making offerings to our ancestors, we should do so as though their spirits were right there before us. This idea has three practical meanings. First, it means that in order to express sincere respect for our ancestors, we must behave properly in life and do good deeds thereby manifesting our respectful intentions toward our forefathers. Second, it means that we must strictly avoid doing harm to others, and that we should desist from engaging in bad behavior, so that we do not bring shame to the whole family's reputation. Third, it means that whenever the entire clan participates together in an ancestral worship ceremony, it gives the whole family a chance to reunite and harmonize family feelings."

Mr. Li continued, "We scholars are not superstitious, so we do not believe that the spirits of our ancestors actually congregate to enjoy the offerings we make. Ancestor worship is really meant as a way to strengthen family solidarity in life, and as such it is an excellent idea that completely conforms with common sense."

The room in which Mr. Li invited me to stay was unusually attractive,

*This is a common Chinese euphemism for death, i.e., "crossing over to the other side" of the river of life and death.

and the bedding, furniture, and decor were all elegantly designed and well crafted. It felt far more comfortable and interesting than staying in even the most expensive hotel. Only shortly before I left did I realize that the room I'd been occupying was not at all the Li family's guest room, but rather Mr. and Mrs. Li's own personal bedroom. As it turned out, it was the only bedroom in the whole house. So during my four-day sojourn in Yulin, the two of them had no choice but to stay temporarily in a guest room at the school. Such generous hospitality is very seldom encountered in other countries.

Everywhere in the world, traditional societies all place great importance on courtesy and good manners, but it is also very easy for courtesy and good manners to degenerate into insincerity and hypocrisy. The hospitality described above was truly a far cry from insincerity; it was something that arose spontaneously from the depths of a sincere heart. Today, very few contemporary Chinese are able to recite by heart the precious gems of wisdom spoken by their ancient sages, but the legacy of propriety and virtue that these wise sages bestowed upon the Chinese world has not yet been totally lost. Throughout the far-flung world of Overseas Chinese communities, there are still many people who faithfully follow the noble virtues taught by the sages of ancient China.

A Lustrous Lama

While I was teaching school in Hong Kong, in addition to my usual holiday travels, every two or three days I took the ferryboat across the bay to visit Yuan-ruo, Fifth Uncle, and other old-fashioned family friends. I truly admired them, and they influenced my life in many ways. Whatever they liked, I too found very easy to like. Among their circle of friends were some members of a Buddhist retreat center in Hong Kong. The abbot of the hermitage was Cantonese and had lived for many years in the mountain wilderness of Japan, where he had learned the rituals and studied the meditation methods of the True

Discourse (also known as the Eastern Esoteric)* school of Buddhism.

This form of Buddhism had originally been founded in China, but during the latter years of the Tang Dynasty (618–906 CE), it abruptly disappeared there. Fortunately, shortly before its extinction in China, the Japanese monk Kung Hai (Ocean of Emptiness) transmitted the tradition to Japan. The abbot of the hermitage in Hong Kong wished to revive this esoteric school of practice in China. Fifth Uncle and Yuan-ruo often took me with them to this retreat center, where I participated with the members in all sorts of teachings and practice.

Before long, however, brother Yuan-ruo's spiritual inclinations shifted, and he entered the Vajrayana path of Tibetan Tantric Buddhism.† I felt certain that my elder brother had sound reason for doing this, so without asking him for any explanation, I simply followed along. Whenever we were together, this sort of unspoken sense of agreement often prevailed.

One afternoon, I went to pay a visit to elder brother and found a venerable Tibetan monk staying at his home. Elder brother invited me to come inside and meet the lama. And there I saw a Tibetan monk dressed in long robes, with shaved head, long whiskers, a compassionate face, and sparkling eyes. As I was introduced to the lama, I bowed my head in respect. The old monk said the he was very pleased to meet a Western Buddhist, and he said to me, "If you ever have any questions about our teachings, I would be very happy to explain things for you."

I naturally felt delighted with the chance to ask him about the teachings, but the language barrier made it difficult. The lama had lived in Szechuan‡ for many years, so he spoke Mandarin Chinese quite well. Among my seven or eight Cantonese companions in the room,

*The Eastern Esoteric sect is Japan's Shingon sect, which was based on the teachings of three Indian Tantric teachers active in China's capital of Chang-an during the seventh and eighth centuries.

†Vajrayana, or the "Diamond Path" of practice, aims at attaining fully enlightened awareness in this lifetime (wisdom), for the benefit of all beings (compassion).

‡Szechuan (Four Rivers) province, located in southwest China and bordering on Tibet.

several understood the Mandarin dialect, and so they tried to explain the lama's teachings to me. But the lama found it difficult to understand their garbled southern pronunciation of Mandarin words, so I felt seriously doubtful that they were able to translate my questions to him in a way that he could really understand. The moment the lama heard my concern, he laughed and advised me that I need not worry about such trifling obstacles as language. He suggested that I and a friend of mine from Hong Kong who spoke relatively fluent Mandarin come back to see him again after dinner.

As I bowed to take my leave, I thought to myself: I must not waste this great monk's time; I must think of some important questions to ask him. After dinner, my translator Mr. Hsieh and I returned together to see him. In a low voice, Mr. Hsieh confided in me that he was really not qualified to translate difficult questions in a way that the old lama would completely comprehend, so he asked me to try to use only the simplest manner of speaking.

Unexpectedly, the moment we had paid our formal respects, and without pausing to inquire about the questions I had prepared for him, the lama immediately began to give me teachings. He seemed to have forgotten that our original arrangement had been for me to raise some questions and for him to reply. Although I had made an intensive mental effort to come up with five suitable questions, it seemed as though my questions would not be raised for discussion.

Soon, I was struck by an amazing wonder. The lama's teaching, although not divided up into separate subjects, nevertheless precisely covered all of the topics included in the five questions that I had not yet asked. Not only did he not leave out a single important point contained in my questions, he also did not utter a single word that was not directly related to my five questions. How absolutely astonishing! He could answer people's questions without the need to first hear them say out loud what was on their minds. Could this be none other than an example of mental telepathy? In any case, his abilities became a source of endless surprise for me. The old lama radiated a feeling of extraordinary tranquillity, as though nothing whatsoever were ever out of order. At first Mr. Hsieh was unaware of the close confluence between what the lama had taught and the questions I had not yet asked. Later, when he became aware of this, he too was deeply awed.

Decades later, when I was in India studying Tibetan Buddhism, I met many Tibetans who were skilled at telepathy. I don't think that it's a technique they learn; perhaps it's an inborn gift from Heaven, or maybe they develop it as a result of their meditation and visualization practices. But even in Tibet, I doubt that there are many others like that old lama, who knew at a glance what others were thinking in their minds.

Some time later, the old lama agreed to a request that Elder Brother had been waiting to ask for a long time—that the lama remain in Hong Kong from February through March in order to transmit teachings and give empowerments to more than thirty recluses at the hermitage. On the day of the initiation ceremony, even though I had not attended the complete series of the lama's teachings, because I was a novice practitioner from afar, the lama nevertheless allowed me to receive his empowerment along with the others.

After the ceremony was over, the lama said to me, "You are now an initiated disciple. How do you feel in your heart?" Forcing a smile, I confessed, "Frankly speaking, although I feel deeply grateful for your kindness and compassion, I do not notice any unusual feeling in my heart. That's probably because this is not vacation time at school, and therefore I have not been able to attend all the daily teachings, and since I do not understand Mandarin very well, and my Cantonese is also not very good, I've been unable to gain a deep understanding of the venerable master's profound words." When the old lama heard all that, he smiled and replied, "Your straightforward manner of speaking is highly commendable. Since you have not yet gained a clear comprehension of the teachings, even though you have received initiation you cannot properly practice the Vajrayana path. When I gave you the empowerment, I sowed the seeds of the teachings in your heart. Never doubt that this will have no effect. After twenty or more years have passed in your life, the seeds I planted in your heart today will surely sprout and grow. These are not empty words: in due time, you will see for yourself." (And so it came to pass! Many years later, I had the opportunity to go to India, where I received many esoteric Tibetan teachings and learned many practices from a great Tibetan master in the Himalayan mountains; and it was all due to the initiation and empowerment I had already received many years earlier that I found the teachings I wanted in India so easily.)

A Deliberate Breach of Etiquette

While the lama was giving teachings in Hong Kong, an unexpected situation arose. At the time, the members of the hermitage were divided into two groups—the Eastern Esoteric and the Tibetan. The former continued to participate in the normal activities of the hermitage as before, but the latter gradually stopped practicing the Eastern Esoteric tradition, although it was not until much later that this group established a Tibetan Buddhist center of their own. Fifth Uncle did not part ways with the Eastern Esoteric group. Elder Brother, however, became a founding member of the Tibetan group. Fortunately, both groups were Buddhist, and therefore their relationship always remained harmonious.

One day, I went to Elder Brother's clinic to pay him a visit. He said, "Some people claim that I follow the old-fashioned manners and traditional way of life to an excessive degree. That doesn't matter to me. I like the old ways, and that's all there is to it. But there are also those who say that I am arrogant. Now that is simply not true! How could someone like me, who believes in the doctrine of negating the ego, be arrogant?" I replied, "I know Elder Brother quite well by now, so I can definitely say that you are not at all arrogant. However, if I did not know you so well, then judging by the skullcap, long gown, and jacket that you always wear, and the meticulous manner in which you cling to your old aristocratic airs, I might also think that you were arrogant. In any case, I firmly believe that Elder Brother would prefer to descend to the deepest realms of hell than to make a deliberate breach of etiquette in the presence of others." He replied, "You really know how to misread a person! All right then, please step outside the door with me right now, and you may witness just how strange and far from the norms of proper etiquette my behavior can be in the presence of others!"

When he finished speaking, Elder Brother led me out the door to stand on the sidewalk beside the road. In those days, there were already lots of cars chugging along the streets, with pedestrians bustling back and forth in the traffic. The next thing I saw was Elder Brother hollering loudly at the people in the street, like a lunatic. People stared at him in amazement, and a small crowd gathered, wondering why this skinny gentleman dressed in old-fashioned clothes was standing there yelling at them. Quickly, Elder Brother used both hands to lift up his gown and undershirt, exposing his bare belly for all to see, then he slowly turned around in circles so that everyone watching could get a clear view. After that, he returned to normal and bowed politely with a big smile on his face. The onlookers, who thought that his behavior was very strange indeed, grunted and gradually dispersed.

After we went back into the house, I still felt extremely agitated by his behavior, but Elder Brother did not look the least bit ruffled. He said, "I really love the old-fashioned etiquette. People today pay less and less attention to social propriety, thereby sinking back into the barbarity of animals. When I was young, I received strict training in the rules of etiquette that prevailed among the families of government officials. For example, upon entering a room, one should always step over the threshold with one's left foot first, then advance a few more steps to offer formal greetings to the host. I also learned to whom I should bow my head, to whom I should extend greetings, before whom I should prostrate fully or just bow from the waist or simply nod my head, and so forth. Regardless of how complicated the code of conduct might be, one can never afford to ignore it and thereby invite ridicule from those who understand these things, or give others the mistaken impression that one has not offered them proper respect. After a long time, these customs simply become second nature.

"As the ancient sages taught, 'Manners are useful, but equanimity is the most precious virtue of all.' A moment ago out there on the street, while I was pretending to be crazy, if by chance my behavior had been witnessed by one of my own elders, it would have made them very angry and prompted their strong objections, while I myself would also have felt that I had done something gravely wrong. Nevertheless, although any sort of behavior that violates traditional etiquette is reprehensible, arrogance is far more disgusting. And perhaps there is indeed some validity to what you said about me being arrogant. Therefore, my pretending to be crazy just now had two purposes. First, since I really do sometimes worry that I might become arrogant in my ways, I deliberately did that to expose myself to ridicule in public and invite the scorn of others. Second, I wished to prove to my younger brother from England that I'm really not arrogant at all."

When I heard his explanation, I felt touched by it and said no more, thinking to myself how well my brother reflected the virtues of all three great philosophies of China. Out of respect for Confucian teachings, he treasured formal etiquette; because he followed the Buddhist path, he rejected the illusions of ego in himself and others; and owing to his deep erudition in Taoist philosophy, he refused to be bound by the fetters of conventional thought and lived his life in freedom.

My Passion for Sojourns in Mountain Monasteries

While living in Hong Kong, I moved constantly between two contrasting circles of people. The school where I taught belonged to modern China, while Elder Brother and his group belonged to ancient China. These two groups were very different, and whenever I went over to the mainland, I entered yet a third circle. Fortunately for me, the cost of travel in those days was not at all expensive; trains, buses, inns, hotels, and food and drink were all very cheap. My salary amounted to only ninety Hong Kong dollars per month, and while that was not much, it was enough to cover all my travel expenses, which on average did not exceed two or three dollars a day. (At that time, seventeen Hong Kong dollars was the equivalent of one-pound sterling, or four American dollars.)

What I liked best of all was to stay in mountain monasteries. Most of the Buddhist monasteries and Taoist hermitages throughout China were accustomed to accommodating travelers. In those days, monasteries did not charge a fixed fee for room and board; instead, guests donated as much money as they wished. The most interesting monasteries were those located in the most famous scenic mountains, in settings of exquisite natural beauty, where "the smoke of human habitation is not seen for miles and miles."

I truly appreciate beautiful natural scenery and poetic settings. I like peaceful places, and I feel a deep love for China's endless landscapes, with their rocky cliffs, ancient monasteries, gigantic pines, maple trees, bamboo groves, mountain streams, waterfalls, deep lakes, floating clouds, autumn moons, and other exquisite elements. A line from an ancient Chinese poem notes, "From deep within the silence, a temple bell sounds in the night." In the early morning hours, before the break of dawn, I was often moved by the sound of a temple bell. At sunrise, guests staying at mountain monasteries also heard the tones of chanting, brass cymbals, "wooden fish" percussion,* big drums, and other lovely sounds.

The guest quarters in these mountain monasteries, although rustic, had a certain elegant charm of their own. The pillows were

*A wooden fish is a hollow block of wood carved like a fish, on which monks tap a rhythm with a stick to accompany their chanting.

stuffed with a fragrant wild grass, and this natural aroma helped people fall asleep and enter the dream state. Buddhist monasteries always prepared succulent vegetarian meals for their visitors, while Taoist hermitages provided both meat and vegetable dishes, cooked with wild herbs and other products gathered in the mountain forests. The great variety of tasty mountain delicacies they served was something that city dwellers could not ordinarily obtain. During the summer, guests could sleep outdoors, and at dawn they could watch the golden rays of the rising sun appear over the mountain peaks and witness the magical display of colors in the early morning sky. The joys of a sojourn in the mountains are well expressed in this elegant couplet by the poet Pai Yu-chan: "Pine cones drop to the ground and birds sing beautiful songs / A clear breeze rises and scatters away my dreams." I only wish that I could describe this scenic beauty, and the joyful feelings it evoked, in Chinese verse.

The hermits living in seclusion in the mountains drank tea made from freshly picked tea leaves. After the evening meal, they sat outside on a moonlit terrace to talk and drink their tea, and this gathering was also one of the great pleasures there, especially in the company of monks who no longer felt any worldy attachments, their hearts serene and completely at peace, and their conversations rich with the flavor and feeling of another world.

Ever since the last emperor abdicated the throne, monasteries in China no longer received the Son of Heaven's* generous financial support. Moreover, with all the social upheaval and constant warfare that prevailed throughout China during the time that I was there, life in the monasteries often became very difficult indeed. Wealthy upper-class scholars rarely took monastic vows any more; instead, they studied Buddhism in small privately funded retreats, or else practiced at home in the cities. But despite all this, those who still lived in the old mountain monasteries were not short on eloquence and charm. Their wis-

*Son of Heaven refers to the emperor of China.

dom sprang from nature, and this was the source of that unique flavor found in their words. Furthermore, some of the monks were extremely erudite, such as Master Tai Hsu, and some were great transmitters of the Dharma, such as the venerable monk Hsu Yun and Master Neng Hai. There were also many Buddhist monks and Taoist recluses who, although not educated at schools, had been close personal disciples of great scholars and therefore understood all of the classical texts written since the Han Dynasty (206 BCE–220 CE), and who, by virtue of their own spiritual self-cultivation, had attained a permanent state of tranquility. Some of them had become highly adept at elucidating the most profound mystical principles in the simplest of words.

One day, I was traveling alone in the Lo Fu Mountains in Guangtung province. By that time my Chinese had already progressed beyond the beginner's stage, so when I met Taoist adepts in the mountains and they explained the basic principles of the Tao to me, it was easy for me to understand. One old Taoist hermit told me that the most important point of all is to always maintain a completely carefree state of mind. The old Taoist said that he had begun to study the Tao when he was fourteen years old. His master taught him to pay close attention to all natural phenomena, such as floating clouds, the reflection of the moon in a pond, flowing water, birds, and so forth, and to take these as models for his own behavior. With the sole exception of the human species, no other species of life on earth ever violates the principles of Heaven. Birds and beasts, flowers and trees, all conform to the primordial principle of "flowing with the wind," and they all follow their destinies as decreed by Heaven. Those species never wonder why stormy winds arise; instead they simply delight in the natural world created by Heaven, without wasting an iota of energy trying to change it. For example, if a tree is growing in a heavily shaded spot, it naturally extends its branches and stretches its boughs to reach for sunlight. In order to enjoy the incomparable joy of such a carefree state, humans should take flowers and trees, birds and beasts, as their teachers.

2

The Place I Love Most of All—Peking

Returning to My Homeland of Previous Lifetimes

During my second year in Hong Kong, by a stroke of good fortune I received a letter from my friend Mr. Li in Yulin. His letter contained the best of all possible news for me. In his letter, he said that he remembered how much I wished to find a job on the mainland, and that my most ideal choice of location was Peking. Mr. Li informed me that he had recently heard that the Hopei Academy of Industry in Tienjin was looking for an Englishman to hire as a teacher there, and that he had therefore asked an old friend of his to contact the academy on my behalf. Not only had the director of the academy immediately agreed to hire me, he had also promised to arrange my teaching schedule to my own convenience, in a way that allowed me to spend three nights each week in nearby Peking.

Mr. Li added, "Please forgive me for not being able to arrange your employment entirely in accord with your wishes," referring to my preference to live in Peking, but I felt quite satisfied as it was, and I could hardly wait until August to go there. Although I found it difficult to part with Elder Brother and his friends, time flowed by swiftly, and if I did not take advantage of this opportunity to move to the mainland now, there was no telling when another such chance might present itself. Therefore, I immediately wrote a letter of reply and accepted the job. Shortly before my departure, I swore a formal oath of eternal brotherhood with Yuan-ruo, and pledged him my everlasting allegiance, as an expression of my lifelong loyalty to him.

In the summer of 1935, I left Hong Kong and headed for Peking. First I took the steamboat to Shanghai, then boarded a train there bound for Tienjin. Upon arriving in that city, I immediately reported to the academy to take up my position there. I was received by the director of the academy himself, and he told me that classes did not begin until September, so there was nothing to prevent me from spending the time until then in Peking.

I bid him farewell and immediately hired a cab to take me to the train station. While purchasing my ticket, I felt a wild surge of joy and kept singing to myself, "Today my most beautiful dream comes true, today I will see the Forbidden City,* today I return to my homeland of previous lifetimes." I felt so crazy with joy that I wondered whether I might be endangering myself, but in any case, never again in my whole life did I feel as completely happy as I did then. And most fortunately, upon my arrival there I did not feel the slightest trace of disappointment: each and every thing was exactly as I'd imagined.

I will never forget that day for as long as I live. Peking made me fall in love at first sight. As the train approached the suburbs of the city, I gazed out the window at the tall city walls, guarded by the towers of more than a dozen great gates, and this sight alone, which so clearly reflected that grand, lofty, sublimely elegant architecture that remains unique to China, sufficed to leave me breathless with wonder. After the train entered the city, I noticed that most of the private homes and shop-houses were simple single-story structures constructed of gray brick, and that even the bigger houses of the wealthy did not much impress the eye from the outside. What attracted my attention most of

*The grounds of the imperial palace in Peking are known as the Forbidden City.

all, of course, was the ancient imperial palace in the center of the city: its magnificent grandeur defied all description. Within the grounds of the Forbidden City surrounding the imperial palace stood all sorts of other beautiful buildings, such as the private residences of the royal family, great temples, and so forth.

Both within the Forbidden City as well as elsewhere, the walls of all the temples were painted in a rich purple-red color, and the roofs were covered with brightly enameled tiles. Most private homes and public buildings, however, had a far simpler, more sedate appearance, discreetly enclosed behind plain gray walls, their roofs hidden from view from the street, with only their red lacquered gates and long gray walls visible from the lanes outside. Of course the homes of wealthy families had elaborately crafted pavilions and beautifully decorated rooms, with exquisitely designed courtyards, but one had to enter the inner premises in order to see them. Pedestrians on the streets could hardly imagine the grandeur and beauty that lay behind those plain gray walls. Later on, I had occasion to visit the home of Professor Li, the friend I'd met in Guangshi, so I discovered all of this firsthand.

Ai, today Peking is totally different from the way it was in those years! When the communist party took power there, one of their first acts was to completely dismantle the great city walls, the soaring gate towers, and many of the famous temples, public monuments, and other ancient structures. This was not the violent destruction of the Red Guards, but rather the official policy of the government. Recently I've heard that the government administration has begun to regret these actions and is therefore in the process of repairing many of the architectural treasures that were destroyed, but I'm afraid that most of them can never be restored.

A Handsome Gentleman of Leisure

Upon my arrival in Peking, I took a taxi from the railway station to the address of a private residence located near the An Ting Gate in the northern district of the city. It was the home of Professor's Li's friend, Mr. Yu, who had arranged my job in Tienjin at Mr. Li's request. When I reached the neighborhood, all I could see were two long rows of walls lining both sides of a residential lane that ran east to west, with red lacquered gates spaced equally apart, one gate for each residence. The gatekeeper at the Yu residence led me through two or three interconnected inner courtyards. The place had once been the official residence of a high-ranking minister in the Ching Dynasty, and its old-fashioned decor still had a very elegant and charming appearance.

Mr. and Mrs. Yu were in the midst of a meal when I arrived, so they invited me to sit down and eat with them. In my eager haste to reach Peking that day, I had not taken a bite to eat since getting out of bed that morning, and yet I had not noticed my hunger. But when I saw all those dishes of delicious food on the table, I suddenly realized how empty my stomach felt. However, after eating only a few bites of food, I began to feel ill at ease. The reason for my discomfort was that although Mrs. Yu had not yet finished eating when I arrived, she had already left the table. I soon understood that this was because traditional Chinese etiquette did not permit women to eat at the same table with a male stranger. I regretted that I had not pretended that I had already eaten, but now there was nothing I could do about it.

Mr. Yu said that he wished to introduce me to one of his nephews, so that we could become friends. This fellow's surname was Pu, and his personal name was Lin-ru. He was in his twenties, and he worked as a reporter for a local English newspaper. I learned that Mr. Pu had plenty of leisure time and that he was very eager to practice his English. Mr. Yu noted that if we spent a lot of time together while he showed me the sights, then this would be of benefit to both of us. Naturally I agreed to this proposal without hesitation. So Mr. Yu immediately telephoned his nephew and asked him to come over.

While waiting for Mr. Pu to arrive, Mr. Yu took me for a tour of his residence. All of the rooms faced onto a central courtyard, and all of the doors, windows, and beams had been intricately carved by highly skilled craftsmen, and further decorated with coats of variously colored lacquer. Within the courtyards stood ancient trees, some of them at least three or four hundred years old, and many varieties of chrysanthemum and other potted plants, plus artificial hills and other features. Because it was nearly midsummer, the servants were busy erecting a canopy to shade the main courtyard. There were many large ceramic pots for keeping goldfish, with many different varieties of these fish, and they were among Mr. Yu's most prized possessions. I asked him whether they were very expensive, and he smiled and said, "You better believe they are! Some of these beloved goldfish cost about as much as they would if they were made of solid gold."

Before long Mr. Pu arrived. He was a handsome and carefree young gentleman of splendid appearance, with a clear white complexion, a soft and seductive manner, and an air of refined elegance. He wore a long gown of brightly lustrous white silk, and his black cloth shoes appeared to be made of the finest velvet. As we were introduced and exchanged courtesies, his whole demeanor reflected utmost sincerity and kindness. I could see that having him for a friend could prove very interesting, even though he might perhaps be just a bit too extravagant for me.

He told me that he enjoyed relaxing pastimes, and that one of them was practicing his English, which he wished to improve, and that this was why he so happily agreed to his uncle's plan. From that time onwards, he often accompanied me in leisurely pursuits. In those days I was still only a callow youth. During my days in Hong Kong, I remained under the influence of Elder Brother and Fifth Uncle, even to the point of cultivating the Tao and practicing the teachings, so I had little occasion to indulge in wicked ways. Here in the north, however, I now had a friend who led me into the world of pleasure, and I soon became a young man in fond pursuit of romantic adventure. On the first day we met, he agreed to take me out to find a suitable apartment to use as a residence there. As we took our leave, Mr. Yu told him to bring me to the Yu residence every day for lunch. I wondered how I could possibly accept such hospitality.

I did not wish to spend my time having such long leisurely meals every day, nor was I willing to waste time taking taxis all the way to the northern end of the city, but at that moment all I could think of by way of reply to Mr. Yu was to murmur, "I dare not accept such great kindness." Later, when I explained to Mr. Pu that I was definitely unwilling to go over there every day, and suggested that he telephone his uncle immediately to politely decline his invitation, Mr. Pu looked very surprised and said, "Surely you're joking! My uncle knows perfectly well that we will not come and disturb him very often." So I asked him, "In that case, why did Mr. Yu invite us in the first place? Is that not rather insincere?"

Mr. Pu replied, "You should not say things like that. If we were in fact to go over there every day for lunch, my uncle would most certainly welcome us. So his invitation was definitely sincere. But he knows equally well that we will not go. Who would want to waste so much time, and who would wish to put their elders to so much trouble? Perhaps you foreigners do not understand our Chinese courtesies. Sometimes I also think that all our polite talk is a bit too much, but one cannot say that it is insincere. Courtesy is a legacy that has been handed down to us by our great sages. The sages taught us the paramount importance of sincerity and trust, and thus they said, 'True sincerity on the inside must always be reflected by appropriate behavior on the outside.' Only those who merely make the superficial motions of being polite externally, while remaining devoid of true sincerity internally, may be described as insincere. It is absolutely essential to manifest courteous manners in harmonious accord with the higher principles of Heaven. Thus it is said, 'Etiquette is a ceremonial form of cosmic principles.'"

Today, it is difficult for me to remember the exact words Mr. Pu used to express this idea, but I do remember the way he said it. He could recite by heart many gems of wisdom from the ancient sages, and he often cited them when we discussed the subject of virtue. His talent for this was something that I could never hope to match.

Amusing Distractions at the Tung An Market

Several days later, Mr. Pu took me out to see the unique varieties of goldfish, chrysanthemums, and pigeons that were cultivated only in Peking. At that time, there were over thirty types of pigeon available, more than two hundreds kinds of goldfish, and hundreds of varieties of chrysanthemum. At the various temple festivals that were held there each month, these particular items were always available for sale. In old Peking, there were so many beautiful things to delight the eye and so many leisurely pleasures to amuse the mind that it would be very difficult indeed to describe them all. Among the city's most famous attractions were the many ancient palaces, the fabulous Forbidden City, and other impressive sights such as ancient memorial arches, tall drum towers, and other unusual old architecture. In addition, there were also public parks that had once been the private gardens of emperors, designed and landscaped with the most elegantly refined taste.

Within the city walls were all sorts of places to go for entertainment, such as the famous restaurants and teahouses, brothels and theaters, and so forth, and there were also countless bookshops, antiques dealers, and many vast market places. There was a great variety of theatrical and other performances to see, including Peking Opera, drum playing, bamboo instrument music, story telling, puppet shows, and much more. Most of these things were completely new to me, so I found them all rather exotic, and everything strongly aroused my interest. Of all the many different kinds of pleasure I have enjoyed in my life, none compare with the pleasure I experienced during my early days in Peking.

(Upon returning there once three or four years ago, I found that not a trace of Peking's old imperial splendor still exists. On the first day of that visit, upon returning to my hotel room for the night, I could not help but weep bitterly for what has been lost.)

After leaving the Yu residence together that first day, we headed toward the eastern district, where Mr. Pu introduced me to a rather grandiose apartment building and suggested that I rent a very large studio there. The building had been some sort of important official residence during the previous Ching Dynasty. The rooms and courtyards were all quite magnificent, and even though the furnishings inside were rather plain and simple, they too retained a certain antique charm. The rent was not expensive, all basic services were included, and throughout the day until late at night one could order all kinds of tasty things to eat from nearby teahouses, have hot charcoal delivered for the heater, and enjoy other amenities. After moving in there, I henceforth had two places to live: an apartment in Peking and the academy in Tienjin.

Among the many places I went for amusement with Mr. Pu was the Tung An Market. This place was chock full of bookshops, restaurants, tearooms, and little stalls that sold a wide range of various and sundry products. All of the tearooms there staged theatrical performances, such as Shanhsi folk music, drum recitals, and other forms, in order to draw customers into the premises. Spending only a few coins, one could enjoy oneself in these places for two or three hours. The restaurants in large markets like this were very inexpensive: for twenty or thirty cents one could buy a simple but delicious meal. If one wished to try some of the famous dishes from other regions of China, or Russian food, or Western pastries, these too were all available there at reasonable cost. The academy paid me a salary of two hundred dollars a month, which at that time was considered to be no small amount, especially since I did not have a family to support, so whatever I wished to buy and whatever I wanted to do were all well within my means. As for Mr. Pu, in addition to his salary, he also had abundant income from other sources, so regardless of what happened, he never seemed to be short of money to spend.

In those days, the residents of Peking were still relatively wealthy. By contrast, the farmers in the countryside suffered all sorts of natural catastrophes, frequent warfare, and the evil oppression of Japanese invaders from the eastern sea. As a result, swarms of refugees came to take shelter in the city, and most of them were extremely poor. Other than these refugees, however, the average inhabitant of the city seemed to be quite prosperous and enjoyed all kinds of entertainment, while also doing brisk business in their shops. My dear reader, please note that my own impressions of Peking's economic situation in those days contrasts sharply with the view described by Chinese novelists at that time. Perhaps the reason for this difference is that popular writers then tended to focus more on themes of social injustice and to dwell on the shortcomings of society. In those days, very few writers supported the status quo in China, and while their indignant criticism of unjust social conditions certainly had just grounds, it nevertheless seems to me that their point of view was perhaps a bit overly biased. I was a foreign observer without any ulterior motives, and although my point of view may have been mistaken, at least I remained open and impartial.

Infatuated by a Singsong Girl

After getting to know Mr. Pu for a while, I noticed that he loved to go to a particular, rather ordinary looking tearoom in the Tung An Market. The place was located upstairs above a bakery. Within this spacious room there was a small stage for dancing and many wooden tables and stools, with all the seats arranged to face the stage. The only things that guests here could order were tea, watermelon seeds, and a few other simple snacks. Unlike the teahouses in southern China, which featured all sorts of delicious dishes, this little tearoom attracted customers mainly with musical performances and various other stage acts.

With one hand tapping bamboo chocks and the other beating little drums, the girls onstage accompanied themselves in rhythm as they acted out plays based on ancient tales, using facial expressions and body language to vividly convey the thoughts and feelings of the characters in the stories, and adapting their tunes and lyrics to describe the strange twists and startling turns of events as the stories unfolded. The first time I witnessed this form of storytelling, I felt deeply moved by the performers' skills. These girls possessed truly excellent theatrical talent! Although I did not understand the lyrics to their songs, I nevertheless fully appreciated the marvelous skill of their performances. Alas, the payment they received for this work amounted to a mere pittance, and therefore they had little choice but to also sell their bodies in order to make ends meet.

At first I thought it was Mr. Pu's interest in musical performances that drew him to this place so often, but before long I realized that the real reason he frequented this particular tearoom was because he had taken a fancy to a singsong girl named "Little Jade." Indeed, one could say that he had become completely infatuated by this girl. One evening, he decided to take Little Jade out to spend the night with him, but because I was his "guest from afar," he felt that allowing me to go home alone that night would constitute a breach of etiquette, and so he suggested that I too select a female companion to accompany me back to my place for some fun. No way! It was not that there was any shortage of attractive singsong girls to choose from, but rather that as far as they were concerned, I was just like a mute. Having arrived in Peking only a few days earlier, how on earth could I possibly speak Mandarin yet? And how could someone who was unable to communicate with a young lady possibly win her heart?

As soon as my friend Pu heard this explanation, his face fell, and it appeared as though he might get angry. Afraid that he would disdain me as a killjoy, I quickly changed my mind and casually selected a girl. To our surprise, she laughed and ridiculed us, and firmly declared that she had no intention of going out with us. She said, "Who would want to become intimate with a foreign devil?" That was the first time I had ever been directly designated as a "foreign devil," although in Hong Kong I had often overheard passers-by use the term "barbarian devil" in general reference to me and all other Westerners. Such talk did not make me angry. After all, I thought, Westerners often use similar terms in reference to people of different races, and therefore I could not blame Chinese people for this habit.

Finally, my friend Pu and Little Jade accompanied me back to my apartment building. However, the landlord was not willing to rent them a room for just one night, and so the two of them bade me farewell and went elsewhere. The next day, Pu apologized for causing me such inconvenience. I told him that henceforth he should no longer regard me as a "guest," and that instead I wanted him to treat me as an old friend. Thereafter, although we sometimes disagreed about things, we always managed to swiftly restore a harmonious relationship.

My First Encounter with a Eunuch

Since arriving in the East, I gradually became ever more accustomed to Asian ways, thanks to the influence of my Chinese friends, but still it was not always easy for me to abandon some of my peculiar Western habits, such as resistance to compromise and refusal to defer to friends. Fortunately, the Chinese readily forgive foreigners for their personal idiosyncrasies, and since Mr. Pu no doubt still viewed me as a half-baked barbarian, he usually tolerated my blunders.

Nevertheless, sometimes my stubborn obstinacy became so overblown that it stretched Mr. Pu's patience with me to the limit. One day, we went to Central Park to view the peony blossoms that were just coming into bloom. I became so deeply entranced admiring their beauty that for a long time I was unwilling to leave and remained riveted to my seat in a small tea pavilion, gazing at the smiling flowers as my soul wandered in rapture among them. While sipping my tea, I noticed an old man stroll by. With his flabby physique, face full of wrinkles, and flaccid muscles drooping down, he looked like an old crone but was dressed in male clothing. My friend Pu remarked that this must surely be a eunuch. He said that during the latter years of the Ching Dynasty, there were at least a thousand or more eunuchs serving in the imperial palace, and that this was an avenue to public prestige for anyone who wished to take this route. Although their status within the palace was quite low, eunuchs nevertheless exercised considerable power, and if they managed to gain the emperor's favor, their position could rise very rapidly indeed. Therefore, ever since ancient times, there was never a shortage in the capital of poor people happily willing to become eunuchs.

After his abdication of the throne, the last emperor Hsuan Tung was at first permitted to continue living in customary comfort in the palace, but a few years later, he was driven out of the imperial palace by General Feng Yu-hsiang and had to move his residence to the foreign concession in Tienjin. There he dwelled in ordinary living quarters, and even though it was quite spacious, there was not enough room to accommodate his large retinue of eunuchs. More than a thousand of them suddenly found themselves without a job, and without anyone to provide them with support. Is this not truly a pity?

That day was the first time I had ever seen this kind of person. Observing that old man made me think of the empress dowager* and recall several books I'd read as a child, in which the authors recorded eyewitness accounts of the empress Tze Hsi.

One of the authors had served in the empress dowager's court after the Boxer Rebellion.† This author felt certain that the old empress was not lacking in virtues, and that it was due entirely to slander from others that she became disliked by later generations. I raised this point with my friend Pu, and furthermore stated that the only reason the Ching Dynasty suffered defeat was because its army and navy were no match for the modern new weaponry of the foreign powers, and therefore China had no way of resisting the rapacious aggression of the Western powers. This disastrous situation could certainly not be blamed upon the Manchu emperor, so how on earth could the empress dowager be responsible for it?

---

*Tze Hsi Tai Hou was the empress regent during the reign of the last Ching Dynasty emperor and wielded effective control of China for many years. One of the best accounts of her reign and colorful personal life is *China Under the Empress Dowager* by E. Backhouse and J. O. Bland.

†The Boxer Rebellion (1898–1900) was a violent uprising by the Chinese people to rid their country of foreigners. It was led by military units in the north called *Yihe Quang* (righteous harmony fists).

Perhaps my point of view sounded too biased, for my old friend Pu just smiled coldly without replying, and he looked a bit annoyed. At this point, it would have been best for me to say no more, but at the time I had not yet cultivated the Chinese attitude of humility, so instead I insisted on defending my opinion. I thus continued to heap praise on the Ching Dynasty, particularly the Kang Hsi and Chien Lung emperors.* Pu just sneered and remained silent. Now I too became annoyed, so I deliberately praised the empress dowager by saying, "You want to know why the old empress did not wish to reform China? Because she treasured China's highly refined civilization, and she regarded the Western powers who were trying to destroy China as uncivilized tyrants. How could she possibly agree to accept so-called science and other things from such barbarians? When you look at it from this point of view, doesn't the empress dowager's attitude seem very reasonable?"

To this day, I still believe that the empress dowager's reactions to the situation she faced had their own rational logic, but regardless of my own views, I should not have offended my old friend Pu. At the time, I was still just a foreigner who had recently arrived in China, so how could I be so shameless as to debate the finer points of Chinese history with a Chinese? No wonder then that he was unable to contain his anger and gave me a scolding! While we were in the midst of a loud debate on the issue, Pu suddenly burst out laughing, and with a big smile on his face, he said, "Enough, enough! It's best that each of us just follow his own way."

---

*The Ching Dynasty was unpopular in the minds of ethnic Han Chinese such as Blofeld's friends because it was a Manchu dynasty, i.e., a "foreign" dynasty. The Manchus were from the northern steppes of Manchuria, and like the Mongols, they were foreigners, not part of the Chinese "Han" ethnic tribe. When the Manchus conquered the Ming Dynasty in 1644 they became, by definition, a "foreign dynasty" but, like the Mongols who ruled China before the Ming, they soon became assimilated in the cauldron of Chinese culture.

However, China reached its zenith of peace and prosperity under the Manchu Ching Dynasty, particularly under the long enlightened reigns of the Kang Hsi and Chien Lung emperors in the seventeenth and eighteenth centuries.

Ai! Such generosity of spirit is so rare; indeed, the Chinese are the only people on earth in whom it's a common virtue. The way he suddenly changed his attitude instantly touched my heart. Grasping both of his hands in apology, I thought to myself, "The wisdom of the Chinese way is truly difficult to surpass. When a friend gets angry with me and yet is still able to give me a happy smile, this most certainly cannot be regarded as a false courtesy. This reflects the utmost sincerity and tolerance; this is the authentic legacy of etiquette bequeathed to the Chinese by their great sages. And this example clearly illustrates how effective it can be as a foundation for harmonious social relations!"

The Charm and Grace of Peking Women

A few days later, I had the good fortune to meet Pu's cousin, Mr. Heng Dao-Nu. It was an unbearably hot summer day, and Pu had taken me for a row in a boat on the lake at the Bei Hai Park. We had just lifted our oars to float idly under the cool shade of an ancient tree, when suddenly we saw someone sitting on the shore reading a book, and Pu shouted out to him, "Third Cousin, who would have thought that you too had come here to relax!" He then invited him to come aboard our boat.

Mr. Heng was an exuberant young man about thirty years of age, smartly dressed. He wore a white silk shirt with a high collar and long sleeves that covered his slender fingers all the way down to the knuckles. On one side of the fine gauze fan he held in his hand was painted an elegant black-ink landscape; on the other side, were inscribed four large ideograms: "The Virtues of a Cool Breeze." He very politely asked me how I liked Bei Hai. In a tone ringing with boundless praise, I replied, "I daresay that in all the realms under Heaven, there could not possibly be a more beautiful park than this."

And that truly reflected the way I felt about the place.

Bei Hai lake lay just outside the western wall of the imperial palace, and it was a favorite leisure spot of the empress dowager, Tze Hsi Tai

Hou, who used to come here often to relax. Her imperial boat could still be seen floating in the lake's limpid water. In all four directions, wherever one looked were ancient cassia trees, among which stood exquisitely ornate pavilions, with balustrades and zigzag bridges made of snow-white stone. Lotus blossoms bloomed profusely everywhere, and their subtle fragrance wafted lightly on the breeze, penetrating to the depths of one's heart. Bei Hai's most distinctive feature was a magnificent white Tibetan-style pagoda, which soared up from the top of a man-made mountain on a small island in the lake. The slopes of this mountain were riddled with many caves and ribboned with half-hidden stairways, making the whole mountain look like a beehive.

The three of us rowed the boat across to the northern shore, where we disembarked and went to eat stuffed buns at the Wu Lung [Five Dragon] Pavilion, which had a beautiful roof of brightly colored enamel tiles. The place was crowded with customers, mostly men and very few women. I asked my friends why so few women from good families ever came out for recreation, and why even fewer were ever seen strolling along with male companions. After giving it some thought, Mr. Heng replied, "In the past, there were even fewer women to be seen in the street than now. Today, however, you will sometimes see female students from Yan Ching and Ching Hwa universities walking alongside young men. Unfortunately, these two universities are run by Americans, and most of the students there come from the southern provinces. So many young people from the south are unruly and lacking in good manners. They advocate radical reform of our ancient code of etiquette, and without the least concern for the consequences, they destroy all of our old customs. However, we Peking people remain polite and modest, and our women still maintain traditional propriety. Do you not agree that this is a very good thing?"

I clearly understood that Mr. Heng was adjusting his attitude to take into consideration my feelings as a foreigner. His real intention was to condemn Western ways, but his actual words evaded this point by berating southerners instead. This sort of careful attention not to offend a foreigner definitely reflected the sort of behavior stipulated by ancient Chinese etiquette.

Chinese men most certainly do not pretend to not indulge in carnal desire, and they do not feel that visiting professional houses of pleasure constitutes any sort of violation of morality, but they demand that the women in their own households strictly uphold their moral virtue. At that time, although there were some men who advocated the idea of complete equality between men and women, the laughable fact of the matter was that the overwhelming majority of women deeply feared this suggestion. After marriage, if a husband were to invite his wife to go out for a walk together, side-by-side in public, a woman who wished to maintain traditional family propriety would almost certainly refuse such a display of "lax moral behavior fostered by foreign devils." If their husbands persisted in asking them to adopt such Western customs, these young wives would only feel all the more embarrassed, and would still refuse to accompany their husbands out in public places.

My friends Heng and Pu firmly believed that the women of Peking were not willing to abandon the old customs. I asked them whether relatively modern young women were also like this after marriage. The two of them looked at each other for a long while before Pu replied, "That's hard to say. My cousin and I are not acquainted with that sort of modern girl. None of the women in the families of any of our friends has ever attended a school to study. Our spouses need only be able to read some novels and understand a bit of Tang poetry,* and that is sufficient. You may ask my Third Cousin to confirm if that is not indeed correct."

Mr. Heng said, "What you say is quite correct. For example, my and my brothers' wives are all women with very little formal education. All of them get along very well with their husbands, but they do not necessarily take much interest in their husbands' discussions. No doubt

*The Tang Dynasty has always been regarded by the Chinese as their "Golden Age" of poetry, and children in good families learned to recite the most famous poems by heart from an early age.

they love to listen to the endless chatter of their maids, but they don't much appreciate the casual conversation of us men. Although that's the way it is, you should not assume that they are ignorant women. As far as doing women's work, managing household affairs, and raising children are concerned, they are all well qualified and very capable. Toward their husbands, by which I mean us brothers, they harbor no dissatisfaction. Our family's background and reputation are quite good, our income is sufficient, and our temperament is easygoing and friendly, so there is nothing that causes our spouses to feel annoyed. Most important of all, we husbands and our wives are always happy and willing to help each other. If something important happens, or we encounter some sort of difficulty, both of us unite our efforts to deal with it."

Mr. Heng continued, "Judging from what I've seen in films, you foreigners place great value on the idea of everlasting love. However, that which lasts forever is extremely rare, and it is not necessarily ours to own. I'm afraid that what's known as 'being in love' is nothing more substantial than a fantasy. What's really important is family tradition, family discipline, family legacy, and family property. The purpose of marriage is not to fulfill personal romance, but rather to insure family welfare and family fortune. Lin-ru, how do you feel about this?"

With a sigh of approval, Pu replied, "What Third Cousin says is absolutely true. I myself have never given much thought to these matters, but I think that what you've just said is not the least bit incorrect." Mr. Heng smiled and said to me, "My cousin's wife is a Manchu aristocrat, which means that she could have become a cherished favorite of the emperor himself. If the emperor still occupied the imperial throne, how could she possibly be willing to become Lin-ru's wife? Who knows whether or not she might have become an empress, or perhaps a precious concubine? Someone like her obviously does not need to waste a lot of time and energy acquiring a heap of learning. All that's required is that she knows how to make herself flawlessly beautiful, that her demeanor is always demure, and that her reputation remains unblemished, and that's enough." Only when I heard these words did I realize that although Pu despised the empress dowager, his own wife was also a Manchu woman. Moreover, while I thought that I knew him quite well, this was the first time I heard that, despite his attentions to Little Jade, he was already married.

While continuing our discussion of these matters, we rowed from Wu Ling Pavilion back to the little wharf at the foot of the mountain of the white pagoda, and after paying the entrance fee, we strolled toward the gate into the park. As we stood upon the cloud-white stone bridge admiring the dense greenery of the lotus leaves, Pu remarked, "Of course it's fine to marry an educated woman, but it's best if she has not received her education at a university, because the female students at universities today develop a lot of habits that women should not have. In my own family, we have a number of women whose calligraphy is beautiful to behold, and who also know how to compose poetry, and all of them know how to win a man's heart as well." I nodded in silence. Even though I felt that these two friends of mine were excessively conservative, I also realized that their opinions reflected the point of view held by traditionalists in those days.

Toward the end of the day, the three of us took a motorcab to Ha Ta Gate Street, where we went to a Greek cafe to try the candied fruits. I still wanted to hear more about family affairs in traditional households, so I asked, "Both of you are well-educated scholars; how is it possible that you do not feel bored with half-literate women? This is something that I find difficult to understand."

With a slight sigh, Pu replied, "*Ai ya,* you just cannot stop talking about that. I tell you truly, if a husband and wife become too familiar with each other, it can easily result in an attitude of mutual disdain and cause them to take one another for granted, and consequently communication between them grows ever more uninteresting. Rather than always discussing everything with one's spouse, it's much better to go out and find a courtesan for amusement. Best of all is to visit a high-class house of pleasure; the courtesans there are very well versed in the art of irony and sarcastic conversation. And if you want them to adopt a seductive manner, then that is precisely what they will do for you." Pu continued, "Or if you prefer that a courtesan be serene and silent, then that is exactly how she will be for you."

Mr. Heng agreed entirely. We spoke for a while longer, then he invited us to join him the following evening to eat crepes at a place outside the main city gate, after which we would go to a "blue house" for some fun. Pu explained that crepes were a favorite food for northerners during the heat of summer, and that "blue house" was a euphemism for a brothel.

A Visit to a Singsong House

The following evening, the three of us went out for dinner at a small restaurant along the big boulevard by the main city gate. After dinner, we took a motorcab through a maze of small lanes where all around I heard the sounds of endless laughter and conversation commingled with the cacophony of voices shouting out "goods for sale," songs being sung, and music playing. All along the sidewalks there were snack food vendors and stands where blind musicians played music to beckon customers. The houses on both sides of the street were mostly of the two-storied residential type, each one with an auspicious literary name engraved on a panel over the gate, and the professional names of the resident prostitutes inscribed on elegant signboards hanging beside the doors, names such as Cassia, Belle, Moon Lover, and so forth.

After a long ride, the cab stopped before a gate over which hung a panel inscribed with three large characters: "The House of Spring Rites." Following my two friends inside, I could not suppress a growing sense of curiosity, but I also worried that my Chinese language skills would prove insufficient to really appreciate the entertainment offered there. My friend Heng was a frequent and familiar patron of this establishment, so it was not necessary for us to go into the front parlor first to select girls. Instead, we were taken directly upstairs and seated in a private room. The furnishings included an Eight Immortals* table with matching chairs carved of solid teakwood, as well as a few curtained couch-beds. An old crone came in and announced, "Number Eight will be here shortly." Meanwhile, a couple of pretty young maids, whose mode of dress and manners were all strictly in accordance with the old customs, served us tea and snacks.

Soon two young ladies with rouged faces entered the room and paid their respects. Turning to face my friend Heng, they said, "Lord and master, you have arrived. Number Eight will be here in a moment to accompany you; meanwhile, we have come first to represent her." Heng introduced them to us, but he did not use their real names. All he said was, "Number Five, Number Nine, these gentlemen are old friends of mine, Master Chen and Master Pu." He then explained to me in English that if I liked one of these girls, I could henceforth become her regular client at this house, and the same applied to his cousin Chen, who, like me, was also here for the first time. Otherwise, we should go out to the front parlor and select another girl. He said that once we'd made our choice, it was completely out of the question to ever select any other girl at this establishment. From now on, if we wished to switch over to another pair of bewitching eyes, we would have to go to another establishment.

I didn't really care, because I felt that the language barrier would make communication very difficult, so it didn't matter who I selected. All the women in those singsong houses were charming and beautiful, but I felt convinced that all of them would regard me as a mute.

Suddenly Number Eight arrived. With her splendidly seductive poses and her sparkling conversation, she lit up my friends' faces with happy laughter. Unfortunately, I could only listen without understanding. What caught my attention the most as these two men and one woman talked and laughed together with such gusto was the extraordinary pleasure they so

*The Eight Immortals are legendary Taoist sages, and such a table would have eight sides, a number that is also auspicious because it corresponds to the eight trigrams of the I Ching (Book of Change).

obviously derived from each other's company. Moreover, as far as their attitude and behavior were concerned, both the men and the women treated one another with impeccable courtesy, just as though they were having a conversation in a respectable home. I never imagined that "roaming the pits"* could be such an innocent pastime.

The door to the room remained open the entire time, covered by a curtain that was frequently swept aside by serving girls as they brought more food and drinks to our table. Number Nine was specifically assigned to take care of me. While we both tried our best to feign pleasure, in fact we both felt quite frustrated. After a while, she took my right hand and pressed it against hers a few times to compare size; pretending to be astonished, she loudly exclaimed, "Your hands are really huge!" I appreciated her good intentions and empathized with her inability to make me enjoy myself. Perhaps my friend Heng noticed my discomfort, for suddenly he stood up and said, "Let's be on our way!"

Immediately the old crone appeared, and with a swift sidelong glance she counted the number of plates and saucers on the table. As in the tea shops, that's how bills were calculated in this sort of establishment. Throughout the evening, while the three of us had sat there accompanied by the courtesans, serving girls were coming and going every few minutes, bringing plates of melon seeds, fruits, and other snacks. During the hour that we spent there, twelve plates had accumulated on our table. At twenty-five cents per plate, our bill came to three dollars. In those days, an average clerk's monthly salary was about thirty dollars, so obviously three dollars was no small amount to spend. However, when you take into consideration all the beauty and talent those girls displayed for us, and all the pleasure we derived from their company, plus the cost of their elegant clothing, as well as the food and drinks on the table and the expensive furniture in the room, three dollars was definitely not a bad deal. Later I learned that the price for spending the whole night there was six dollars per person.

---

*"Roaming the pits," or *guang yao-dze,* is a Chinese slang term for visiting brothels.

That evening my friend informed me that the clients who patronized the courtesans in these high-class houses were not lacking in basic human kindness and social courtesy. A customer had to become a particular courtesan's regular patron for quite a long time before actually going to bed with her. So even if their feelings for each other did not run very deep, at least it was a lot better than having sexual relations with a complete stranger. Furthermore, if a particular high-class courtesan disliked a particular customer who was courting her, she retained the right to refuse a sexual relationship with him. My friend asked me whether bordellos in foreign countries also had such rules. I replied with alarm, "God in Heaven, how would I know? When I left England, I was just an innocent youth. How could I be familiar with such things?"

Perhaps my contemporary readers might think that my friends should not have taken me to a singsong house for entertainment, but back in those days Chinese men did not think this way. Traditional Chinese values strongly stressed the importance of protecting the chastity of young women, especially in good families, but the Chinese also realized the fact that young men have an intensely powerful sexual drive that could sometimes become uncontrollable and therefore needed to somehow be released. Besides, in the old society, singsong houses also served a function other than sex.

While there were always those virtuous individuals who never set foot in a bordello throughout their entire lives, most males, regardless of whether they were married or single, were accustomed to taking their friends to these places for entertainment. Among the courtesans were those who excelled in clever conversation, singing songs, playing the lute or zither, and even some who could compose poetry. Therefore, even university professors, government officials, and others who were conscious of their public images felt absolutely no qualms about breaking up into small groups after a dinner party or reception and going out to a singsong house for further entertainment. One should not view such behavior as being bawdy. In those days, the women in good families did not participate in the entertainment of male guests in the house, much less sing songs and play music for them, and so forth. The moment the women in such households heard that their fathers, husbands, or brothers had brought a male visitor home, they immediately scattered and hid themselves away from view. Consequently, if a host wished to take his guests somewhere to enjoy female company, the only place to go was a singsong house.

An Old Couple's Love Grows Stronger with Age

I soon learned that in the traditional Chinese family system it was not until a couple reached old age that the ideal relationship of mutual intimacy and companionship between husband and wife began to manifest itself. During their younger years, most couples did not see very much of each other in their daily lives. It was only when they reached middle and old age that husband and wife became close companions. Mr. Heng tried to convince me that this was a normal and proper development in marriage. He said, "Passionate love does not last very long. True love between husband and wife grows like an evergreen tree: it develops surely but slowly and lasts forever." He then cited his own parents as an example to illustrate his point. His father was sixteen or seventeen years old when he married, and his mother was only fifteen. As a young man, his father was very fond of consorting with courtesans and pursuing romantic pleasures of the night, and though his mother felt hurt by his behavior, there was nothing she could do about it. After reaching middle age, both of them began to feel much closer to one another, and thereafter a very strong bond of conjugal love gradually grew between them. As his father got older, he took less and less interest in managing family affairs, and instead he let his wife make all the decisions. As time went by, the two of them became as harmoniously tuned as the strings of a lute, while his mother handled all the external matters to which his father became increasingly inattentive.

Mr. Heng's description of the deep matrimonial bond between

his parents moved my heart. However, I still reserved a few doubts about the old-fashioned Chinese family system. From time to time, the English language newspaper Pu worked for reported cases of family abuse against young wives. Mr. Heng often told me that family traditions arose from the teachings of the great sages and were of benefit to old and young alike. My only reservation about all this was the possibility that a father or husband could easily abuse his male authority within a family household.

One day, as we were discussing this point, he acknowledged that in fact both men and women sometimes abused their positions within the family. In small family households, if the husband's mother disliked his new wife, the wife's life became very difficult indeed, but in the larger households of big extended families, family affairs were very rarely under the control of one particular individual. He cited the example of his own family, in which there were six unmarried girls, four mature married women, and several wives who were still quite young, plus some chambermaids and many young servant girls, and none of them were subject to any sort of unbearable pressures. The family elders in particular were all very kind and friendly people, and the whole household echoed from morning till night with their endless chatter, as though there were a flock of ducks in every courtyard. Except for the ancestral shrine room, the only quiet room in the house was the library.

Most of the older men in the family kept busy with their work, while everyone else—male and female, young and old—spent most of their time in pursuit of pleasure. Under these circumstances, women very rarely suffered humiliation or abuse from men, and husbands hardly ever interfered in the affairs of their spouses. This sort of separation did not in any way diminish the mutual love between husband and wife, but rather enhanced it. If a couple were to spend the entire day together, it would inevitably cause them to sink slowly but surely into a state of mutual boredom. No matter what, passionate love never lasts long, so if newlyweds remain excessively attached and inseparable, they can easily become disillusioned and dissatisfied later. On the other hand, if a couple only sees each other at night, not only will this preserve their conjugal love, even their carnal desire for one another will last much longer.

Mr. Heng spoke on about this with great enthusiasm, very pleased with his own explanation. He said, "Frankly speaking, I generally don't like most foreigners, but I am very fond of you. We all know very well that you have respect for Chinese people who have not allowed themselves to become westernized. You have not come here to promote your so-called scientific civilization. You are a modest young man. You are a very special sort of Westerner that we Chinese very rarely encounter. And because I like you so much, I want to make sure that you don't get the wrong impression of our humble nation's culture and society. Therefore, since we are now discussing the topic of family tradition, I want you to clearly understand just how precious our ancient family traditions really are. Ordinarily, Chinese people never discuss the personal feelings between husband and wife with outsiders, but in this case, I'm going to tell you some of my most private family matters, in order to illustrate the foundation of our family traditions."

I lowered my eyes, not daring to say a word, and listened intently. Mr. Heng continued, "On the surface, Pan [his wife's name] and I share very few interests in common. She loves to play *ma-jiang*.* And anyone who wishes to become her friend must have some special qualifications, such as a thorough familiarity with all the complex strategies of ma-jiang, and a detailed knowledge regarding the personal histories of the world's most famous movie stars, including the names of all their former lovers, who was whose eighth husband or ninth wife, and so forth. Now isn't that rather annoying?

"Sometimes I really feel like discussing certain matters with her, but I'm always afraid that it would interfere with one of her ma-jiang games, and so I simply refrain from asking her. She too is afraid that her

*Ma-jiang (mahjong) is a favorite game in Chinese households, and plays much the same role as bridge in Western society. Played with tiles and dice, ma-jiang games can sometimes continue for two or three days running.

extravagant personal interests might drive me crazy. I dare not provoke her, and she feels she cannot afford to offend me, so what can we do? All we can do is agree that prior to bedtime, neither of us will demand any sort of social contact with the other! But despite this situation, we are nevertheless regarded as a model husband and wife. Ever since our first night together in the wedding chamber five or six years ago, when our eyes met in an expression of our mutual devotion and lifelong loyalty to one another, until today, the feelings we hold for each other in our hearts have not changed. My dear Pu, do you understand what I mean?" I could only shake my head back and forth in reply.

Mr. Heng smiled and said, "Within the basic context of our immutable loyalty and devotion, we do of course also feel romantic love and carnal passion for one another, but the two aspects are very different. The basic foundation of our relationship also does not preclude my private extramarital affairs, our selfish interests, and other flaws of this sort. Such things are decreed by fate and are closely connected with one's family background, ancestry, and descendants. Foreign couples are so strange, and their relationship is so lamentable. Their sole concern is to cling to the personal emotion that they call "love" (that most fleeting, blind, and vague emotion), and thus they choose to live all alone as an individual couple, isolated from everyone else. They stay together day and night, and eventually this causes them to grow tired of one another. Their children too are to be pitied, for they are deprived of that special affection and comfort that only grandfathers can provide. And where are the old aunties, the grannies, and other relations to prepare tasty snacks for them, and take them out to play? Where are all the siblings and cousins to serve as their playmates?"

Although I was nearly persuaded by his reasoning, I still could not resist mentioning an important point of dissent, and so I said, "I quite agree, and I have always felt a sense of regret that in my own childhood I could not be part of a large extended family household. However, China also has its small nuclear families. Just recently I read a short story called 'A History of Laughter,' written by Chu Tze-ching, and similar stories often appear in the newspapers, describing the bitter tribulations suffered by new brides in Chinese families. In these stories, the role of the 'villain' is always played by a cruel and despicable mother-in-law."

Mr. Heng thought this over for a while before replying, "Yes, I'm afraid this sort of thing happens quite often. But frankly, since almost all of my close friends come from large extended families, I don't discuss this aspect with them very often."

A moment later, he suddenly asked me, "And you? Why have you not yet married?"

This time, it was I who had to pause and think awhile before responding, and I came up with quite a long list of reasons.

First, a young Englishman of twenty-two years definitely did not feel that marriage was a pressing matter. Second, I still felt a very strong urge to explore the mountains and river ways of China, and I did not wish to be held back by the obligations of family life. Third, I hoped to marry a Chinese as my wife, and in those days it was still extremely rare to find girls from good families who were willing to marry a Westerner. Fourth, above and beyond these three reasons, and much deeper yet, was the fact that my father would never permit such a marriage. If I were to inform him of my intention to marry a Chinese girl, the old man would surely feel deeply hurt. Even though I was not a particularly filial son, I would not do something as dishonorable as that.

Upon hearing my fourth reason, Mr. Heng expressed his complete agreement, and said, "Excellent! Your filial piety has earned you my utmost admiration. Now I'm certain that our ancestors will thank us for helping you to become a true Chinese convert."

Romantic Charms of the Four Seasons

At the time that I was just getting acquainted with Pu, Mr. Heng, and other friends, it was the middle of a scorching hot summer, and the seasonal heat was overwhelming.

In the courtyards of most households, high mat awnings were erected to provide a cover of shade. The poles that supported these awnings stood higher than the roof, allowing the awnings to block the sunlight without obstructing the free flow of air below. Early every morning, most of the city's residents flocked to public parks that had formerly been imperial gardens in order to enjoy the cool air and view the flowers. The blossoms that appealed most to the eye were the peonies, which came in countless varieties. During the peak of the peony season, the railways offered special discount train tickets to encourage people from the countryside to come to the city and savor the beauty of these flowers. I heard that for hundreds of years the imperial family had been carefully cultivating and improving the qualities of the peony blossom, gradually developing many new varieties of exquisite beauty, shape, and color that had never existed before. After the peak of the peony season had passed, there were still all sorts of other beautiful flowers formerly cultivated within the imperial gardens to be appreciated, including the lovely lotus blossoms that bloomed so profusely in Peking's six lakes.

The clothing worn by the men and women, young and old, who came to enjoy the flowers was as colorful as the blossoms. Most of the men wore long silk gowns of white, light green, or sky blue color, while the women were dressed in *chi-pao** gowns of delicate silk brocades, or short silk jackets and long pants, all in rainbow colors. Some of the older people carried birdcages, while others held slender ebony tobacco pipes that were so long that they needed to bring young servant boys with them to light their pipes for smoking.

Sometimes I arose very early in order to accompany my friends among the crowds who went to enjoy the cool morning air, and to drink tea in the ornate pavilions in the parks, or to view the myriad varieties of goldfish on display in huge ceramic urns. I was told that

*Also known as *cheong-sam*, these elegant hip-hugging dresses were designed on the model of traditional gowns worn by Manchu women during the Ching Dynasty.

there were at least three or four hundred different species of goldfish in the hundreds of ceramic fish jugs that were scattered among the potted plants or placed beside the pomegranate trees and bamboo groves.

Peking had so many pleasant attractions that every Sunday afternoon, when it came time for me to return to work in Tienjin for four days, I always felt reluctant to leave. My life in Tienjin was also not at all unpleasant, however. Although it was no royal palace, the teachers' dormitory at the Hopei Academy of Industry was comfortable enough. The teachers who resided at the academy all did their best to treat me with kindness and respect. If it was difficult for them and me to cultivate a closer relationship as confidantes, that was only because their interests were focused not on literature and calligraphy but rather on industry, not on the grandeur of ancient culture but rather on the troubles of contemporary times. My contact with the students there was the same: although they treated me very well, not a single student established a close friendship with me during my entire two-year tenure there. Because they felt so deeply concerned about the present dangers facing their nation and the cruel aggression from Japan, they sometimes boycotted classes in conjunction with the students at other schools in northern China, and participated in large public demonstrations to vent their anger. Their dark-blue school uniforms looked very similar to those worn by students in Japan ever since the Meiji Restoration.* In China, wearing this sort of modern uniform had originally represented a deliberate break with the traditional Chinese system of education. I, however, loved wearing the traditional style of Chinese clothing, complete with short jacket worn over a long gown, as though I were an old-fashioned Chinese professor.

Some of the students liked me for being a Westerner who preferred to wear traditional Chinese attire, while others regarded me as an oddity. One time, just before class, I was afraid that I would be late, so I started running in my long gown. An elderly teacher saw me doing

*The Meiji Restoration in 1868 marked the beginning of the modern era in Japan.

this and said, "A teacher should always remain dignified and unhurried. If you are so fond of wearing Chinese clothes, then you should also observe traditional Chinese manners, otherwise you shall become a laughingstock." I totally agreed with this advice.

Most of the teachers who lived in the dormitory ate their meals at ordinary restaurants, where the cost of meals for a whole month came to only five *yuan*.* But there were also more than a dozen teachers, including myself, who went to eat at a "special restaurant," where our meals cost twelve yuan per month and the chef was from Fujien. Every day we enjoyed two gourmet meals there, including sea cucumber and other such delicacies. Those of us who dined together also went to the city's French district once or twice a week to have lunch at a Western restaurant instead, and sometimes we arranged big banquets there.

In those days, ten to fifteen dollars sufficed to pay for a full table of the choicest cuisine, plus some very fine wine, and this also included some food and drink for each guest's taxi driver or rickshaw puller. After our meal, we split up into three or four smaller groups and went to the pleasure district† for further entertainment. Other than this sort of gathering, I had very little contact with my colleagues at the academy, and therefore, whenever I was in Tienjin, I couldn't stop thinking about my good friends in Peking, and I always rejoiced each Thursday when it was time to return to the capital.

From the beginning of autumn until the first winter frost, all of northern China was plagued with sand storms. Whenever the north wind blew, yellow dust filled the air and penetrated all seven apertures,‡ and shutting the doors and windows did nothing at all to block the dust from getting indoors. Except for this, the autumn season in the north was always very refreshing to the spirit. The chrysanthemums in

*The yuan is the basic Chinese denomination of money, similar to the dollar in America. In those days, one yuan was equivalent to about ten cents.

†Blofeld uses the poetic term *hwa jie liu siang* for "pleasure district," which literally translates as "flower streets and willow lanes."

‡"Seven apertures" refers to two ears, two eyes, two nostrils, and the mouth.

northern China were incomparable. Every house and home abounded with pots of various types of chrysanthemum displayed on wooden stands, both indoors and outdoors.

According to *The Annals of Yenching*,* over a century ago there were more than 330 varieties of chrysanthemum in Peking, with names such as "Lovely Lady's Morning Rouge," "Spring Swallows in the Apricot Grove," "Lingering Light of Sunset," "Golden Willow Threads," and so forth. These exotic names were rich in poetic nuance, and they reflected the highly refined degree of creative imagination cultivated by the ancient Chinese.

Although the weather grew quite cold during the winter season, it was also beautifully bright and clear, so different from today, with dismal factories belching clouds of black smoke into the air, polluting the sky so much that children no longer even know the meaning of the term "clear day." By midwinter, whenever it came time to depart Tienjin, I found myself reluctant to leave the cozy warmth of the dormitory's central heating. In my apartment in Peking, the only way to ward off the cold was with a small charcoal brazier. Fortunately I had a winter gown, jacket, and pants that were padded with silk wadding. Not only was this outfit very elegant, it was also much warmer than wool, as well as lighter and far more comfortable than Western winter coats.

The sheer beauty of the winter landscape in Peking was ample compensation for the burden of the numbing cold. During the coldest weather, Bei Hai Park became very animated with crowds of people ice-skating on the frozen lake, while clumps of snow clung to the enameled eaves of the pavilions and hung from the branches of ancient pines—a scene whose beauty could only be compared with the towers and gardens of Chang Eh's† palace on the moon.

Pu introduced me to the proprietor of an antique shop whose name was Li. One day this old gentleman took me for a tour of the

---

*Yenching was a literary name for Peking.

†Chang Eh is the "Lady in the Moon" of Chinese fairy tales.

incomparable snowscapes in Chung Nan Hai Park.* Arrayed along the eastern shore of Chung Nan Lake stood a row of linked pavilions that seemed to be floating on the surface of the water. That day, strands of snowflakes sparkled like gems where they had collected between the humps of the enameled roof tiles. The breathtaking beauty of this vista made my soul turn somersaults.

Overwhelmed with boundless joy, I said, "While this exquisite scene shall remain forever imprinted in my heart, I also feel a deep sense of grief hanging in the air that makes me shiver with sadness. Why is that?" Seeming to suspect some sort of hidden meaning in my words, the old gentleman paused for a while, then asked, "You really don't know?" I shook my head to confirm that I really had no idea. Then he said, "This is the place where the empress dowager imprisoned the young emperor Kuang Hsu. *Ai,* the poor emperor had been led astray by the hasty and ill-conceived advice of his loyal ministers. During his solitary confinement here, even his most beloved concubine was refused permission to visit and give him comfort. He was the crown prince of China, and yet he had to endure the jeers and teasing of eunuchs. Only one or two people dared to express sympathy for his plight. How could one possibly enjoy this snowscape, when one is gazing at the very place where he died?" Even before the old gentleman had finished speaking, we both felt an overwhelming sadness descend upon us.

The most festive time of year was always the annual Chinese New Year holiday. Because I was a single person living there all alone, I was never able to participate in the traditional family New Year celebrations, but to this day one unusual thing still stands out in my memory.

On the second day of the new year, I joined the throngs of people who crowded into the White Cloud Temple, which was the principal Taoist temple in the entire country. Within the temple garden there

*This was formerly the private lake and garden complex of the imperial family. Mao Tse-tung and his entourage chose to live there during Mao's reign in China.

was a depression in the ground. During the New Year festival, three or four Taoist adepts would sit in silent meditation in this cavity, remaining motionless all day long, without emerging from their pristine state of stillness for even a moment. I was told that each and every year several old Taoists sat there meditating like that from dawn to dusk, beginning on the first day of the new year and continuing until the fifth day, never budging from their stillness, stable and immovable as stone towers. If you looked at them very carefully without interruption, you could see that during those twelve hours they sat there without the slightest movement, and even their eyelids didn't quiver. Before leaving the altar where these old Taoists sat absorbed in meditation, almost everyone who came to see them felt compelled by admiration to toss a copper coin as a token donation. Although in those days a copper coin wasn't worth much money, because so many people came the income for the whole day still amounted to several hundred dollars.

After the beginning of spring on the lunar calendar,* the winter cold gradually dissipated, and the ice and snow melted away. In those days, the alleys and lanes of the city's residential districts were not yet paved with brick or cobblestone, and so they easily became rivers of mud at this time of year. It was difficult for pedestrians to avoid getting both feet stuck in the muddy surface of the roads, and sometimes their cloth shoes would be completely swallowed and disappear. Then, as the days passed, the weather changed again, and a balmy breeze blew in, drying the surface of the streets, and signaling that spring had really arrived. The spring light made everything look clear and bright, reflecting from the magnificent mansions and courtyards of the imperial palace like sparkling jewels.

Along the shores of Peking's six lakes and the banks of the many canals within and outside the city walls hung the dangling branches of thousands of weeping willow trees. Before their buds burst into bloom, the willows sprouted tender green tendrils that grew into long

*This usually occurs between the 5th and 18th of February.

limbs stretching to the ground and swaying elegantly in the wind. At this time of year, poets liked to row their boats out onto the lakes and compose spontaneous lines of verse in praise of the willows' beauty. In the mind's eye of these poets, whenever the spring breeze stirred, the jade green willows looked like bewitching women, smiling and dancing without a care in the world.

Eat, Drink, and Be Merry

I've already mentioned the special features of the four seasons that were unique to Peking, so now I'd like to discuss some of the diversions the city's residents pursued in their leisure time.

Chinese people everywhere have always savored the delicious flavors of fine cuisine, and the residents of the ancient capital were certainly no exception. Indeed, their social life revolved primarily around the banquet table. For everyone in society, from merchants to writers, the discerning ability to properly compose a meal in restaurants by ordering the correct combination of dishes was an indispensable skill that even I studied a bit, and so you can well imagine how important this was for high-ranking officials and other dignitaries in former times. Prior to the War of Resistance against Japan, anyone who wished to taste the very best in gourmet Chinese food could pick no better place than Peking. Strangely enough, what's known today as so-called Peking Cuisine never existed before as a category in the culinary arts of China. Of course Peking Duck has always been a dish uniquely associated with the capital, but other than that, northern Chinese food consisted mainly of the culinary style of Shantung,* and therefore "Peking Cuisine" is really a misnomer. Since Peking has served as China's capital city for many centuries, it naturally attracted the best chefs from every province and region in the country. Moreover, the great men who

*Shantung, known in ancient times as Lu, is one of China's oldest and most historically prominent provinces. Located on the northern coast about 150 miles south of Peking, it was the homeland of Confucius.

came to the capital from distant provinces to serve as ministers of state would have certainly included among their entourage of assistants and relatives talented chefs who were skilled in the preparation of their native homelands' finest delicacies.

(According to what a friend told me, the original meaning of the phrase "to feast in Guangjou"* was not that "Cantonese cuisine is superior to all other provinces." As a matter of fact, most people from the northern and western regions of China feel that Cantonese food is far too bland and cannot compare with the grand cuisines of Szechuan, Hunan, Shantung, and Suchou. If that's the case, then why did this phrase spread so far and wide? The reason is that ever since the latter years of the Tao Kuang emperor's reign, Guangjou had become the center of foreign trade, and thus the city of Canton was full of wealthy tycoons who liked to vie with each other in providing their guests with strange, unheard-of delicacies. While these exotic dishes reflected the host's wealth and status, they were not necessarily the most palatable foods.)

Chinese banquets always included fine wines, but according to longstanding etiquette, one must never lose one's sense of decorum after drinking. Chinese people become intoxicated quite easily, and therefore they are very fond of drinking games and can become quite boisterous at banquets, but very rarely do they allow themselves to get roaring drunk in public. According to scenes described in old Chinese novels and the works of famous poets, the ancient Chinese were accustomed to frequent drinking. However, an acquaintance of mine, Mr. Chu Chian, who had served as a senior official in the capital, informed me that back in the days when the emperor was still on the throne, even though officials and ministers of state were required by custom to do a lot of drinking whenever they were entertaining guests or attending formal receptions they always used beverages with very light alcoholic content.

*Guangjou is a southern province in which the city of Canton is located, and is famous throughout China for its exotic cuisine.

It's most unfortunate that since the late Ching Dynasty the sort of self-control exercised when drinking liquor has not been applied to smoking opium. Prior to the reign of the Tao Kuang emperor, Chinese people were not in the habit of smoking opium, until shameless Western merchants started peddling large quantities of it to China. Opium is far more addictive than alcohol, and also far more dangerous. Prior to the War of Resistance, both Peking and Tienjin had many "smoking groves," a term used in reference to opium dens. Among my own circle of friends, there were very few addicts, but after attending banquets, some of them liked to visit opium dens or brothels in order to enjoy a taste of "black rice." Sometimes I joined them.

One time, a professor named Fan took me along for a smoke. I had smoked opium once before in Canton and had quite enjoyed it, but I was very afraid of becoming addicted. Mr. Fan took note of my discomfort and said, "Nothing can be judged as being either good or bad in itself. Whether something is harmful or beneficial depends entirely on how it is used. While common people may find it difficult to control themselves, gentlemen know when they've had enough and are quite capable of exercising restraint and avoiding danger." His reasoning convinced me, and so, rather than refusing his offer, I smoked a few pipes with him and enjoyed the sensation of entering a totally different world. However, the next day I received an unexpected scolding from my friend Pu. He said, "That professor is probably a hopeless opium addict. People like him always say things like that in order to persuade others to believe their story, but their real purpose is simply to entice people to join them without arousing any doubts." I later discovered that what Pu had told me was correct. Professor Fan had already been addicted to opium for a long time. Only his wife knew the real truth, and one day she inadvertently let his secret slip out.

Today, people may well believe that visiting brothels and smoking opium are shameful activities, but I don't agree. During the time that I lived in Peking, I was only twenty-two years old, and though

I was not particularly promiscuous, I was nevertheless quite attracted to the beauty and tender charm of young women. That goes without saying. However, in those days it was impossible to find a girlfriend from a good family. Even for a young Chinese lad, living alone in the city was always a very lonely experience, and this was even more so for a Western youth. At least young Chinese men all had sisters and other female relatives back home to whom they could sometimes turn for female companionship, but how could someone like me find such solace? The girls in singsong houses were skilled in using sweet words to make a man feel happy, and they were trained to carry themselves with a highly refined sense of elegance. In fact, they were often even more sophisticated than girls from good families.

After I had learned sufficient Mandarin to understand basic conversation, these girls warmly welcomed me to become their "language student." Contrary to my expectations, singsong girls were not necessarily greedy for money. According to my own experience, rarely did any of these girls demand excessive payment, and some of them displayed considerable depth of feeling. It was only due to the misfortunate treatment they received from society that they were compelled to sell their smiles and sell their bodies. How could one possibly look down on them for that? You could even say that these girls became my benefactors by using the simplest words and phrases to help me slowly but surely learn a well-cultured style of conversation. In those days, my male friends, such as my colleagues at school as well as Pu and Heng, found little interest speaking Chinese with a beginner like me, and so they always conversed with me in English. Thanks only to the companionship of a few singsong girls did my Mandarin gradually grow smooth and proper, and not only did my manner of speech become more fluent and courteous, but it even began to draw praise from strangers. How on earth could I not be moved to gratitude by such efficient tutelage from these "lady professors?"

Occasionally my friends invited me to go with them to listen to opera performances. Although I could not understand the words, I soon began to like Peking Opera, but since I found it difficult to appreciate the finer points of this performing art, it did not become a passion for me. Many people in Peking were deeply devoted connoisseurs of opera, and some of them could recite by heart all of the lyrics in the most famous operas, and could even accompany themselves on the *hu-chin** as they sang. What I loved most of all was ancient Chinese music, especially the seven-stringed zither. In those days, there were still a few old masters who played the zither with such consummate skill that it entranced the soul.

In the singsong houses there were some girls who excelled in playing the Chinese lute. Even today, whenever I read the lines of *The Lute Girl's Lament,*† my eyes fill with tears of nostalgia for the past. It's clear from this poem that the great poet Pai did not look down on singsong girls, and I feel exactly the same way, although I must admit such a viewpoint has changed over time. For young people today, relations with the opposite sex have become far more convenient than in the past, and therefore singsong girls have lost the important social function they once served. Unfortunately, even though most people today may no longer visit singsong houses, this does not necessarily mean that they are any more chaste than their ancestors.

Another highly refined leisure activity was the game of Chinese chess.‡ Although I was very fond of playing chess, I never became an adept. As for archery and other pastimes favored by my Manchurian friends, I remained completely unskilled. Mr. Heng introduced me to an old Manchu bannerman§ whose surname was Chu. This venerable old gentleman informed me that the reason the Manchu nomads were

*The hu-chin is a stringed instrument used in Peking Opera, drawn with a bow.

†The Chinese lute is called pi pa. The poem *The Lute Girl's Lament (Pi Pa Hsing)* was written by the famous Tang Dynasty poet Pai Chu-yi, after he heard a lute girl playing her heart out on a flower boat.

‡Known as *Wei Chi* in Chinese and *Go* in Japanese (literally "encircle chess"), this game is played with black and white stones on a large checkered board.

§"Bannermen" were the aristocratic class of Manchu society, and during the Manchu Ching Dynasty, they comprised the highest social class in China.

able to conquer and control all of China was due entirely to their peerless mastery of the bow and arrow. He willingly agreed to teach me the art of archery, but after only two attempts, I found it so difficult that I quickly lost my determination to practice. Alas!

The sports that the residents of the capital liked to practice most were tai-chi-chuan and all sorts of martial arts. Groups of spectators often gathered in the Tien-chiao district* to watch martial artists and jugglers practicing their skills. Before my arrival in Peking, I had never witnessed such wonderful skill. As I stood there watching, slack-jawed with amazement, every time I heard a bystander shout "Bravo, bravo," I too shouted out with all my might in order to express my boundless appreciation. At the time, I would never have imagined that only a few decades later, Chinese martial arts would gain popular international acclaim as it spread far and wide throughout the world.

Indeed, there are probably more tai-chi-chuan teachers in Europe and America today than there are in China, and most of them are native residents of those countries. Now in my elderly years, whenever I consider this situation, I cannot help but feel saddened to think that just as foreigners in the Western world are beginning to appreciate some of the most advanced arts of ancient China, the Chinese themselves seem to be abandoning them, or else taking sudden notice of the precious heritage left to them by their ancestors only after seeing Chinese martial arts featured in foreign films.

Before I finish my discussion of leisure activities, I would like to mention the pleasure of visiting bathhouses. Not only in Peking, but also throughout northern China, residential homes very rarely were equipped with hot water facilities. Anyone who wished to have a bath with hot water had to go to a bathhouse for it. Whenever the weather turned cold, customers swarmed to the bathhouses, and many came only to relish the warmth.

*Tien-chiao was a not-quite-respectable district just outside Tian-an-men where all the carnival types would gather: fortune tellers, jugglers, strongmen, brick smashers, balancing acts, swordsmen, and hustlers of all types, trying to pick up a few coins to make a living.

Most bathhouses had three pools: a warm pool, a hot pool, and an even hotter pool. They were about the same size as a small swimming pool. Unless one first entered the warm pool, the temperature of the hot pool was difficult to tolerate, not to mention the heat of the hottest pool. While soaking in the warm pool, one could call for a bathhouse attendant to come scrub one's back. First he placed a large cross-shaped wooden frame into the pool, with the bottom part braced against the bottom, the center part propped against the wall of the pool, and the top part sticking up out of the water. The customer then leaned at an angle on this framework, as though he'd been sentenced to the punishment of dismemberment on the rack. The scrub boys had to exert an extraordinary amount of muscular effort in order to perform this sort of work. Most of them came from Shantung, or had been apprenticed to Shantung mentors. First they wrapped a towel tightly around one hand, and used it to briskly rub out the black particles of dirt trapped in the pores of the customer's skin. No matter how clean you might have thought your own body was, an amazing amount of dirt always came out in the wash.

After this treatment, the customer stepped into the second or third pool to soak for a while, then went to the lounge room to rest. The lounge room was equipped with dozens of cots, and there you could lie down comfortably and ask for another attendant to come over and give you a massage, while young manicurists came to trim the nails of your fingers and toes. Fine tea, stuffed buns, steamed dumplings, fresh fruits, and other snacks were available at your beck and call. Since the cots were placed quite close together, the reclining customers merrily engaged one another in casual conversation. For me this was one of the most enjoyable aspects of going to a bathhouse.

While traveling around China, whenever I first arrived in a new town along the way where I had no acquaintances to receive me, I immediately went to a bathhouse to relax, and killed two birds with one stone. On the one hand, there were always local residents there who were happy to tell me all about the town's more interesting diversions, and on the other hand, the bathhouse was always very warm, whereas the inns seldom had any form of heating other than a small charcoal brazier. Upon first arrival in a town, one always felt freezing cold from head to foot, so if one didn't go to a bathhouse, it was almost impossible to ever get warm.

3

Roaming the Famous Mountains and Monasteries of Northern China

The Winds of War Compel a Long Journey

When I first came to Peking, the charms of the city completely captivated my soul, but after a while I realized that the political situation there was becoming a matter of serious concern. Japan had already occupied three provinces in the northeast. Northern China, comprising the five provinces of Hopei, Shaanhsi, Heilungjiang, Shantung, and Shanhsi, was nominally still under the control of the central government, but in fact all of these provinces fell within Japan's sphere of influence. Japanese and Korean thugs blatantly provoked trouble there, especially in the countryside, where they stopped at nothing—from peddling narcotics and raping women to killing innocent civilians and other criminal activities—and these events were frequently reported in the newspapers. At the time, the government still maintained a policy of appeasement toward the aggressors. However, everyone knew that Japan was only waiting for a suitable incident to use as a pretext for extending its tyrannical dominion over all of northern China.

Consequently, during the two to three years prior to the Lu Kou Bridge incident,* the people of northern China felt extremely uneasy.

*This was a skirmish between Japanese and Chinese troops at a place called Lu Kou Bridge, which the Japanese used as an excuse to invade Peking.

Students frequently went on strike and boycotted class in order to participate in anti-Japanese demonstrations, and these protest campaigns suddenly provided me with many extra periods of spare time. Considering that I was a young foreigner who had just arrived in China and was unable to offer any assistance to the striking students, I thought I might as well take advantage of this opportunity to travel around the country. Therefore, I decided to start by exploring the mountains and river ways of northern China.

Except for my worries about the current state of affairs in China, my good fortune reached its zenith during those two years. However, in June 1937, I received a letter from my father asking me to return briefly home to England to deal with some family matters. Therefore, when the Lu Kou Bridge incident occurred on July 7, I was sitting on a train crossing the steppes of Siberia. Hearing the alarming news on the radio that invading Japanese troops had begun to occupy all of northern China, I felt an overwhelming sense of tragedy and could not stop myself from weeping openly in front of my fellow travelers. Later I heard reports that China was beginning to mount resistance. During the following eight years, the bitter suffering endured by the Chinese people defies all description. Such woe!

After our family affairs had been settled, my father did not try to prevent me from returning to China, so in September I set forth but with no idea where to go, for obviously it was now impossible for me to return to northern China. When I arrived in Hong Kong, I stayed over at Elder Brother's home, and after discussing the situation with my old friends, I decided to head for Guilin.

Allow me first to describe some of my travel experiences prior to the war. Throughout the two years prior to the Lu Kou Bridge incident (1935–1937), the anti-Japanese student strikes mentioned above became a frequent occurrence. With the additional leave provided by weekends and holidays, I had abundant leisure time. During these vacations, I liked to roam around northern China, particularly in the provinces of Shantung, Hopei, Shaanhsi, and Shanhsi. Besides Peking and Tienjin, I visited many famous places of historical interest in northern China.

The train ride from Tienjin to Shantung was very convenient. The fabled sights of that province were very exotic, and the seascapes along the coast seemed like a realm of the immortals. No wonder the ancients believed that the magic isle of Peng Lai* was located somewhere in the misty waters between the two seas of Po Hai (the Gulf of Chihli) and Huang Hai (the Yellow Sea).

I often saw two very different types of landscapes in Shantung. One consisted of richly planted plains full of orchards and gardens, and the other was barren mountain regions convoluted with craggy peaks. The range of fruit trees included peach, plum, cherry, pear, and other varieties, and their branches, leaves, blossoms, and fruit each had their own special beauty. The rural people who cultivated these fruits for a living seemed to enjoy a very good life. But for the minorities who lived up in the desolate wild mountain areas the situation was quite different. In my eyes, those barren rocky cliffs had their own enchanting beauty, but those who lived there could barely maintain subsistence, and sometimes the weak could not even survive. The proclivity of Shantung people to invoke the aid and protection of gods and demons, and the fact that so many of them chose to become sorcerers or bandits, may stem from these unfortunate conditions.

The first time I visited Shantung, I started with an excursion to the Ling-yan Monastery. This monastery was established during the Jin Dynasty, in the year 357 CE. Such an ancient temple was a rarity even in China. Its pagodas were built during the Sung Dynasty, and they were very elegant structures. What attracted the eye of the visitor most of all, both inside and outside the monastery, were its qualities of natural simplicity and tranquil grace. To the front and the back could be seen the two types of landscapes described above. The fruit orchards on the front side of the monastery extended out as far as the eye could see. The mountains and hills on the back side looked like

*Peng Lai was a mythical island, believed to be located off the coast of Shantung, where immortals dwelled.

gourds. The entire monastery was enveloped by steep cliffs, linking it seamlessly with the mountain ridges. Even more marvelous was the way the monastery's main temple hall was placed right in the center of the mountains, making it look like an extension of the mountain range. It was difficult to distinguish between the architectural features and the natural landscape, producing a scenic vista of extraordinary wonder.

At the time, there was only one old monk living all alone in the monastery, but fortunately, neighbors often came over to take care of him. Late at night the sound of him striking the wooden fish reminded me of my brother Yuan-ruo, Fifth Uncle, and other fellow practitioners in Hong Kong. They were all totally devout Buddhists, pure and true of heart, and they were all highly accomplished scholars as well. As far as I could see, that old monk was also this sort of person—plain and simple as a country bumpkin on the outside, but richly endowed with sublime wisdom inside his heart.

Mount Tai's Eighteen Stairways to the Gates of Heaven

The next time I visited Shantung, I made the journey to Mount Tai. Unfortunately, at that time my Mandarin was still limited to only a few sentences, so I was unable to inquire about the famous sites there; all I could do was rely upon my own two eyes for guidance. Nevertheless, I wasn't worried about getting into any trouble along the way. When I was young, I loved China truly with all my heart, and even in my dreams it never occurred to me that Chinese people would ever do me any harm. And in fact, no matter how carefree I was in my travels through China, not once from beginning to end did I ever come to any sort of harm.

On the first day of that journey, the train arrived at Tai An very early in the morning. As I approached the Tai Temple, I felt a bit disappointed by what I saw. The ambience of the place did not reflect the grand dignified style of an ancient temple, and the main shrine hall had been transformed into an extremely vulgar little museum, while the nationalist slogans printed all over the walls definitely did not express the precious spirit of ancient tradition. Later I discovered that this sort of artistic destruction had become very common throughout China, and it deeply saddened me. Countless emperors and great ministers of state had come to Tai Temple to offer prayers and sacrifices to Heaven, and now that it belonged to the Republic, why was the integrity of this ancient treasure and its ancestral traditions no longer treated with respect?

After coming out of the temple, I went to a small restaurant and ate two bowls of steamed Shantung dumplings, then headed toward the mountain. The ancients claimed that Mount Tai was the greatest of all sacred sites, and that its magnificent grandeur had no peer.

There upon that broad expanse I saw many monastic sanctuaries, pavilions, extremely ancient trees, waterfalls, caves, memorial tablets inscribed by famous men, and countless other precious relics. At the foot of the mountain I found a winding stairway that ascended step by step all the way up to the distant peak of the mountain. The stairway was forty-five *li** long. Near the peak, there were several sections of stone steps so steep that they made the climber's head dizzy and vision blurred. This segment was known as the Path of Eighteen Platters.

All along the way came flocks of pilgrims with offerings, some of them walking on foot, others sitting in sedan chairs. What left me most awestruck was the sight of so many old women with tiny feet bound into "Golden Lilies,"† crawling up the mountain on their knees. I could see from the coarse faded blue jackets they wore that they could not afford the cost of riding in sedan chairs, so their only option was to sew kneepads onto their pants and, grinding their teeth against the pain, crawl wearily up the mountain. *Ai ya ya!* It took a young person seven to eight hours to reach the peak of the mountain, so imagine how long it took an old

---

*One li equals about one-third of a mile, so the stairway was about fifteen miles in length.

†The bound feet of Chinese women were known as Three-Inch Golden Lilies, and they reduced a woman's gait to a painful hobble, while many older women were only able to crawl without assistance walking.

woman with bound feet! Even four to five days were probably not enough! To think that they were ready and willing to risk death in order to make this pilgrimage makes me feel amazed that women with such ardent devotion exist in this world. Fortunately, there were plenty of places along the way to provide them with food and shelter.

The steps passed through many gateways, the last of which was called the Gate of the Southern Heaven. Beyond it lay a piece of flat land and a very short lane. The shops along the lane sold incense and food and provided pilgrims with overnight lodging. Before proceeding onward to offer incense, travelers stopped here first to rest. The facilities at these little inns were very rustic, and the prices were geared to the impoverished conditions of most of the pilgrims. Wealthier travelers, however, could afford to stay at the more luxurious guest quarters provided by some of the monasteries.

I arrived at the Gate of the Southern Heaven in the afternoon and stopped to rest at a small inn. Although I had no companions I did not feel lonely there, and after a meal and some fruit, I got up and continued on my way. Crossing over a small stretch of grass, I headed uphill and arrived at three large temples. This place, which was located at the peak of the mountain, was the central spot for ceremonial worship. Pilgrims filled the temple grounds, and in the middle of the courtyards stood enormous bronze incense urns from which clouds of fragrant smoke unfurled in all directions. I think that those flocks of old women with their feet bound into Golden Lilies must surely have believed that the scented smoke would carry their prayers all the way up to heaven. They obviously did not feel that their efforts to get there were made in vain, or that the difficult journey they'd undertaken brought them no benefit, for as soon as they reached the summit, their faces grew radiant with rapture and reflected their boundless joy.

After sunset, the travelers stayed overnight at the inns, where they ate their evening meal and went to sleep. Just before the break of dawn, everyone climbed up to the place known as the Sun View Peak and stood there gazing at the distant ocean to the east. Soon the vast sky brightened, and the swirling clouds and mist gradually grew resplendent with color. Looking out toward the eastern sea, all we viewers could see were the blurred boundaries of endless ranges of lofty steep mountains; and then the far distant seascape slowly unfolded as golden rays of light illuminated our view, creating an imaginary vision of the jade realms of the immortals.

The Prophesied Utopia of a Woman's World

Descending the mountain did not require much effort, and by noon I arrived back at the foot of the mountain and entered a grass shack to have tea. Suddenly, a Western missionary followed me inside and stood there staring coldly down at me with an extremely rude air of grave accusation that startled and bewildered me. He said that the previous evening one of his Chinese converts had seen me paying reverence to the great god of Mount Tai, and in a chilly tone of voice that missionary said to me, "How could you be so shameless?" He then announced, "Westerners who behave like this shall surely be rejected by their own race." After he finished speaking, I asked him what concern of his was my good or bad behavior, and he replied that Westerners should not encourage the superstitious beliefs of "uncultured races."

Trying my best to contain my anger, I answered him by saying, "I'm afraid that you, sir, are the one with a rather thick-skinned face.* It is neither they nor I who indulge in superstition, but rather it is you yourself. You have never met God, and yet you believe that there really exists such a supreme being, and that is superstition. Your sort of belief doesn't have a shred of evidence to support it. As for me, although I do not firmly believe in the existence of gods, nor do I deny the possibility that they do exist. Perhaps there is no such thing as one great god, and perhaps there are millions of great gods as well as little gods, but how on earth would I know? If I were to observe everyone in one of your

*The Chinese term for "shameless" is *lien-pi hou,* literally "thick-skinned face."

churches worshipping Jesus, I would not hesitate to worship together with them, and the reason is that I would not wish to be disrespectful in their presence. Yesterday I observed everyone bowing their heads in reverence to the great god of Mount Tai, and so I too bowed my head in reverence and offered incense. Please do not forget the fact that this is China, and that you are obliged to follow the local customs and respect the national ways. Is it not true, in fact, that you missionaries have come here expressly to destroy the beliefs of others? Please think this over carefully!" When I'd finished speaking, I nodded my head and left him standing there amazed and speechless. Glaring at me with ice-cold eyes, the missionary followed me down the steps, simmering balefully with the huge grudge he held against me.

Just then I encountered an old woman passing by selling magic talismans, and in order to deliberately annoy that missionary I pulled out a few coins and bought three or four of them. After returning to Tienjin, I asked a colleague to take a look at those talismans and tell me what they meant. Taking out a small booklet printed on yellow paper, he flipped through each inscription, then roared with laughter and said, "Incredible, really incredible, these come from my own native home, and they were written by a yellow-cap Taoist.* These are not talismans. The inscriptions written here are prophecies. The first one is hilarious, so I shall translate it for you."

Although I've long since lost that little booklet, I still recall the general meaning of the inscription, as follows:

Once upon a time, there was a sorceress who transmitted this message while possessed in trance by a spirit: "The Land of Women in the Eastern Sea disappeared long ago, but in the latter years of this century, there shall appear a land in the Western world called The United Nation of Women.

"For the first five hundred years, the United Nation of Women

*Yellow-cap Taoism, sometimes referred to as "yellow turban" in English, refers to the Taiping Tao, or "Way of Supreme Peace," an early school of Taoism founded in 175 CE. The founder was famous as a healer whose method was based on magic.

shall be governed by a select committee, and all members of this committee shall be female. After this period, a female angel shall come to take charge of the nation's affairs. In terms of intelligence, integrity, physique, health, elegance, and all other aspects, every member of the governing committee shall be a true beauty. All members must take office before the age of seven. Every year, a select number of young women shall be tested for their intelligence and then be designated as Candidates-in-Waiting. On the day of their inauguration to office, they will be required to enter a hospital for surgical removal of the uterus, clitoris, breasts, and all female glands, in order to eliminate the unique traits that make women receptive and tender. After surgery, owing to the elimination of sexual passion, the committee members will be able to overcome all emotions that are not beneficial to the nation, and because they will be free of the emotions that arise from sexual passion, they therefore will become unbiased, and because they will be unbiased, they may therefore generate unconditional love and thereby become virtuous leaders. After completing the ritual removal of the clitoris, the young delegates shall receive the most advanced education, and at the age of ten they shall be tested once again, in order to determine whether they qualify to remain as members of the highest select committee, or, if they fail to qualify for the highest posts, whether they should be assigned to another less important office. Not until the age of eighteen shall they receive formal confirmation of their posts.

"A nation of women does not require soldiers. As the Old Sage* said, 'Because one has no enemies, therefore one needs no soldiers. A nation that maintains a large army will not have sufficient resources to meet the needs of the people. A nation of women also does not need police and lawyers in order to maintain peace and order. If too many laws are declared, it is difficult for people to avoid violating the law, and the more prohibitions there are, the more criminals there shall

*"Old Sage" refers to Lao-Tze, author of the Taoist classic Tao Teh Ching, from which the quote that follows is a paraphrase of a passage on government.

be. Thus it is said that governing a great nation is like cooking a light meal.'

"Those who govern a nation of women need not fear Heaven, nor need they fear Earth. Their only fear is the male gender, and thus they will contrive to reduce its numbers for the greater good of the nation and the benefit of the people. For every three males that are born, they will suffocate two of them, and thereby they will limit the number of males to less than a third of the population. After five hundred years, when the governing angel descends from Heaven, she shall announce that the nation of women no longer requires males among the people. Except for five hundred prime male studs to be kept for the purpose of propagation, all males shall be expelled, old and young alike, each and every one shall be exiled from the nation, or sold into slavery abroad, or simply executed. When all males have been eliminated from the populace, the United Nation of Women shall become prosperous and strong, healthy and happy, and shall unify the whole world under its dominion."

After my colleague finished translating this passage from the little booklet, I asked him in which period of history the Taoist who wrote the booklet lived, and I mentioned that in ancient times there was no such thing as a select committee of governors, and that therefore it was clear that this Taoist was definitely not a historical figure. The professor said that he had no way of knowing about this, but that he too believed the author must be a contemporary figure. And then he speculated, "Perhaps that Taoist was a female. . . ."

Do you believe this or not?

The Dignified Simplicity of Confucius' Tomb in Shantung

Two or three weeks later, I again traveled to Shantung to visit the tombs of the two great sages, Confucius and Mencius. First I went to Chufu.

Chufu was like one of those ancient towns depicted in old Chinese paintings, full of colorful artifacts that have now become extinct. At that time, Confucius' direct descendent, the venerable Kung Teh-cheng, still lived in the family manor there.

I really wanted to meet the seventieth-generation descendent of the great sage. I'd heard that he was a very refined gentleman who was even younger than I. Perhaps he would not feel averse to receiving me, but what if language barriers made it impossible for us to communicate? What then? Why should I pointlessly make myself a laughingstock? Thus I dared not to pay him a visit.

The train station was located some distance from Chufu, and after reaching town, I told the rickshaw puller to take me to a suitable inn. When I arrived at the inn, a waiter came out and brought my luggage into the tearoom, then took me in to open my room. *Ai ya!* I never thought that the facilities would be so crude. The bed quilt was filthy, the mattress was stained, and a big woman with dirty clothes and a runny nose followed me into the room without even asking my permission. What a mess! The inn was utterly disgusting, but I did not wish to offend anyone, so I decided to tolerate the place for just one night.

It was still early, so I ate a bowl of millet gruel and some fried breadsticks before walking over to the temple. The magnificence of the temple structure was beautiful to behold, and only later did I learn that it had been totally rebuilt at the beginning of the Ming Dynasty. The main hall stood on a two-tiered terrace of white jadestone. The grandeur of this stone terrace matched that of the ancient imperial palaces. Beneath the front eaves of the hall's roof were seven enormous white jadestone columns carved into the shape of dragons. The garden, which opened out toward the back side of the hall, was called the Grove of Confucius, and this was where the sage's tomb was located. Arrayed along both sides of the pathway leading to the tomb stood rows of gigantic stone animals and ancient cypress trees that captivated the eye. It struck me that most visitors would regard these stone animals with awe, and that the sight of them would leave the viewer speechless with wonder. I felt particularly fond of old cypress trees and let my spirit wander freely among them. Fortunately the ancient Chinese believed that the beauty of nature surpasses anything produced by man, and therefore the famous sites of northern China were richly endowed with these enchanting old trees.

As for the works of art and craft produced by the human hand, no matter how exquisite they might be, none could compare with this natural beauty. The main path passed by a five-arched memorial gate sculpted in floral motifs, carved with impeccable stone craft that far surpassed the decor of any other memorial gate I'd ever seen elsewhere in China. Contrary to my expectations, Confucius' tomb was relatively pristine. Its elegant simplicity and solemn dignity transcended the exceedingly ornate and complex style of the tombs of famous people in contemporary times.

With a feeling of deep reverence, I stood before the tomb for a long time, and then reluctantly took my leave.

Any ancient relic, regardless of how commendable it may be, can only hold one's attention for a short while. After gazing upon it for too long a time, one's enthusiasm gradually diminishes and the spirit grows weary; so I went to a restaurant for some food, and after wandering around the old section of the town, I returned to the temple to have another look around. While walking down the street, I encountered three scholars heading toward a bookshop.

Elegantly attired in long gowns of white silk, with high collars and beautiful black satin shoes, the three scholars presented themselves with model Confucian demeanor and a courtly attitude that reminded me very much of my honorable elder brother Yuan-ruo. One of them, who was still in the full bloom of youth, with a creamy white complexion, particularly resembled my elder brother, and he was truly a handsome young man. Looking at him again, I suddenly thought: could this possibly be the great sage's direct descendant, Kung Teh-cheng? My heart leapt with joy, and I really wished to approach him with a greeting and engage him in conversation, but then I reconsidered and thought to myself: "Old Pu, what's wrong with you? What's the point of intruding upon this worthy young gentleman? Do you really believe that he would welcome being approached by a stranger, especially a foreigner? Don't stir up trouble for nothing!" With this thought in mind, I silently turned around and walked away.

That evening at dinnertime, I drank a few extra cups of warm, strongly distilled liquor, in order to help me forget about that filthy bed quilt. When I returned to the inn, I felt relieved to see that the woman with the runny nose was nowhere in sight. It seemed that most of the guests at that inn did not take rooms there in order to sleep. Many of the bedrooms echoed with the sounds of stringed instruments and high-pitched singing voices, as well as the clickety-clack of ma-jiang tiles. Intermittently came the hoarse cries of men and women laughing uproariously, as well as the loud voices of men cursing and the coarse words of women angrily refuting. I thought to myself: although the room rates at this inn are indeed conveniently cheap, overnight stays here are certainly very inconvenient.

The next morning I first took a train, then rode a rickshaw, passing through a large flatland of parched yellow earth, until I arrived at Dzou County.* As I recall, the tomb of Mencius there seemed very plain, and all I can remember about it now was a great crane resting on a branch of a nearby pine tree. This was a common sight throughout northern China. That I now cannot remember anything about the style of Mencius' tomb strikes me as rather strange. Perhaps that's because during the time before and after Mencius' death his disciples always viewed him only as the shadow of Confucius. But never mind, for Mencius himself would never have wished to compete with or surpass Confucius.

On my way back to Tienjin, an old professor shared the same train carriage with me, and we quite naturally struck up a conversation together. He asked me what I thought of Confucian philosophy.

*This was an ancient principality in Shantung.

Perhaps my response left him feeling dissatisfied, for at that time such questions did not much interest me. In a solemn tone of voice, he then expounded upon the precious legacy of the sage's teaching, as follows:

"People today generally take a dim view of ancient Chinese society, regarding it as full of misfortunate flaws. In fact, none of those shortcomings arose from the original intentions of the sage, but were rather the result of distortions perpetrated by later generations. Among them, even emperors and Confucian scholars twisted the sage's teachings to their own advantage. Kings, fathers, husbands, and elder brothers disregarded the mandates of Heaven and did not conduct themselves with propriety, thereby causing grievous harm to their ministers, children, wives, and younger brothers, and forcing them to bear the brunt of inhumane treatment. Thus they made it extremely difficult for people to properly apply the true teachings of Confucius and Mencius.

"Furthermore, the contemporary situation today is something that the ancient sages could not possibly have foreseen. Therefore, their original principles cannot possibly cope with present conditions. However, one certainly cannot use this as a pretext for disrespecting their ideas. And why not? Because for two thousand years prior to this century, China surpassed every other nation on earth in every aspect. Thus the way of the sages can only be regarded as peerless throughout the world. It was precisely because the scholars of ancient times applied the teachings of the sages, and rigorously implemented their virtues, that China was able to become the foremost nation under Heaven."

The words of this old gentleman left a deep impression in my heart. Even though the passing years, like flowing water, have washed away so many of my memories, I can still remember the vitality of spirit and power of language with which he expressed himself to me that day.

The Unforgettable Jade-green Pines and Vermilion Maples of the Western Hills

Within three months of my residence in northern China, although my command of Mandarin terms and phrases remained rather simple, I nevertheless was able to carry a fluent conversation. Because I had previously learned some Cantonese, my progress in the Mandarin dialect was relatively swift.

I had heard that during the autumn season the scenic regions around the Western Hills* near Peking became resplendent with autumnal colors, with thousands of maple trees forming a tableau of blood red. It was not very far from the city, and usually there were few people there, but in the autumn season the place attracted a lot of sightseers, though not enough to ruin the tranquil atmosphere. As soon as I heard about this place, I immediately decided to go and savor the scenery there. It was on a weekend that I boarded a bus in Peking and went on my way, arriving there a short time later to spend the whole day enjoying the place.

The entire area was canopied with maple trees, and all around blazed a flaming sea of autumn color. The jade-green tint of the pine trees provided a contrast for the fiery hues of the maple leaves, which glittered with exceptionally red tones. I liked this setting very much, and it left a deep imprint in my memory. Although I'm sure that similar scenery exists in many places elsewhere in the world, this was China, the land I'd been dreaming of morning and night since the age of twelve, and while this was the first time I'd ever seen this place, I nevertheless seemed to recognize it from long, long ago and felt obsessively attracted to it. As I stood there gazing at this picture-perfect scene, I knew for certain that China could never fall short of my expectations.

As evening approached, I took lodging at an old monastery nearby. The roof tiles were covered with green moss, green grass sprouted

*One of Peking's most scenic sights, this is a gentle range of hills located to the west of the city, where many ancient temples and other historical sites are located.

John as a young man in Hong Kong, shortly after his abrupt departure from China.

(Photograph courtesy of the Blofeld family)

John in robes, posing with the abbot of a Buddhist monastery in Hong Kong.

(Photograph courtesy of the Blofeld family)

Chungliang Al Huang gives his good friend and colleague John Blofeld a warm hug.
(Photograph courtesy of Ko Si Chi)

from the seams between the stone slabs in the courtyard, and the great bronze bell was coated with layers of tarnish as green as the moss. There were no monks in the monastery, but there was an old Taoist in plain robes living there, along with his twelve- or thirteen-year-old disciple, who addressed his teacher as "Grandpa," although I had no idea whether he was the child's real grandfather. I also could not tell whether the youngster was a boy or a girl, for while his attitude and manner seemed like that of a male, his facial features seemed more like a female. The old Taoist was very solemn and rarely spoke, but his eyes reflected the wisdom and serenity within his heart. After the evening meal, they both retired to bed, but I found it difficult to sleep, and so I sat up alone to enjoy the moonlit setting. The tranquil atmosphere of that ancient monastery enraptured my soul. As the fragrance of incense mingled with the scent of pine, I felt the energy of the Tao flow in gentle harmony with the breeze from the cypress trees, and the whole place came to rest in silent serenity.

The Old Taoist Who Could Fly

Feeling happy and content, with my whole body calm and comfortable, my spirit soared as though intoxicated. Early next morning, the young acolyte brought me tea and pastries, and told me that Grandpa had sat meditating all night long and had not yet emerged, and that he often continued sitting like that all day and to therefore forgive him for failing to bid farewell to his guest. I acknowledged his words with a grunt, then asked whether the young disciple was a boy or a girl.

He looked offended and replied gruffly, "Think it over yourself! Surely you don't believe that Grandpa would want a silly, giggling, bed-wetting girl to serve him?" So I asked him, "Are all young girls bed-wetters?" In a voice ringing with disdain, he replied, "They most certainly are! Even after getting married, my older sister still wets her bed, and it drives her mother-in-law crazy." He paused to think for a moment, then continued, "Even my eldest brother is unable to serve

Grandpa. All of my brothers have gone off to school. How could someone who studies to become an ordinary person possibly aspire to become a practitioner of the immortal way, and how could such a person ever serve a great immortal adept?" I asked, "Where on earth does one find an immortal adept?"

The boy expressed great surprise, and with a big smile on his face, he answered, "There's a great immortal adept right here, he's my Grandpa. Everyone here on this mountain knows that Grandpa can fly, and that he can make himself suddenly disappear. If only I could show you, but unfortunately Grandpa doesn't like to reveal his spiritual powers. I'm eager to become an immortal adept too, and to become a living aircraft like him, but Grandpa isn't willing to teach me so quickly how to fly up and play at the pole star. Whenever I mention this to him, he tells me that I must adopt the patient attitude of a man of excellence. He says that flying to the moon is not as good as staying indoors, and that ignoring everything that happens outside one's window is the best way to perfect the practice of meditation. This is the method of Lao-tze's precept, 'To know the world below is to witness the way of Heaven above.' But I think that meditating and concentrating the mind must be extremely difficult. Even little birds can fly through the air, but they cannot meditate."

I suspected that this young lad was excessively superstitious, so in order to find out how much he understood about real Taoist studies, I asked him, "Little brother, do you know the meaning of the term 'eternal Way' in the line 'The way that can be named is not the eternal Way?'"* Without a moment's hesitation, and with an air of great satisfaction, the boy replied, "How could I possibly name the unnamable Way? If you ask me to name it, what words could I use?" At the same time, his eyes beamed with an expression of having won a victory over me, and he added, "Grandpa taught me all this. He says that the Great Way is the origin of all things, the mother of all things, and the essen-

---

*This is the first line in Lao-tze's Tao Teh Ching (The Way and Its Power), the classic bible of Taoist philosophy.

tial nature of all things. Our language cannot describe the Great Way; it can only be revealed in meditation." The child's manner of speech had a bit of the pedantic air of an old professor. He obviously delighted in the opportunity to show me that a Chinese, even if only a small child, could easily defeat a foreign devil. Although I detested this sort of combative attitude, I also realized that boys often display this kind of temperament, so why should I blame him? For in any case, he was an intelligent and quick-witted young scamp.

The boy said that yesterday a visitor's mule had dumped a pile of stinking feces in the garden. He told me that he'd once asked Grandpa whether or not the basic nature of stinking feces also partakes of the Great Way, and that Grandpa had replied, "Yes indeed. Only an idiot would have any doubt about that." Grandpa had further noted, "The color of feces is not inferior to that of amber." The boy had then remarked on the foul smell of feces and said, "The smell of the Great Way couldn't be that foul!" The old Taoist was annoyed by this remark, and glaring at the boy as though he were about to slap him, he said, "You ought to go wipe the snot from your nose. Unless your five sense organs are clean, how could you smell the fragrance of the way of donkey feces?"

As the boy related his grandpa's words to me, his attitude reflected even more of the pomposity of an old academician, and I could not suppress my laughter. Angrily he berated me, "You foreigners are really barbaric! How could Chinese people respect the likes of you? We are extremely conscious of courtesy, so how dare you laugh at the precious words of a great immortal master? It's perfectly normal for Grandpa to tell me to wipe my nose. And if I were to first wash out the wax from my ears before asking questions about Taoist teachings, that too would be normal." And at the same moment, hot tears came pouring from his eyes! *Ai ya,* now I really regretted laughing at him, so I quickly apologized and tried to soothe him by saying, "Please pardon my offense, young Taoist. I beg you to grace me with further teaching." But he adamantly refused to forgive me, and silently turned around and walked away.

More than fifty years have passed since this encounter, but in my mind's eye the scolding I received from that child seems to have happened only yesterday. I can still hear his tone of blame ringing in my heart. Whenever I recall how I made him cry, I once again feel remorse. The lesson he taught me certainly had a lasting effect. Later, a good friend of mine further expounded upon the method of "Washing Clean the Five Sense Organs," and as a result I sometimes gained a glimpse of the light of the Tao, heard an echo of the sound of the Tao, or caught a whiff of the fragrance of the Tao; and thus I finally understood the profound meaning of "All things great and small contain the essential nature of the Tao."

Although I do not often experience such rare and precious realizations, I still reap great benefit from them. For example, whenever I feel disgusted by a particular person or thing, I remind myself that the fault does not necessarily lie in the object of my disdain, but rather that my own senses have become distorted with pollution, and that I should therefore clean them and clarify my perception. I find two advantages in being able to overcome my own mental aversions: first, it prevents me from doing harm to others; second, it prevents me from incurring the ill will of others. Looking at it from this perspective, that young lad definitely led me a step further toward understanding the Doctrine of the Golden Mean.*

The Thrilling Risk of Climbing Mount Hua in the Snow

During the winter holidays in 1935, I took a trip to Sian.† At the time, I still did not know much about Chinese history, and so I had no way of appreciating the significance of the many historical sites there, dating from ancient times, when the city was known as Chang An.

*The Doctrine of the Golden Mean refers to the "Middle Way" or "Middle Path" in Chinese philosophy, and it applies to all three of China's "great teachings": Buddhism, Taoism, and Confucianism. The essence of all Chinese philosophy is to always take the middle way between any extremes.

†An ancient city west of Peking, Sian served as the imperial capital during the Tang Dynasty, when it was known as Chang An (City of Eternal Peace)

Although the high city walls and tall gate towers that still surrounded Sian left me wide-eyed with awe, I was not particularly moved by the city's ancient relics from the past, and after only a three-day sojourn there, I departed.

While sitting on the train en route back to Peking, about two or three hours along the way I suddenly saw a sight of such magnificence that it tumbled my soul. It was a high and mighty mountain that soared like a tower straight up to the sky. Someone informed me that this mountain was one of the Five Sacred Peaks revered by Taoists, and that its name was Huashan (Mount Hua), also known as the Western Peak. *Ai ya!* One glance left me feeling topsy-turvy, for this lofty, rugged mountain was unlike any other, and its vistas were spectacular beyond description. Even before the train began to slow down at the next station, I had already decided to disembark and go have a look, and I quickly jumped up from my seat to grab my luggage. The train had not yet come to a halt when I leaped onto the platform and immediately left the station on my way to the foot of the mountain. As I walked ahead, I looked around for a local countryman who might be willing to carry my bags and serve as my guide.

The weather was extremely cold, and the surface of the earth was frozen solid. There were hardly any people afoot in the fields, and very few pedestrians on the street. After a long while, a young man strolled by. The moment he saw me he stopped in his tracks and stared at me wide-eyed and dumbfounded, as though he'd encountered a strange animal. I asked him whether there was anyone willing to accompany me up the mountain. He thought about it for a long time, then said that from the beginning of winter until the break of spring no one ascended the mountain; that reaching the mountain peak was extremely difficult at that time of year, as well as very dangerous; that the mountain trail was completely covered with snow and ice and the dwellings along the way might all be snowbound; that wild beasts were roaming about up there and sometimes even bandits; and that with so many dangers lurking along the way, who would dare to venture up there?

Just as I felt my heart grow dim with disappointment, the expression on his face suddenly shifted, and with a smile he said, "How about me going along with you? Anyone with experience from around here would surely be unwilling to go, but I'm a local resident who has never been up to the top of the mountain. I've only ventured about halfway up once or twice, so I'm not familiar with the trails toward the top. So I can carry your luggage, but I cannot lead the way. Would you like to take me along?" He noticed my hesitation and told me that if we got lost along the way, we could simply follow the little trail upwards for a while, and since the trees grow quite sparsely near the top, we'd sooner or later find our way back to the main path. I mulled it over and figured that since he was willing to take the risk, he was probably telling me the truth. And if I didn't hire him, then who could I hire? Finally I agreed to pay him a relatively generous fee, but only gave him half of it in advance in order to make sure that he didn't change his mind along the way. Thereupon we immediately set forth up the mountain. Before long we encountered two or three of his acquaintances, and he asked them to relay a message back to his family, to avoid causing them worry by his absence. They addressed him as "Little Chen," and so that's the name by which I also called him.

At first the weather was clear and bright, and though the stone steps were slippery, there was a handrail, which made it quite easy to move along at a slow pace. Toward dusk, we stopped at a hermitage to spend the night. A group of Taoist adepts were in the midst of their evening meal when we arrived. The aroma of warm wine, coming on top of our extreme hunger, almost made us swoon.

I hadn't had a bite to eat all day, so my belly felt like an empty bun. As soon as the Taoists heard of my condition, they immediately led me into the dining room to eat. The dinner they served me that evening was quite tasty, with huge steamed buns and well-prepared dishes. Little Chen and I devoured the food like hungry wolves and tigers, and we didn't stop until we were full. Little Chen patted his belly and smiled at me with satisfaction. I realized then that he very rarely had the opportunity to eat his fill, much less to enjoy countless cups of good wine. That evening he got quite drunk and lost consciousness, so a young Taoist boy helped him take off his clothes and steered him into bed. I too felt like a well-fed tiger and fell sound asleep without awakening.

During the night the weather grew severe, and the next morning the whole place was dense with swirling clouds and fog and covered with falling snow. The Taoists did not want us to depart and continue on our way up the mountain. But because my winter vacation was almost over and time was growing short, I decided to risk the weather and move on. The stone steps were even more slippery than the day before, so it was impossible to walk quickly, and we could hardly cover ten li of ground in a day. The gates of most of the little monasteries along the way were tightly shut, and it seemed that no one was there to provide overnight shelter during the winter. We'd brought along some food from the hermitage for lunch, and other than the wine they'd given us, the only thing we had to drink was snow. By nightfall the peak of the mountain was still far from sight. Little Chen started to feel afraid, and every time we passed a shrine post, he touched his head to the ground and begged the gods for help. Just as I was getting desperate and on the verge of complete exhaustion, a red wall appeared in the mist through the clouds in the distance. With an enormous sense of relief, we forged ahead with renewed effort.

The red wall enclosed an ancient hermitage, and the gate was shut tight. Only after we banged on the door for a long time did it finally open. Scrutinizing me carefully, an old Taoist inquired in great detail about where I'd come from and why I was there, and only after a long while did he finally allow us to enter. At first, the Taoist feared we might be bandits, but when he realized how unlikely it was that a Westerner would be in league with local thieves, he relaxed. As it was winter, there were only three old Taoist recluses and a few young acolytes in the hermitage. The three Taoist hermits were all charming old men of warm and friendly character, with a strong regard for old-fashioned courtesies, and this was precisely what I myself liked best. Thanks to the training I'd received in the old ways from Elder Brother Yuan-ruo, I was no stranger to such traditional etiquette. Polite terms such as "so honored to meet you," "grace me with your teaching," "your esteemed name," "your honorable home," "your venerable age," "your noble profession," "your good self," and similar honorifics came easily to my tongue. I was also quite familiar with the style of personal conduct required by old-world etiquette. Very few Westerners ever bothered to learn these civilities, and even most young Chinese remained unfamiliar with them.

The three old hermits made me feel warmly welcome there, no doubt because we all observed the same ancient code of propriety, but Little Chen's conduct was very different. He was a scrawny, underfed orphan who had never had a chance to eat and drink to his heart's content, so he spent all his time at the hermitage sleeping, eating, and drinking as much as he possibly could. The three Taoist gentlemen understood his situation and did not begrudge allowing him to eat and drink as much as he wished, but at the same time, they made it clear that they did not approve of this sort of undisciplined behavior.

Listening to a Gentleman's Lecture

Two more days went by, and still the clouds and mist hung thick and heavy, before finally scattering on the third day. During these two days I could not go outdoors, and instead I spent the whole time in my room keeping warm by the fire and reading books, but I did not feel the least bit lonely. From time to time the old Taoists came in with cheerful faces to prepare tea for me. Sometimes we had a chat, sometimes we played chess, and sometimes they took me into another room for a bite to eat or a glass of wine.

I noticed that the Taoists were quite frugal, though not excessively ascetic. They certainly did not limit their diet to dew and moonbeams, for they enjoyed two or three meals each day of tasty food, and though they knew that getting drunk was reprehensible, they were also not averse to drinking a few cups of strong spirits to help combat the cold. Out of curiosity, I inquired whether a taste for good food and fine wine might be harmful to the refinement of spirit and cultivation of the Tao.

They smiled and told me that among the teachings included in the Tao Teh Ching are the precepts to "eliminate conflict, eliminate extravagance, and eliminate excess," and that the meaning of this advice is that one should always cleave to the Golden Mean by avoiding extremes. They said that the scriptures also cautioned one to "observe purity, maintain simplicity, eschew profit, and relinquish desire." This means that one should cherish the plain and simple, dispense with the grand and opulent, and delight in the tranquil and refined, while also practicing generosity and nonattachment. Moreover, in all the entire thousand volumes of the Tao Tzang,* there is not a single sentence that tells people that they should not enjoy the simple pleasures of life.

I then asked how one might overcome the myriad difficulties involved in cultivating traditional Taoist teachings in today's modern society. The three Taoist worthies exchanged knowing glances; then one of them replied in very simple terms in order to make it easy for me to understand: "Society consists of people, including you, me, and our neighbors, plus the neighboring districts and the neighboring countries. If you wish to rectify society, you must first rectify yourself." I felt that this statement was excessively simplistic. Back in the time when the sages Lao-tze and Chuang-tze were born, the world did not yet have enormous cities, so how could the old sages envision the situation we live in today, much less think of ways to improve it? Later, however, whenever I recalled that old Taoist's words, the more I thought about it, the more I understood his profound meaning, until finally I began to agree with him.

When the weather turned clear again, I was anxious to get back to

*Literally "Treasury of the Tao," this is the complete collection of all the classical Taoist scriptures.

school and dared not waste any more time. Although I had not reached the mountain peak, I now had to resign myself to going back down. Little Chen took me to the train station, collected the balance of his fee and, cracking a big smile on his face, ran back home. The station master informed me that the train would not arrive until midnight and led me into a small shop next door to warm myself by the fire. Inside the shop, an old woman sat by the stove selling lamb and noodle soup, and the aroma was wonderful. Many other local people, including various street vendors, were also in the shop waiting for the train. Some lay on the *kang** smoking, some played cards, some were gossiping, some sleeping—the atmosphere was very cozy. The setting and ambience there typified the winter habitat of country villages throughout northern China.

Despite their poverty, shabby clothing, and illiteracy, that group of men and women, old and young alike, reflected an attitude of modesty and respect, and they were all admirably well-mannered, guileless, and kindhearted. If I were to select a term to describe them in English, I'd call them "nature's gentlefolk." Physically, they were not particularly clean, and some of them reeked heavily of garlic, but that didn't bother me because I also have a fond taste for garlic. The main point here is that although they had no formal education of any sort, they nevertheless manifested the finest virtues of thousands of years of Chinese culture.

Regrettably, at that time the rural folk in northern China were, despite their endearing charm, also extremely distressed, and the hardships they endured are almost beyond description. For example, almost every household raised chickens, but very rarely did anyone ever have a chance to taste a chicken egg, much less chicken meat! Chicken eggs and meat were marketable commodities, so to consume them at home was regarded as a waste. *Ai, ai, ai!*

Soon after returning to the school in Tienjin, I received a copy of

---

*A kang was a heated brick platform, common in most houses in northern China, used to keep warm by day and night. It served as both couch and bed.

an English translation of the Confucian classic, The Great Learning.* After reading the first chapter, I discovered that the admonitions of the great sage did not differ from the essential points of advice given to me by the Taoists at Mount Hua. The first chapter contains these words: "Those who wish to govern the nation must first bring order to their own families. Those who wish to bring order to their own families must first correct their own conduct. Those who wish to correct their own conduct must first rectify their hearts."

As I took these words into consideration I thought: the fact that Confucius and Mencius held precisely the same point of view on this issue as Lao-tze and Chuang-tze could not possibly be a mere coincidence. And according to what Elder Brother Yuan-ruo had told me, Buddhists also hold the same view. In other words, the basis of Buddhist spiritual practice is to "correct your conduct and rectify your heart." Although for Buddhists the purpose of this principle is not entirely limited to reforming society, but also to helping all beings end suffering, find happiness, and gain salvation, nevertheless one could say that the basic meaning is, "If you wish to rectify others, first rectify yourself."

Buddhists cultivate their conduct by observing the precepts to refrain from killing, stealing, and immoral sexual behavior; they cultivate their speech by refraining from telling lies, making empty promises, slandering others, and not saying what they mean; and they rectify their hearts by refraining from greed, anger, and doubt. From this it's clear that the most fundamental principles of the Three Teachings of China (Taoism, Confucianism, and Buddhism) do not depend on the strength of faith in gods but rely instead on one's own strength to overcome one's own flaws. From their inception, the Three Teachings have always transcended superstition, as evidenced by Confucius' advice to "respect gods and demons but keep them at a distance," and by the passage in the Tao Teh Ching that

*Ta Hsueh (The Great Learning) is one of the sacred Confucian texts that every scholar in traditional China studied meticulously, and had to be committed to memory by those who wished to pass the civil service exams in order to obtain a post in the imperial bureaucracy.

states, "All things originate from the Great Tao, but the Great Tao takes no credit for it." According to the interpretation of Professor Yang Chia-luo, this means that all things in the world are created by the Great Tao and ultimately return to the Great Tao, but the Tao creates and receives all things naturally without preconceived intent and does things without deliberately doing them.

Buddhist scriptures also reflect the nonsuperstitious nature of the Three Teachings, such as evidenced in the passage, "All Buddhas and all sentient beings are of one single mind, and there is no other dharma than this." In Buddhist studies the word "dharma" in the phrase "there is no other dharma than this" means "phenomenon." From this we may surmise that if all Buddhas and all sentient beings are of one single mind, then there cannot possibly exist any beings beyond this one mind, and thus how could there be any gods? Therefore, what people commonly refer to as the great almighty God, if such a being does indeed exist, could not be anything other than our own essential nature. It was only due to the way that later generations misinterpreted the original meaning of the great religious teachings that they degenerated into superstitious beliefs.

Some of the most advanced thinkers in modern physics have discovered that the basic principle of truth proposed by traditional Asian religions (especially Buddhism and Taoism) that "everything that exists is produced by consciousness, and nothing exists beyond this" accords precisely with the basic axioms of science. This essential truth has only recently begun to be understood by conventional contemporary scientists. I'm quite certain that these newest scientific revelations have already come to the attention of traditional scholars in Asia.

Datung's Golden Lily Pageant

Toward the end of July 1936, during the summer recess I set out for Mount Wutai in Shanhsi province. My original plan was to stay there for a little over a month, but unexpectedly, shortly before the next semester began, all the universities and academies in northern China suddenly stirred with a big wave of strikes. Hearing of this while still up on the mountain, I decided to take advantage of this opportunity to extend my stay there for a few more weeks. Including the time it took for my return trip, that journey lasted almost three months, and I'd say that the experiences I had along the way constituted the most extraordinary holiday of my entire life.

China abounds with fabled mountains, which people there believe are the sacred abodes of bodhisattvas and great gods, and thus there is an old adage that states, "It is not the height of a mountain that counts; it's the presence of immortal spirits that make it famous." Among the many famous mountains in China, there are nine of special distinction, known as the Nine Great Mountains of Fame, and these nine legendary mountains include the Five Peaks (the fabled mountains of Taoist lore) and the Four Lofty Mountains (the sacred dwelling places of Buddhist bodhisattvas). The Five Peaks are Mount Tai, Mount Hua, Mount Heng, Mount Hung, and Mount Tsung, and the Four Lofty Mountains are Mount Wutai, Mount Omei, Mount Putuo, and Mount Chiouhua. Although I have not yet gone to see all nine of these great legendary mountains, I have visited most of them.

I had the good fortune to climb and pay my respects at the sacred sites on the southern, western, and northern summits of the Five Peaks (namely Mounts Tai, Hua, and Heng), as well as Mounts Putou, Omei, and Wutai. According to the impressions I still carry in my memory, Mount Wutai in Shanhsi surpassed all the others in terms of scenery, interesting sites, and spiritual ambience. Perhaps that's because the longest sojourn in all of my travels was there. Prior to my trip to Mount Wutai, I'd already heard quite a lot about this place. Friends had told me that its history extended back prior to the Tang Dynasty, that a number of structures dating from Tang times still remained there, and that there were over three hundred temples, large and small, located on the mountain. Due to a major expansion of construction during the Ching Dynasty, most of these temples were Tibetan lamaseries.* Among the monks living on the mountain, more than ten thousand were Mongolian and Tibetan lamas, but there were only a few hundred Chinese monks.

In those days, transportation to Mount Wutai was very inconvenient. Although Mount Wutai stood only 261 miles from Peking, it took over ten days to get there. First I boarded the afternoon train headed due north, arriving at Chiang Chia Kou late at night, then the train headed southwest, reaching Datung the following morning. After disembarking there, I checked into an inn, and the innkeeper informed me that the road to Mount Wutai was so heavily infested with bandits that it was essential to travel there with a group. Fortunately, a big group of merchants was departing soon, and in addition to the merchants, a large number of Mongolian pilgrims were also traveling along with them. The innkeeper said they would depart the day after tomorrow and that he would make arrangements for me to join the group, asking me also whether I was willing to ride a horse or if I'd prefer to hire a cart to carry me. Since carts were drawn by mules, this would also require me to hire a pair of strong mules, as well as a muleteer to follow on foot.

Datung was a midsized town and quite interesting. According to the innkeeper, this town had three distinctions: first, it had served as the imperial capital two thousand years ago; second, the local women here claimed that their Golden Lilies were more petite and more beautifully shaped than any others and that indeed they were unrivaled throughout the nation. (Opportunely, a Golden Lily pageant was scheduled for the following day, during which all young women who were not yet engaged to be married sat in front of the gates of their homes and allowed passersby to admire their tiny feet, thereby attracting the attention of young men who might become potential suitors.) Third, near Datung were the famous granite caverns in which thou-

*The emperors of the Manchu Ching Dynasty (1644–1912) had a particular affinity for Tibetan Buddhism and generously subsidized construction of Tibetan temples.

sands of Buddhas were sculpted in solid stone during the Wei Dynasty of the Three Kingdoms Period (220–265 CE), a sight of incomparable wonder.

Although I had not anticipated lingering in Datung for a few more days, I felt I could not waste the chance to relish these remarkable sights. To fully appreciate the awesome artwork in the stone caverns, as well as examine the display of hundreds of pairs of pretty Golden Lilies, I would surely need at least three days there. Of course, I wasn't fond of bound feet and felt great pity for the suffering it caused those young girls, but this sort of pageant was an extremely rare sight. Picture hundreds of young maidens sitting there while passing crowds casually inspected their little feet bundled up in colorfully embroidered shoes, feigning complete indifference to the scrutiny of wayfarers. They pretended to chat and laugh merrily among themselves, but we could clearly see that most of those girls found it difficult to endure such indignity.

Not until the day of departure did I find out that I was traveling together with over sixty other people, some of whom were riding on horseback, some sitting in carts, and others walking. My muleteer was a stout young man surnamed Ma, with a pleasant disposition and a friendly, courteous demeanor. Beyond town, the road became very rough, narrowing to the width of a small trail. Every twenty or thirty li along the way, we found the road flooded by swollen rivers, with water rising to the height of the horses' chests.

Those on horseback crossed the rivers with ease, but those of us riding in carts had to disembark and wade across on foot. I watched as others took off their pants without hesitation, hitched up their overcoats, trudged into the water, and waded across to the other side, but I felt too bashful to strip off my pants. My muleteer took note of this, and with a big laugh he said, "You need not disrobe, sir, I shall carry you across on my back." I saw that most of the lamas and merchants were being carried across on the backs of their servants, and that only the local peasants were wading bare-bottomed through the water.

The mules carrying our cargo and drawing our carts were all afraid of the water, and since they had no riders, they could not be spurred to make them ford the rivers. So each mule had to be dragged across with great strain by two or three people. Besides this, several other things slowed down the pace of our journey; for example, every day at noon the entire entourage of merchants insisted on stopping over at towns and villages along the way to have lunch, after which they tarried for another hour or two to give themselves and their horses a rest. Consequently, each day the merchant caravan traveled no more than forty-five Chinese li (about fifteen miles). Modern motor vehicles, if the roads are fairly good, would take no more than twenty minutes to traverse this distance.

The Florid Carpet of Color Covering the Slopes of Mount Wutai

Eight or nine days after leaving Datung, we finally arrived at the foot of Mount Wutai. The summit towered more than eight thousand feet above sea level, while the base of the colossal mountain spread wide and far, with each of the five separate peaks soaring up from the broad expanse of a high plateau. Most of the more than three hundred temples and monasteries there, as well as the local government offices, shops, markets, and a very tall white pagoda, were all located on this plateau. The shrine halls in most of the temples were extraordinarily ornate, and their architecture and decor easily matched the grand style of the most famous sites of ancient times. On the streets of the small town, and along the mountain trails, it was common to see people dressed in splendid attire. Most of the ten thousand lamas living there wore the purple-red Tibetan-style monastic robes, but some of the lamas were dressed in the elaborately floral garments worn by officials and eunuchs during the Ching Dynasty.

The ornate facades of the shrine halls, the multicolored robes of the lamas, the jade-green silhouettes of the distant peaks, the vivid variegated hues of the countless wild flowers on the mountain slopes—the whole tableau made one imagine that the entire mountain was covered with a florid carpet of color, without brink or border.

When I first arrived at Mount Wutai, I immediately sighed with awe at its flourishing luxuriance. Later I discovered that none of the other famous mountains of China matched this rich abundance, and I found this rather strange. Prevailing conditions in northern China at that time were not conducive to such plenitude. In fact, even when Japanese aggressors began to plunder the region, the Buddhist monasteries of Mount Wutai still managed to avoid the ravenous greed of corrupt officials and the pillage of bandits.

How could this be explained? There were probably three reasons for this. First, according to Buddhist belief, Mount Wutai was the sacred abode of the bodhisattva Manjusri. Manjusri represents the Buddhist virtue of wisdom, or enlightened mind, and he was particularly revered by Mongolian and Tibetan devotees. Second, Mount Wutai was located closer to Inner and Outer Mongolia than the other sacred mountains of China, and therefore countless Mongolian pilgrims came there each year to worship, and Mongolian lamas constituted the majority of the resident monks on the mountain. Third, from the beginning of the Ching Dynasty until the War of Resistance against Japan, China carefully avoided any action that unnecessarily provoked the people of Mongolia. Not only did the Manchu emperors adhere to the so-called Lamaist school of Buddhism (i.e., Tibetan Tantric Buddhism), they also needed the assistance of Mongol leaders to help them control China, and therefore they treated Mongolian and Tibetan lamas with special favor.

Although the Chinese government did not grant special preference to the Mongolian people during the early years of the republic, it also did not wish to stir up any trouble with them. If they had tried to seize control of Wutai, this would inevitably have incurred the wrath of the Mongolians and thereby increased the threat of civil unrest that gripped China at that time. Neither the government nor the people of

China wished to provoke this sort of calamity. Because of these factors, Mount Wutai was able to enjoy several hundred years of uninterrupted peace and prosperity.

Our merchant entourage made the journey without encountering a single raid by bandits and arrived safely at Mount Wutai. As soon as we entered the little town there, the members of our group scattered in all directions and did not regroup again. As I disembarked from the cart, a huge Buddhist monastery loomed before my eyes. Above the main gate hung a wooden tablet, and on the tablet were inscribed the words "Bodhisattva Summit." The Tibetan-style pagoda that towered outside the gate marked the center of the town. Located near the pagoda were numerous little workshops that produced various Tibetan handicrafts. Although at that time these items were not regarded as particularly rare or precious, today it would be difficult to find them anywhere outside of museums. Because I was extremely fond of this sort of traditional handicraft (bronze statuary, paintings, and so forth), I decided to lodge at the Bodhisattva Summit in order to browse around and inspect the craftsmen at work.

In that enormous Buddhist monastery even the guest bedrooms were sumptuous, because in the past, high-ranking officials and other social luminaries often came to stay there. At the time of my visit, there were no important guests, and therefore I was able to stay in a very luxurious suite. The kang was covered with beautiful wool blankets, and on the three walls adjoining the kang was painted an exquisite work of art—a hunting scene (even though hunting was an infraction of Buddhist ethics). The bedroom furniture was made of birch wood, the bowls, cups, and other utensils were all superbly fashioned, and the uniforms of the service staff were as elegant as those worn by eunuchs in the imperial palace.

Since this was a frontier region, I felt concerned that perhaps I'd be required to eat the sort of diet that prevailed beyond the Great Wall. I'd heard that Mongolians only ate food products made from domestic animals and wild game (such as meat, milk, butter, and fresh blood), and that they ate no rice, noodles, vegetables, or fruits. Fortunately, when meals were served, all of what I saw set before me was the sort of food preferred by Chinese people.

This beautiful environment was richly endowed with things of interest. Most interesting of all was observing the ritual activities of Mongolian pilgrims. One of them was "circumambulation," whereby devotees walked in a circle around a pagoda, while using their hands to spin scores of huge prayer wheels arranged around the base of the pagoda. Some of them circumambulated the white pagoda ten thousand times before resting, while others performed grand prostrations before the pagoda, first kneeling down to touch their foreheads to the ground, then quickly stretching their whole bodies forward until their toes, knees, bellies, chests, and chins all touched the ground at the same time, and finally holding their palms together above the crown of their heads to express their reverence. After standing up again, they repeated the entire sequence over and over, hundreds of times per session, many sessions per day, continuing day after day until they'd performed from ten thousand to one hundred thousand prostrations. Many pilgrims came from Heilungjiang and other faraway places, walking the entire distance on foot, and after staying there for a few months, they walked all the way back home. They came like this to worship at the sacred mountain every three or four years.

The Mysterious Phenomenon of the Bodhisattva Lights

It's a pity that I couldn't speak Mongolian, because after a few weeks at Mount Wutai, I began to yearn for the company of friends. Therefore, I decided to visit a place where travelers of Chinese descent stayed. A local resident informed me that there were very few ethnic Chinese monks living on the mountain, but that there was one special monastery called the Lodge of Supreme Beneficence. The founder was the renowned grandmaster Neng Hai. He had lived for a long time in Tibet, where he had become highly proficient in the Tibetan language, and he had mastered the Vajrayana (Tantric Tibetan Buddhist) teachings.

Grandmaster Neng Hai had studied the entire heart of the Tantric Tibetan school of Buddhism and transmitted its essential teachings to disciples who were not literate in the Tibetan language, enabling them to practice the path of Tantric Buddhism. He had thirty to forty close disciples, all of whom were highly talented and well-disciplined monks. During the time of the Tang Dynasty, China had its own school of Tantric Buddhism, but toward the end of the Tang period, it fell into decline and disappeared, and only a branch sect in Japan continued this tradition. Grandmaster Neng Hai wanted to revive the Chinese Tantric school of the Tang era and to further enrich it with Tibetan Tantric teachings. My local informant also told me that every year during the summer season, Chinese practitioners came to live in retreat at the Lodge of Supreme Beneficence. Happy to hear this, I decided to pay a visit there.

To my complete surprise, among the lodgers was an acquaintance of mine from Tienjin, Dr. Chang. He said that I'd come just in the nick of time, for in a few days he and some of his friends were going to explore one of the mountain's Five Peaks (I think it was the West Peak, but perhaps my memory is wrong) to see the so-called Bodhisattva Lights, and if I wished to join them, nothing would please him more. Naturally I felt very happy to accompany them on a visit to such a famous sight, but when I accepted their invitation, I could not foresee that the Bodhisattva Lights would become one of the most unforgettable and mysterious phenomena I've seen in my entire life.

Before departure, we hired a few mules and horses. As we set forth on our journey, the sky was gray and overcast, and the mountain peak stood dim in the distance, sometimes shrouded in white mist, sometimes completely concealed by clouds. Before long, our clothing grew damp. The road was slippery and difficult to traverse, slowing the mules and horses down to a plodding pace. That evening we lodged at a small monastery, and the next morning we continued our ascent in the rain. The mountain trail was even more slippery than the day before, so we had no choice but to dismount our horses and proceed on foot. Originally we had anticipated viewing the Bodhisattva Lights that evening, but the groom informed us that during inclement weather there were no unusual phenomena of any kind to be observed there.

Just as we were sighing with disappointment, the sky began to clear. As the sun set in the west, the clouds dissolved and the mist scattered. When night descended, the entire sky filled with stars. Upon arrival at the peak, we took lodging at an ancient mountain monastery, where there were only three or four monks, but lots of rodents. After we'd finished a vegetarian meal and the kitchen lamps had been extinguished, the monks led us into the kitchen to have a look. Inside, it was pitch black, and in the darkness we could feel soft bodies bumping constantly against our feet with a shrill squealing sound that gave us the creeps. A monk struck up some sparks on a flint stone outside, lit a small torch, and came inside. *Ai ya!* All we could see was the entire floor completed covered with a seething mass of rats, so densely packed that not a sliver of space separated their bodies. I'd often heard that remote monasteries were like this, and since monks were forbidden to kill any form of life, they had no choice but to tolerate it. Every winter the mountain monasteries were sealed off from the outside world by snow, so they had to store sufficient supplies of rice to prevent the monks from starving to death. This attracted swarms of rodents, and other than killing them, what else could be done to eliminate them?

The monasteries at the peak of the mountain had very few bedrooms, so our only option was to sleep on the floor planks of the reception room; and even though it was the summer season, the nights up in the high mountains were still very cold. The monks lent us a pile of their thickly padded bed quilts, and since our little group slept closely nestled together, we slipped comfortably into sweet slumber.

Late in the night, we were suddenly startled awake, and as we opened our eyes we saw a monk standing in the doorway and shouting at us, "Get up, get up, hurry out to the terrace to see the Bodhisattva Lights!" The moment we heard that, we scurried to our feet and threw on a few pieces of clothing, and though we draped ourselves with quilts as substitutes for our padded coats, we still felt very cold. We ran out to the terrace, where it was even colder, making our bodies shiver from head to foot, but our hearts were filled with excitement as we focused our attention on viewing the mysterious phenomenon of the famous sight before our eyes.

That peak was Mount Wutai's central pinnacle, and it stood relatively aloof from the other four peaks. Viewing them all from the vantage point of the level plateau halfway up the mountain, the five peaks looked like five separate mountains. But looking into the distance from the terrace, with the main peak's summit behind us, the other four peaks were concealed from view, and the high plateau was spread out thousands of feet below us—so gazing out at the view from here, all we could see was open sky.

As we stood on the terrace outside the monastery, scanning the expanse of the horizon, we saw thousands of strange objects floating slowly above the terrace. These extraordinary globe-shaped entities approached from faraway and disappeared again into the distance, continuously radiating golden beams of light, as though the whole sky were filled with countless glowing lanterns. Their shape, color, size, and other features were all exactly alike, without any noticeable variations. These mysterious orbs moved across the sky at about the same speed as goldfish swimming calmly in water.

However, because there was no way to judge the distance between these curious objects and the terrace, it was difficult to determine their size. According to my conjecture, they seemed to be about the size of footballs, but they could also have been as large as observation balloons. In the midst of the darkness, distances were impossible to verify.

The Bodhisattva Lights could not have been etheric objects. Instead, they appeared to be physical entities with both substance and duration, and one could clearly discern that they were light and delicate, otherwise how could they float in the sky? Only those with strong faith in Buddhist doctrine would think otherwise. They would believe that these things were neither light nor heavy objects, but rather that they were the radiant light emanating from the enlightened heart of Manjusri Bodhisattva. What I have said above is all based on later conjectures. At that time, we all just stood there astounded beyond bounds, stammering at each other, speechless with wonder. Not yet able to even speculate on the possibility of such a mysterious phenomenon manifesting in the sky, we simply stood in awestruck silence in order to appreciate its unfathomable nature.

That was fifty years ago and I still find it very difficult to explain this phenomenon! In those days, most people believed that it really was an emanation from the luminous awareness of a bodhisattva. And perhaps this was in fact the case, for I have no grounds to dispute such a claim. People in modern times, even if they are Buddhists, generally find it difficult to really believe in the existence of supernatural phenomena in this world. Even I, while actually witnessing this startling marvel, felt no doubt in my mind that it was an arcane mystical phenomenon. Later, however, when I tried to analyze it with reason and logic, I found myself searching for a theoretical basis to explain the origin of this phenomenon. But in all this time, I still have not found a suitable scientific answer, only a lingering doubt.

Of course, it's true that countless other travelers have also seen the Bodhisattva Lights, and naturally many of them are not Buddhists. Perhaps they ask themselves whether this phenomenon is simply produced by marsh gas. Personally, I think that's definitely not the case. How could marsh gas discharge from a high plateau halfway up a tall mountain, rise several thousand feet, then dissipate into the vaults of heaven? Moreover, those countless thousands of glittering golden globes clearly drifted in from the far distance, then floated away again into the distant horizon. I've never heard of any marsh gas that can rise up high into the sky and drift dozens of miles, all without the slightest change in their original shape and size. How could that be possible?

Those who have never witnessed this fascinating spectacle might guess that it's an illusion produced by some sort of deceptive technique. But how could anyone up on the mountain possibly produce those countless thousands of luminous spheres? To produce thousands of "lights" each and every day would cost a fortune, and to make them fly high and far would definitely not be an easy task, and would require spending an even greater sum of money. What would be the point of wasting money like this?

At the time, I did not inquire whether or not the Bodhisattva Lights occurred in all four seasons, but in any case, it was certainly not limited to any particular days. When Dr. Chang and his group invited me to travel with them, they did not specify a special day to ascend the peak of the mountain. In fact, they postponed our departure several times in order to attend some teachings given by Grandmaster Neng Hai. Nor did I ask whether the Bodhisattva Lights were only to be seen on one peak, or if they could also be observed from the other peaks. I think someone from a big travel agency in China would know. Ever since the Buddhist monasteries on Mount Wutai were wrecked by the Japanese army, and the suppression of religion by the Red Guards that followed later, very few travelers went to that mountain. Only recently have people once again begun to mention the various famed sights of Mount Wutai. During the intervening decades, the situation at this sacred mountain has no doubt changed. People today may not even know that Mount Wutai has such a marvelous phenomenon as the Bodhisattva Lights. Nor have I asked anyone lately whether people still climb up to the peak to witness this extraordinary display.

Meeting the Old Man of the Northeast

After our visit to the peak, I bid farewell to Dr. Chang and his companions and returned to my lodging at the Bodhisattva Summit. One day an old Mongolian man appeared and invited me to his hostel for tea. I didn't know his name, but we had met while traveling together in the merchant caravan. Whenever I think of him, in my mind I always refer to him as "the Old Man of the Northeast."

His homeland was in Chilin province, and his village was located more than four thousand li (about thirteen hundred miles) from Mount Wutai. He was already more than seventy years old, but he was still able to walk that distance on foot. He was illiterate and had very little money, and the only luggage he carried was the wooden bowl commonly used by Mongolians, a pair of chopsticks, a small knife, and a toothpick made from ox bone. At night, he stayed either at monasteries that provided food and shelter free of charge, or else he slept outdoors; sometimes he did a few days of labor in order to earn a bit of money; and sometimes he had to depend on begging to survive. After reaching Datung, he joined the merchant caravan, and before long we became acquainted.

After our departure, I started paying close attention to him. The reason was that he walked in giant strides at a speed that kept pace with the carts, and while he strode along he often chatted with my muleteer. Every time we forded a river, he took off his pants and helped my muleteer pull the cart as well as one of the mules across to the other bank. Strange as it may seem, although mules are afraid of water, as soon as they heard the sound of that old man saying, "all right, all right," they no longer resisted and obediently crossed the water. He never asked for any money, and I instinctively stayed near him, inviting him to eat with me whenever we stopped in small towns for lunch. One time he said, "I don't like begging for food, and except when I'm so hungry that I cannot bear it any longer, I don't impose on others due to hunger. But I love to do odd jobs for people, and in return, they never fail to toss me a few coins, or a couple of steamed buns. That's very good."

The Old Man of the Northeast had an enormous appetite. When ordering food, I usually asked for two entrees, one soup, plus two large steamed buns, or one or two bowls of rice. But he could eat countless buns and then consume several bowls of rice or millet porridge as well. Although the stuffed dumplings served in the countryside regions of the northeast were huge, if we were having lamb dumplings, he could easily eat three platters (seventy-five pieces) plus a big bowl of soup. Despite his astonishing capacity for food, his physique was relatively slim. After arriving at Wutai, I lost track of him and did not anticipate that he would come to find me.

As I walked with him over to the Manibhadra monastery for tea that day, I thought to myself that even though the old fellow could not afford the cost of inviting me for a little drink, he nevertheless wanted me to be his guest at least one time.

Why? He was the sort of character I referred to earlier, a "rustic gentleman from the northeast." His line of thought may have gone something like this: "I helped get those hydrophobic mules of yours to cross the river many times, and you invited me to eat my fill at numerous meals; since this doesn't differ much from hiring an 'odd-job man' for a short period of time, one could say that I merely served as your hired hand. Nevertheless, you invited me to eat, and now I have come especially to take you out for tea—this is a mutual expression of our friendship. From this you can clearly see that I regard you as my friend, not just as my employer." How totally true! The old fellow was beset by hardship and poverty, and had no education, but still he did not view me as "superior," nor himself as "inferior." He was a guileless, unpretentious, good-hearted man. I took it as an honor to have gained his friendship.

The monastery where he stayed was so fully packed with poor pilgrims from Mongolia that some of them couldn't even find enough space there to spread out a mat, and had to sleep instead in a cave beside the monastery. When the weather grew very cold up on the plateau, most of the pilgrims departed and returned to Inner Mongolia, Ching Hai, Chilin, and other places. Those who remained at Wutai were therefore able to sleep in borrowed beds within the monastery. As for the Old Man of the Northeast, I never asked him where he lodged, but shortly he led me into a sumptuously appointed room full of antique furniture and fixtures, which may well have been lent to him by a lama so that he would have a suitably fine place to entertain a foreign guest from the West.

After steeping the tea, he brought out an extremely beautiful porcelain teacup and was just preparing to pour, when he noticed that the inside of the cup was dirty, whereupon he politely stuck out his tongue and licked the interior surface of the cup completely clean. Then, after showing me with great satisfaction that the cup was now spotless, he poured in the tea and handed it over to me to drink. All I could do was force myself to express my gratitude.

The moment I noticed the color of the tea, I nearly fainted! I already knew that Mongolian custom was to boil brick tea and add butter, but what I did not expect was that the butter he added to the tea was not only made from camel's milk brought there from a great distance, but was also of a yellowish-green color, with a smell that stank even worse than stinky bean-curd,* as though the butter had been left to go rancid for several months.

Ai ya, the stench of that butter was really hard to bear. As soon as I smelled it, I felt like throwing up, and immediately I thought to myself, "Old Pu, you must behave like a 'rustic gentleman,' you must pretend that the beautiful fragrance of this tea surpasses even that of the sweetest nectar served in heaven! This man is treating you with such sincerity and good will, that to hurt his feelings and make him unhappy would be a shameful disgrace." Thereupon, I forced myself to drink down a full cup in one big gulp, as though swallowing a bowl of bitter medicine, while at the same time expressing a euphoric attitude of ecstatic pleasure. The Old Man of the Northeast's face lit up with delight, and he immediately poured me another cup! In the end, I drank four cups in a row (each cup with many spoonfuls of that extraordinarily smelly butter stirred into it) before I was permitted a respite from drinking. After that we shared a very enjoyable

---

**Chou tofu,* literally "stinky bean-curd," is a fermented northern Chinese delicacy that smells and tastes somewhat like Limburger cheese.

conversation, during which I continuously begged him not to boil another kettle of water to make more tea, and after a long while we parted on a happy note. While that was one of the most unforgettably difficult trials of my life, winning that old man's heart made it all very worthwhile for me. This too is something I shall never forget.

Senior Lamas Traveling in Cortege

The most colorful festivals at Mount Wutai occurred over a period of several days in the middle of the seventh month (August) on the lunar calendar. On one of those designated days, thousands of lamas performed a ceremonial celebration in which they all lined up and traveled together in cortege. The prayer ceremony was a grand sight to behold, as lamas with their ritual instruments arrayed themselves in perfect formation. In addition, there were solemn musical recitals, sacred dances (known in Chinese as "ghost casting" dances), public oracles performed by specially ordained lamas, and explanations of difficult points in Buddhist teachings. Many varieties of this sort of activity were featured at this festival. From the scores of vending stands that sprang up along both sides of the route traveled by the cortege of lamas, fragrant clouds of incense rose up and filled the sky. The route extended over a distance of more than ten li, passing by many of the most important Buddhist monasteries.

On the day of the cortege I went to observe and participate in the festivities. The robes worn by the monks were very florid and beautiful. The leader of the procession, who rode on horseback, was the highest ranking lama on the mountain (I heard that he was usually a grandmaster from Tibet), and the horse he rode was snow-white, with saddle and reins inlaid with silver. Three or four steps in front of the horse, two young monks walked ahead holding up a tapestry stretched horizontally across the path and supported on a pair of wooden posts, moving along in stride with the horse's pace. The fringe of the tapestry was only about two feet from the ground. Woven in five bright colors, with silk tassels dangling along the bottom edge, the tapestry was magnificent.

As the grand monk rode ahead on his horse, many of the devotees along the way cast themselves to the ground in front of the tapestry, touching their foreheads to the earth in full prostration. But the young monks carrying the tapestry did not break stride, and it passed by in a moment, so the devotees had to quickly leap away in order to avoid getting trampled by the horse. Performing full prostrations with head to the ground was a way of obtaining the blessing of the lama and earning merit. On impulse, I suddenly strode forward a few steps and prostrated myself before the tapestry. As it passed by my head, I saw that the horses' hooves were just about to stamp on my body, and fearing that I could not stand up in time, I quickly rolled over and lay sprawled in disarray by the side of the path. The crowd roared with laughter and shouted out loud, "Bravo, bravo, you've earned your merit!"

Regarding merit, some people believe that those who sincerely cultivate compassion by giving alms when they come to worship at the temples on Mount Wutai eventually develop the ability to see Bodhisattva Manjusri with their own eyes. It is said that the Bodhisattva customarily disguises himself as a beggar in order to test the hearts of the pilgrims. Those who give alms generously can earn boundless blessings and divine protection. Because of this tradition, beggars on this mountain are treated with great generosity. Some people dismount their horses and approach the beggars with big offerings of alms held respectfully before them in both hands. In the old days, the beggars who came to Mount Wutai definitely did not regard their fate as unfortunate!

One day I read in a newspaper that the student strikes were coming to a halt, so I prepared for my return journey to Tienjin. Dr. Chang and a group of his friends had also decided to return home before the weather turned extremely cold. We therefore joined a group of travelers heading for Pao Ting prefecture. At the time, people said that the eastern route was easier to travel than the northern route, with fewer river crossings and more inns along the way, and that the trip could be made within seven days.

En route, an adept named Li, who was totally infatuated with the game of chess, insisted on stopping to challenge anyone he saw sitting by their doorway playing chess, at every town and village through which we passed. By the time he finished a game of chess, he had barely enough time to catch up again with the rest of us. As the sky turned dark at dusk, we worried that Mr. Li would not make it to the inn at which we were lodging; but fortunately, late after dinner, he finally straggled into the inn, wheezing and panting, soaked with sweat, and thoroughly exhausted. Luckily, he never encountered any serious mishap.

I hear that today Mount Wutai is only a half-day journey from Peking, which is certainly far more convenient. However, travelers today cannot enjoy the unique pleasures experienced by travelers in former times. Enduring difficulties and occasionally facing a few dangers, if they are not too extreme, enhances the flavor of travel, does it not?

4
Studying Zen and Seeking the Tao While Wandering in the Southwest

A Rare and Beautiful Lute Player

As noted above, when the Japanese army first invaded northern China, I was still overseas. In mid-September, I decided to return to China and boarded a ship bound for the Far East in Marseille, France. By that time, Tienjin had already fallen to the Japanese, so I had no idea where it was best to go. Luckily, there were two Chinese passengers on board who befriended me, one named Li and the other named Guo, both of whom had just graduated from college in England and wanted to return to their homeland to serve the nation. However, they did not know yet whether or not they could go back to their native region to visit their parents, and had therefore decided to disembark in Hong Kong in order to observe the situation. I resolved to do the same.

Upon arrival in Hong Kong, I heard that the Chinese government had relocated its wartime capital to Wuhan,* and that due to the military situation millions of civilians had migrated to the rear of the war

*Wuhan is an important industrial city located at the confluence of the Yangtze and Han rivers, about five hundred miles west of Shanghai.

zone to find work or attend school, including a great number of teachers and students. After some consideration, I and my two newfound friends decided to go first to Guilin* and take it from there.

From Hong Kong we took a steamboat upriver to Wujou, then hired a sailboat in preparation to continue upstream along the Gui River (known today at the Li River) to Guilin. We did not anticipate any difficulties on this stage of our journey. Toward evening the next day, after stowing our luggage in the cabin of the sailboat, the three of us went to a restaurant for a light meal.

We figured the oil lamps aboard the boat would not provide sufficient reading light, but still attract swarms of mosquitoes, and since the boat would not set forth until the crack of dawn, we may as well wander around Wujou for a while, then reboard to sleep. We were just in the midst of our deliberations, when the autumn breeze brought to our ears the beautiful dulcet tones of a *pi pa* lute.† The moment Mr. Li heard it, his spirit soared with joy, and with a big smile he said, "The sound of that lute is definitely coming from a flower boat. The player could well be one of our Sujou girls—this tune comes from my home region. Let's run over there and have a look."

Along the riverbank we could see a few flower boats floating on the surface of the water. A small rowboat took us over to the boarding plank of one of the flower boats, where a floridly dressed madam greeted us and loudly announced that guests were coming aboard. A group of music girls hurried out to welcome us. Several of them played the lute, but none of them were local girls. One of them took us into the cabin of the boat to entertain us with her singing and lute strumming, accompanied by another girl playing a violin. Mr. Li was completely enraptured by the music. Mr. Guo and I exchanged knowing glances, as though to ask whether or not our friend would be willing to return to the sailboat with us tonight. After a long while, two more rouged girls came over from another boat, summoned by the proprietor of our boat, who announced that they were

*Guilin is a scenic city located in Guijou province in southwest China.

†The pi pa is an ancient Chinese stringed instrument, similar to a Western lute.

both genuine Guijou girls. Mr. Li expressed no reaction whatsoever to this, for it was obvious that his heart and soul had already been captivated by the little enchantress playing the lute.

The two girls were both from Guilin, seventeen or eighteen years old, dressed in short white satin jackets with high collars and glossy black silk pants. I also felt infatuated by the girl playing the lute. Her jade-like complexion, pretty as a flower, her seductive gaze, and the exquisite beauty of her voice and music, plus the scent of jasmine blossoms in the boat and the reflections of the boat's multicolored lanterns on the water outside the windows—all made me feel extremely exhilarated. If only Mr. Li had taken a liking to the girl playing the violin, for I felt myself being drawn with an overwhelming emotional attraction to the girl playing the lute. She had bangs combed down over her forehead, with long hair hanging down her back and a spray of jasmine flowers arranged on her head. Rarely in my life have I ever encountered such an enchanting beauty.

Even though what I'm recording here happened forty-nine years ago, the image of her beautiful demeanor still lingers with perfect clarity in my mind. The strangest thing of all is that although I really liked her, I felt so befuddled in her presence that I completely neglected to speak with her. Perhaps it was because I felt inhibited to express my feelings in the company of my friends, or didn't wish to compete for her favor with Mr. Li, that the entire time I didn't utter a single word to her. After all these years, who could know the real reason?

After the two girls had finished singing a few tunes, it was already quite late, and Mr. Guo kept yawning continuously, indicating that he wanted to go back and sleep. It was obvious that Mr. Li was not at all happy about leaving, but we really had no other choice. The two of us felt extremely reluctant to part company with that beautiful girl, but the sailboat was scheduled to cast off before dawn, and it wouldn't do to return too late and awaken the captain, so all we could do was leave the flower boat with Mr. Guo. After boarding the sailboat, we climbed into our bunks in the cabin to sleep.

For a long time I could not sleep and just lay there staring at the top of the cabin. Suddenly, after much introspection, I realized that the beautiful young girl's eyes curved upward in the form known as "phoenix eyes." Gloomily I admitted that something impure lurked in my heart, and felt a foreboding that my future might be fraught with trouble. I asked myself, how and why could I become so infatuated that evening with a girl whom I'd never seen before? Most people define so-called beauty in terms of a pretty face, elegant limbs, and a refined demeanor, as well as interesting conversation, copious knowledge, and righteous character—this is what they would call the ideal beauty. But this sort of woman has never aroused the slightest passion in me; indeed, I'm more inclined to feel distaste for such types.

On the other hand, even though a particular woman may be quite ordinary, with little education, flawed character, and various other shortcomings, as long as she possesses a pair of phoenix eyes, such as those of a beautiful actress in Peking Opera, I'm very inclined, for this one and only reason, to fall completely in love with her. Obviously what motivates my passion is totally beyond any logic and reason. Are most people like this when it comes to love—that is to say, is this sort of passionate love nothing more than fantasy? This is something I had no way of knowing; all I knew was that because my own passions ran like this, they were extremely disturbing. The more I thought about it, the more I feared that this defect would cause me a lifetime of suffering and sorrow. With these thoughts in mind that night, it was a long time before I finally fell asleep.

The Exotic Natural Landscapes of Yangsuo

The captain of the sailboat was a stout fellow over forty years old, and with him were his wife and one-year-old son. With the boat moving upstream, the sails were useless, so instead the boat had to be towed with ropes attached to the front. Each morning at the crack of dawn, two boatmen went ashore to pull the boat forward by ropes. A third boatman stood on the back of the boat to steer the rudder.

The distance covered by our journey was nearly two hundred miles and would take about nine days. The rope pullers had to plod along a small path strewn with boulders, and each step required great effort. Despite the difficulty of treading the narrow track, they bent their backs into it and moved forward step by stolid step, rarely showing any signs of distress, as though their nerves were numb. During the day they only stopped once to gulp down three or four bowls of rice and take a short rest, and not until sunset did the boat drop anchor for the evening meal.

I often watched them as they carefully chose where to set down each foot between the rough boulders and smooth river stones, and I could see how much effort went into each and every step. Despite these conditions, they often sang and joked, and I truly admired their spirit of determination. Whenever the boat towing job shifted to the captain's wife, even she showed the same strength of spirit, and the moment she climbed aboard again, she immediately went back to take the rudder, without the slightest sign of fatigue. When we dropped anchor in the evening, the men all lay down to rest, but that woman still had to prepare food for six hungry people. With each day passing just like this, it must have been very hard to bear.

We passengers sometimes lay in our cabins reading or enjoying the scenery passing along both sides, and sometimes we went ashore to walk for a while. But we didn't have to trudge along the boulder-strewn banks; instead we strolled on a small trail covered with grass and wildflowers a short distance from the shore.

During these few days on the sailboat, it seemed as though we had severed all connections with the outside world, spending the whole day leisurely traveling along, enjoying the splendid views, and chatting with one another; national affairs and family matters drifted ever further away. The mountain landscapes grew more magnificent day by day. As we approached Yangsuo, it felt as though we were entering a magic realm. Now I understand the meaning of the old saying, "The landscapes of Guilin are the finest under Heaven, the landscapes of Yangsuo are the finest in Guilin." This saying not only notes that these two regions are the most beautiful places on earth, but it also indicates that they have the most exotic and unique mountain scenery in the world. When looking at most Chinese landscape paintings, one cannot necessarily identify the location of the beautiful scenery in the painting, but when the subject is the landscapes of Guilin and Yangsuo, one can tell at a single glance.

When we dropped anchor at Yangsuo, the rosy rays of sunset were shining down on the town, which was tucked in a mesmerizing tableau between mountains and water, and the strangely convoluted peaks and crests looked like a scene in a dream. By the time we stepped ashore, the sky was already growing dark, and soon the shadows enfolded into the night. We went into town for a meal and drank copiously in order to encourage poetic inspiration. Unfortunately, we drank too much and found ourselves incapable of grasping the lines stirred by the wine in our poetic imaginations. As we swayed our way back to the boat, a full moon suddenly rose up in the sky, flooding the mountains with radiant silver light. I said, "Foreigners easily make the mistaken assumption that the landscapes painted by your artists, beautiful as they may be, are far too exotic to reflect reality, and that the mountains they depict are completely unnatural. The mountain scenery here is no doubt the most extraordinary on earth, but it is still totally natural." Mr. Guo laughed drunkenly and said, "Don't speak nonsense! What do you mean by unnatural? All phenomena are completely natural, otherwise they would not manifest at all!" Mr. Li quoted an old Latin adage, "After wine one spits out the truth," then added, "Your noble self has just spoken the truth."

I interrupted to say, "In the Sung Dynasty, there lived a learned scholar, I don't recall his name, who integrated Buddhism with the teachings of Confucius. His thesis was that all things originate from the essential nature of the Tao, and that all existent phenomena are nothing more than products of consciousness. Consciousness is infinite and immeasurable, so how can there possibly be any distinctions within it? Reality and fantasy all spring from the same essential source of Tao, and therefore there is not the slightest difference between the two. Do you two gentlemen feel that this point of view makes sense?"

Mr. Li seemed displeased by our inebriated verbosity and said, "Enough, enough! I beg you both to shut up so that we may quietly enjoy the moonlight, all right?" Upon hearing these words, Mr. Guo's face flushed and he fell silent. Agreeing with what Mr. Li had said, I too said no more and gazed at the "most beautiful view under Heaven" in reverent silence. Regrettably, before long the wine rose to our heads and we had to lie down to sleep, leaving the lovely landscapes of Yangsuo unappreciated for the rest of the night.

The next morning at the break of dawn, with the mountain peaks cloaked in glowing mist and the fog drifting aimlessly over the water, a fleet of fishing boats set sail from the shore. Savoring the riverscape alone, my heart filled with joy beyond words.

People Are More Frightening Than Ghosts

A few days later, we arrived in Guilin. My two friends were eager to find jobs serving the nation and busied themselves preparing to travel onward to Wuhan. Unwilling to pass up the exquisite scenery of Guilin, I decided to stay there for a while, and think about the problems of finding work and earning a living later. First I rented a place with three rooms and temporarily established myself there as a private English language tutor. Contrary to my expectations, I soon discovered that the situation in Guilin left me feeling very disappointed. The landscapes had not changed since ancient times, that goes without saying, and the houses in the city still reflected the grace and beauty of traditional style, but these elegant external appearances did not suffice to satisfy me, for this place retained very little of the old Chinese culture. I'd heard that during the Taiping Rebellion* the city had been

*The Taiping Rebellion was a prolonged and very violent rebellion against the Manchu Ching Dynasty in the mid-nineteenth century, led by a quasi-Christian sect opposed to traditional Chinese culture. The rebels destroyed many old cities in southern and central China.

laid to waste many times by both the Taiping rebels and government troops. After the rebellion had been suppressed, although the buildings had been reconstructed, it was not possible to restore the highly refined civilization of the past.

In addition to this, the entire province was controlled by warlords. Li Tzung-jen and Pai Tsung-shi's* policies reflected strong militaristic elements. All residents of the city, men and women alike, were required to cut their hair very short and wear gray military uniforms. Nine out of ten scholars as well as other educated people could only find employment as government clerks, while suitable work in other professions was virtually nonexistent.

This sort of situation made conditions in the city and the province seem not much different from the regions controlled by the communists, although this had nothing whatsoever to do with Marxism. However, if one were to compare Generals Li and Pai with Fascist leaders, this would certainly be a reasonable comparison. To my mind, their way of doings things was truly deplorable. For example, several important military officers who were followers of Islam destroyed Buddhist monasteries throughout the entire province. This sort of arrogant barbaric behavior was so rampant there that it's impossible to describe it all. After discovering that the culture in Guangshi had suffered such severe damage, I decided not to prolong my stay there and prepared to move on to live in another region.

Before my departure, I traveled outside the city to see the mountains and waterways. One day as the rays of the setting sun slanted between the mountain peaks, I was startled to hear the rhythmic "chock chock" sound of a wooden fish and heard someone chanting the Diamond Sutra. This was something I had not heard since my arrival in Guilin, and I could not help but feel astonished. Walking further ahead, I saw a deserted stone cave, and in the cave an old monk sat secluded with his legs crossed in the lotus posture, tapping

*These Nationalist Chinese generals ruled as warlords in southwest China.

a wooden fish and chanting sutras. When the old monk saw a "foreign devil" appear, his face expressed a sense of shock, and his voice began to falter.

The old monk nevertheless completed his recitation of the Diamond Sutra, before he stopped tapping the wooden fish and took a rest. I bowed formally at the mouth of the cave to pay my respects, and he responded by placing his palms together at his heart, then signaled me with a gesture of his hand to come inside and sit down. After exchanging greetings with him, I inquired, "Are you not risking trouble, dear sir, reciting sutras in this area?" The old monk replied, "Here only ghosts can hear me. I daresay they might even enjoy listening. Do you think so?" I couldn't help but burst out laughing, and laughing along with me he said, "You don't believe there are ghosts in these mountains? Fine, fine, so you wouldn't believe in the existence of ghosts. Ghosts are products of one's own mind. How could there exist anything whatsoever outside the mind? However, some people are even more frightening than ghosts. Did you know that?" I quickly answered, "Isn't that indeed the truth! That's exactly what I think." He nodded his head thoughtfully for a while, then said, "Precisely. It's for this very reason that I have come out to live in the wilderness. However, lately things are not the same as they were a year or two ago. For example, if an old monk like me were to go into the city wearing these blue robes and carrying a wooden fish, loudly chanting sutras in the streets, probably no one would try to stop me. But if I were to start giving public sermons on the teachings contained in the sutras, that might really lead to big trouble."

He poured me some tea, then continued, "The people of this province are not very fond of religion. That's not surprising. Eighty years ago, Hung Hsiou-chuan* was driven mad by his overwhelming belief in a foreign creed, and thus he raised an army that slaughtered people

*The leader of the Taiping rebels, he claimed that he was the younger brother of Jesus and that he had been appointed by God to convert China by force to his megalomaniacal version of Christianity.

indiscriminately. Moreover, he declared that he and his clique were all celestial monarchs, celestial generals, and celestial warriors. Their scheme was to conquer the entire world. The destruction and loss suffered by the entire nation as a direct result of their behavior are beyond calculation. The consequences of that gang of long-haired wastrels' campaign to overthrow the Ching Dynasty by force of arms continue to this very day. Those who suffered the most severe damage are the people of Guangshi province. In the past, Guilin was distinguished as the most important cultural center in all of southern China, and the local dialect here was known as the 'official language of the south.' However, after our city was repeatedly ravaged in turn by the so-called celestial warriors and the opposing government troops, the rice fields and pastures, the crops and livestock, and all the people throughout the entire province suffered enormous damage and depredation, not to mention what happened to our highly advanced civilization!" With a woeful sigh he once again fell silent.

After a long time, the old monk fixed a penetrating gaze at me and asked, "Are you an Englishman?" I nodded my head in acknowledgement. He then said, "During my youth, I heard it said that the Taiping Rebellion was provoked by your English queen, Victoria. Is that true?" Startled by what he had said, I looked at him awkwardly and replied, "What on earth are you saying, dear sir? I'm afraid you've heard wrong." He repeated what he'd just said again, and added, "What drove Hung Hsiou-chuan and his clique mad? It was the deviant influence of fanatic English missionaries! Crazed with manic fury, the rebels defeated wave upon wave of imperial troops sent by the throne to subdue them."

The old monk continued, "After a few more years, the two patriotic generals, Tzeng Kuo-fan and Tzuo Tzung-tang, recruited soldiers and trained them to form the Army of Immortal Victory, and only then were they able to defeat the rebels. I heard that they relied on the assistance of General Gordon, who was sent to China by the government of England. At that time, your domineering queen was constantly interfering in the affairs of our country. First she used missionaries to provoke their fanatical converts into rebellion, causing the Chinese people to shed their own blood almost to the point of destroying the entire nation—then she sent an English general to help the dynasty subdue the rebellion."

I found it difficult to believe this senseless talk, and asked, "Why would the queen engage in such evil schemes?" With a sardonic smile, the old monk replied, "In order to grab control of our country, first she secretly sent missionaries to induce countless Chinese to slaughter one another, after which she pretended to sympathize with our nation's plight and offered to assist our government. This of course made our emperor feel grateful for her kind intentions, and believe that your queen was a reliable friend!"

My face flushed red with the realization that during the nineteenth century, the government of England often utilized missionaries to provoke trouble in other countries. Even though what the old monk had said may have been somewhat oversimplified, it still contained a significant element of truth. Queen Victoria's government certainly did harbor the intention of splitting up China like a ripe melon in order to gain control of several key provinces along the Yangtze River as colonies of England. Although the old monk's statements were not entirely accurate, they nevertheless described some real facts, and in any case it's absolutely true that England frequently intruded upon China's sovereignty. At the time, the reason I reacted so negatively to what he'd said was probably that he seemed to hold all Westerners in contempt, and he spoke quite rudely. Most Chinese, when speaking with a foreigner they have never met before, would never openly criticize that person's country directly to his face. This sort of behavior fell far short of traditional etiquette. On the other hand, the old monk seemed to be very naive, and he certainly had no intention of deliberately offending me, so I really had no reason to fault him.

After a long while, I rose to bid farewell, but as it was already dark outside, I feared that finding my way back through the mountain trails would be difficult. Fortunately, there were plenty of extra blankets in the cave, so staying there overnight was not a problem. The next morning I expressed my thanks and went on my way. Two or three days later, I left Guilin and returned to Hong Kong.

The Story of Why the Chinese Sit in Chairs

On the day of my departure, I caught a large sailboat heading for Wujou, with eight or nine boat hands and a few dozen passengers on board. The return journey was all downstream, so there was no need for tow ropes. Traveling down the Gui River, we didn't even need to raise sail, for the current was swift and strong, and the boat flew downriver like an arrow released from a bow. But there were many hidden shoals, and the captain kept shouting, "Watch out for submerged rocks, you old mother, why don't you be more careful?" So the journey was really quite dangerous! Our lives hung entirely in the hands of the helmsman. When the boat left the dock, the boat hands killed a rooster for good luck, splashing fresh chicken blood all over the surface of the boat, while praying to the dragon king of the river for his blessing and protection; otherwise the ghosts of those who'd previously drowned in the river might have tried to conspire to drag us down to our deaths!

Finally, without running into any sandbars along the way, the boat arrived safely at Wujou on the fifth day. There I transferred to a steamboat on the West River, and the next day I reached Hong Kong, where I stayed with my pledge-brother, Dr. Tsai Yuan-ruo. My reunion with him, Fifth Uncle, and other dear friends filled me with boundless joy.

In the spring of 1938, I took an ocean steamer to the port of Haiphong, in order to catch a train bound for Kunming (also known then as Yunnan prefecture). En route, the train stopped over briefly in Hanoi. In those days, Hanoi was still a very charming place, with an atmosphere much like old China, although it also reflected a certain degree of French influence. The city was centered around a large public park, and on a small island in a lake within the park stood a Buddhist temple. Its elegant architecture differed in style from Chinese temples, reminding me more of ancient Japanese temples, but also expressing the unique style of traditional Vietnamese civilization. I believe that due to the strong classical influence they received from China during the Tang and Sung dynasties, both Vietnam and Japan avoided the excessively ornate tendencies that dominated Chinese style during the Ching Dynasty, but I'm not certain if this is in fact the case. Vietnamese monks still followed the monastic customs that prevailed during Tang times, and when conducting ritual ceremonies, they did not stand before the altar, but rather sat with their legs crossed and bowed their heads down to the floor.

Speaking of this reminds me of something that one rarely hears anyone mention. Before Asia became westernized, China was the only Asian country that used chairs. In other Asian countries, the custom was to sit on mats spread on the floor. Originally, it was the same in China, until the Tang Dynasty, when this custom changed. By that time, the bureaucratic system of government was already well developed, with an enormous number of functionaries, a highly complex administration, and hundreds of clerks constantly coming and going to and from the many ministries. Many officials were summoned to appear before their superiors dozens of times a day. Before chairs came into use, every time they entered an office from a courtyard, they had to take off their shoes to avoid soiling the mats, and after completing their reports to their superiors, they had to put their shoes on again to cross the courtyard and return to their own offices.

How troublesome this must have been! Therefore, within the ministerial offices, wooden chairs began to be provided for seating as substitutes for floor mats. Thereafter, visitors were not required to take off their shoes every time before entering a room, thereby saving a lot of wasted time. The type of wooden chair used in the offices usually had rails along the back and on the right and left sides. The host and his guests sat on these chairs with small tables placed on both sides, and set upon the tables were brush and paper, ink and inkstone, tea utensils, and other requisite items. The chair rails and the table tops were about the same height, so that it looked as though they were all connected together as a set of linked armchairs. From this prototype, it's easy to see how armchairs later developed. Ordinary chairs also evolved from this forerunner.

The information given above is based on what a friend who specializes in the study of traditional Chinese furniture told me. If one were to ask about the origins of the wooden chairs that first appeared in the Tang Dynasty, that would be fairly easy to surmise. Northern China gets very cold in winter, and therefore they began using heated brick kangs in early times. When a clerk entered a room with an elevated kang in it to hand a document over to his superior, the sitting mat would be spread on top of the kang, not on the floor, and therefore the visitor need not take off his shoes before entering the room. So when officials from northern China were assigned to posts in the southern regions, it would have been a simple matter for them to have wooden chairs made as substitutes for the brick kangs of the north.

Staying at a Pair Lodge in Kunming

Returning now to my main narrative, I couldn't resist staying over for a few more weeks in Hanoi. In those days, each Asian country still had its own distinctive flavor: the garments, architecture, cuisine, handicrafts, music, dance, all had their own unique regional style. Vietnam was no exception, but by the time I arrived there, it had been occupied for a long time by Westerners, and there was little left of its ancient atmosphere. *Ai, ai,* truly is it said, "life passes by in a flash," yet even within the span of my own brief life, I have witnessed many venerable Asian cultures, thousands of years old, vanish like bubbles, oh such painful woe!

From Hanoi, I took a train and crossed into Yunnan province.* Before long, from the window of the train carriage, I saw an ancient

*This is the southernmost province of China, bordering on Vietnam, Laos, and Burma to the south, and Tibet to the west. "Yunnan" means "south of the clouds."

city surrounded by tall city walls, and felt a strong impulse to disembark and go have a look. The name of that city was Mengdze,* and I remembered that the founding emperor of the Yuan Dynasty (1260–1368), Khublai Khan, sent his army here en route to invade Burma, so many of the inhabitants of this city must have been of Mongolian descent. After subjugating the king of Burma, many soldiers remained to live in Yunnan, so possibly the name "Mengdze" derives from this time. In any case, its ancient appearance greatly excited my imagination, and appealed to my passion for vestiges of antiquity.

Friends sometimes accuse me of being "unrealistic." Their reasoning is that everyone knows that worldly affairs are impermanent, so my deep regret regarding the westernization of the East does not accord with the reality of the situation. This sort of criticism certainly makes sense, but my point of view has been determined by my destiny. While I was still very young, an idealized vision of China had already taken shape in my mind, and its beauty and perfection were boundless. When I first arrived in the Far East, I had the good fortune to meet several gentlemen who cultivated virtue rather than chasing after profit, such as my pledged elder brother Yuan-ruo, Fifth Uncle, and several other intimate friends. They were men of truly refined character, the sort of highly cultivated gentlemen no longer found in the western world, and this provided me with ample proof that the China I had fantasized in my mind and the real China of traditional times were not that far apart.

After arriving in Kunming, I could see that this place would not disappoint me, and indeed the longer I stayed there, the better it impressed me. Yunnan has a temperate climate, cool in the summer and not too cold in the winter. At that time, the city walls and other major architecture still retained the style of ancient times, and all the homes and shops were built of mud brick that had an apricot-yellow

---

*"Meng" is the Chinese word for "Mongol." The Mongol emperor of China, Khublai Khan, established the Yuan Dynasty, in 1260 CE, and it was he who incorporated Yunnan into the Chinese empire.

color. Spreading out in all four directions beyond the city walls, the mountains, lakes, and fields unfolded in a green tableau, the fertile land and scenery weaving a floral tapestry of beautiful colors—red, yellow, black, violet, and every shade of the spectrum. The people of Kunming were very warm and friendly. Since the city was located very far from the sea, not many Yunnanese, except for a few local merchants who sometimes went to Burma and Vietnam to do business, ever traveled abroad, and therefore they expressed an insatiable curiosity about the outside world.

The women of Yunnan were especially competent. In most of the local shops, the proprietor almost always seemed to be female. If a customer came in and asked a male clerk about the price of a particular item, he usually had to consult the woman of the house before replying. Occasionally I looked into their kitchens, and always saw men cooking at the stove, taking care of the children, and doing other household chores. Outside of town, I often saw women working in the rice fields and doing other heavy labor.

Travel expenses from Hong Kong to Yunnan were quite high, and soon I'd spent all of my money. Fortunately, while looking for work, I was able to stay in the cheapest type of accommodation, the so-called pair lodge. A pair lodge was an inn where single travelers could occupy just half a bedroom. Each room had two beds, and single guests therefore had to share a room with a stranger.

The most frequent sort of guests in pair lodges were truck drivers and muleteers. They were all very kind to me, and since the Kunming dialect was quite similar to Mandarin, conversation was not difficult. Guests usually ate their meals together, so it was easy to make friends. Every morning and evening, a lavish but inexpensive selection of dishes was served on a few round tables set out in the courtyard, and the flavor was always very pungent. Not only was chili pepper used to season all stir-fried dishes, chili was also used as a condiment for eating rice, and the food was so fiery that even the chili-loving people of Hunnan and Szechuan found the cuisine of Yunnan to be excessively hot.

Going into Seclusion at Hua Ting Monastery to Learn Meditation

My original intention had been to seek a teaching position at the United University of the Southwest (the temporary wartime university jointly established by Peking University, Ching Hwa University, and Nan Kai University), but I had not yet secured a letter of appointment. At the time, I heard about a classical Zen seminary located outside the city, called the Hua Ting monastery, so I decided to take this opportunity to study Zen meditation there. I also heard that several decades earlier this ancient monastery had been renovated by the famous old monk Hsu Yun. While living in Hong Kong, I had accompanied my friends several times to hear this venerable monk give teachings, and though I did not understand much of what he said, I nevertheless took refuge* with him and received the dharma name "Ocean of Wisdom" (Chih Hai).

One day, I walked beyond the city walls and took a cargo boat across a large lake called Yunnan Lake. Arriving on the other shore, I hiked up a mountain trail and entered a forest, and after passing through a series of memorial archways, I reached the gate of the monastery. On both sides of the gate stood a pair of enormous guardians cast in clay, with ferocious faces and intimidating poses that would frighten off any demons and prevent them from daring to come there to disturb the Buddhist adepts inside. Entering through the front gate, I crossed a broad garden and found an inner wall stretched across the way before me.

In the center of this wall was a gate into the entrance chamber, and passing through this chamber gave access to a large courtyard within, from where one could visit all of the large shrine halls inside. The roof

*To "take refuge" in the Triple Gem (Buddha, Dharma, and Sangha) with a revered Buddhist master is a simple ceremony whereby a person formally becomes a Buddhist, or reconfirms his existing status as a Buddhist, and receives a dharma name (*fa ming*) from the master.

of the entrance chamber was covered with enameled tiles and had a very grandiose appearance. In the middle of the entrance chamber sat a very impressive gold lacquered statue of Maitreya, the Laughing Buddha, on an octagonal dais. The Buddha image radiated a living spirit, and his beaming smile seemed to welcome visiting pilgrims to step inside. The four great kings of Heaven stood in the four corners of the chamber, like four brave warriors standing sentry.

When I walked around the lacquered dais and stepped into the large courtyard, I saw two memorial archways on the left and right sides. In the center stood a large ornate shrine hall with a roof of brightly enameled tiles.

Inside the shrine hall there were three enormous statues of the Buddha, all of them coated in gold lacquer, with a very dignified appearance. Nearby stood figures of the Eighteen Lohan,* depicted with marvelous expressions and looking very lifelike, and created with such superb craftsmanship that they immediately captivated the viewer's attention. Because the expressions on the faces of the Lohan were always rather facetious, they resembled the playful demeanor of children. I've often noticed that the artisans of ancient China seemed to enjoy depicting the Lohan as excessively self-satisfied monks. I once heard someone explain that this odd tendency derived from the difference between the Hinayana and Mahayana schools of Buddhism. Followers of the Mahayana path believe that helping others to attain liberation is the most important goal of a Buddhist practitioner, and that devoting all of one's time and energy exclusively to the goal of one's own liberation definitely does not suffice. On the other hand, adherents of the Hinayana path believe that a person can only liberate himself, and that helping someone else attain liberation is absolutely impossible; therefore, even if one aspired to this good intention, it would never succeed, and thus one should devote all of one's effort to

*Lohan is the Chinese term for "arhat," a saint who has attained enlightenment through the practice of Zen meditation.

the more realistic goal of self-liberation. During their incarnate lives in the world, the Eighteen Lohan were all practitioners of the Hinayana path, and consequently the Mahayana Chinese artisans looked down on them and depicted them as superficial practitioners.

As soon as I entered the shrine hall, a young monk asked me why I was there. I replied that I wished to meet the abbot of the monastery, and asked if that were possible. He led me through a series of the monks' private meditation rooms, all of which were very clean and orderly and much simpler than the outside area. The abbot lived in a suite of small rooms located in a tranquil courtyard, and the plain and simple style of his quarters evoked my esteem. He met me at the gateway and led me inside a room to sit down. He was big and strongly built, and had a robust vitality, but the expression on his face seemed to reflect a sense of displeasure. He looked surprised when he saw a Westerner perform the ceremonial formalities of respect, and after I finished touching my forehead to the floor before him, I noted that his attitude relaxed a bit. It was obvious that he was not accustomed to receiving Western visitors, and perhaps he had assumed that I was a missionary who had come there in order to debate religious doctrine with him. After watching me perform the formal ritual of respect, he seemed more at ease in my presence.

However, when he heard that I too believed in Buddhism, he immediately shook his head, as though saying to himself, "No Westerner would ever believe in my faith, so could this foreign devil be the sole exception?" I considered how I might persuade him to believe me, and so I mentioned that I'd taken formal vows of refuge with the venerable master Hsu Yun. The abbot seemed extremely surprised by this, as well as deeply moved, and it was clear that any doubts he might have had about me had vanished. He then asked, "What dharma name did the venerable master bestow upon you?" I told him that my dharma name was "Ocean of Wisdom." The abbot smiled happily and nodded, for he obviously knew that during the particular year that I took refuge, Hsu Yun gave all of his new disciples a dharma name containing the word "wisdom," and setting aside all his skepticism about me, his manner became very warm and friendly.

This gave me hope of fulfilling my goal, so I asked him how this monastery taught Zen meditation. He told me that there were currently forty young monks and novices learning meditation there. They all lived together in the meditation hall, unlike the older monks, each of whom had his own bedroom. Except for their participation in the morning and evening classes in the shrine hall, the young monks had no other concerns outside of the meditation hall. Sitting in meditation, reading scriptures, cleaning the hall, eating, and sleeping were all group activities, with meditation practice of central importance.

Noting the consistently friendly attitude the abbot now showed me, I mustered my courage and asked him to let me stay for a while in the meditation hall and participate in the various aspects of Buddhist study. At first he firmly refused permission, stating that a layperson could not live together with ordained monks. I nodded respectfully and murmured, "Yes, yes, of course. That's correct, quite correct." For a while, we both remained silent. Because I had taken refuge vows with the venerable Hsu Yun and was therefore a bona fide Buddhist, at least in name, he seemed on the one hand reluctant to refuse my request, and on the other hand still unwilling to break the old monastic rules; so he felt himself placed in a difficult position on the matter. In a very humble tone of voice, I said, "I've heard tell that two or three years ago, Master Hsu Yun allowed an American woman to learn Zen meditation at the Hua Nan monastery. She too was not an ordained monk." The abbot laughed sardonically and said, "Ha-ha, I was afraid you'd mention this example and cite it as a precedent. All right, since the venerable master showed her such compassion, I can only treat you with the same spirit of compassion. However, I must first stipulate a few conditions."

The conditions included the following: "First you will move into the monastery, but you may not immediately live in the meditation hall; after a few weeks, we'll see what our two senior teachers, Master Wei Na and Master Dang Jia, have to say about the situation. If they agree to let you stay in the meditation hall, you will have to have your head shaved and wear monk's robes, but you may not wear cassocks. When entering the shrine hall, you shall simply wear plain blue robes. In addition, you must observe all the regulations within the meditation hall, and you must not break any of your monastic vows. The only exceptional condition for you is that you shall not attend classes together with the young monks. While they are studying together, you will be separately taught by several of our older monks." When the abbot had finished speaking, I agreed to his conditions and expressed my sincere gratitude, then took my leave and returned to the city to make preparations. Two days later, I came to stay at the monastery.

Morning Recital and Evening Recital

The meditation hall was located in a tranquil shaded courtyard, and was a long, square single-story building. Except for the two words "Meditation Hall" inscribed on a plaque over the main door, the exterior had no other decor. Along the four walls on the inside of the hall was a broad sleeping platform, three feet high and eight feet wide. The platform was covered with a clean straw mat. This platform served as communal sleeping quarters for the several dozen monks living there. Before sunrise each morning, they rose and stored away their blankets, socks, and other items in cabinets, leaving only the glossy straw mat. While sleeping, the monks lay with their feet toward the wall and their heads toward the center of the hall.

A sitting platform ran around the four walls in line with the sleeping platform, and this was where they practiced meditation. About the same height from the floor as an ordinary stool, it was wide enough for each monk to sit crossed-legged with eyes facing toward the center. The meditation hall was square, and therefore both the sleeping and sitting platforms were also four-sided. In the center of the hall, enclosed by the sleeping and sitting platforms, was a large empty space that served as a sort of exercise area. After each period of two to three hours of still sitting meditation, the monks needed to do some exercise to stimulate blood circulation, so at specified intervals a bell sounded to signal them to rise and walk around. At this signal they all lined up on the floor and walked around in a circle, at first very slowly, then faster and faster, until they were running. After a while, the bell rang once more, and the monks sat down again to continue their meditation practice as before. This pattern was repeated several times before it was time to disperse.

While lined up and circumambulating around the hall, the monks had to walk with their right shoulders facing inward toward an octagonal pedestal set in the center of the hall. On the pedestal sat a statue of the bodhisattva Manjusri, symbol of Supreme Wisdom. The fruit of Zen meditation was the realization of this sort of wisdom.

The monks living at the monastery were required to attend two important ceremonies each day, known as "morning recital" and "evening recital." Every morning before dawn, someone using an implement like a drumstick rapped the stone slabs on the ground in the courtyard, producing a sound like the Cantonese exclamation, "*duh, duh, duh. . .*" The beat gradually accelerated from slow to fast. After a while, big cymbals began to chime in, so that the cadence became "*duh, duh, duh, dang, duh, duh, dang, duh, dang,*" until one no longer heard the "*duh*" sound, only "*dang, dang.*" Then a huge drum thundered in with a "*lung lung*" sound, creating a percussive tempo of "*dang, dang, dang, dang, lung, dang, dang, lung, dang, lung,*" and after a while only the thump of the drum could be heard, beating faster and faster, booming louder and louder, until finally the thunderous peal abruptly stopped. At this moment, the entire congregation of monks began the morning recital, chanting in chorus with a dulcet sound that was very pleasing to the ear.

The time between their abrupt awakening by the sound of rapping on the stone slabs and the beginning of the morning recital amounted to about half an hour. During this time, they all rose from their beds, put on their underwear, stored away their bedding, rinsed their mouths and washed their hands, donned their blue robes, slipped on their cassocks, walked to the shrine hall, entered, and bowed their heads to the ground before the image of the Buddha.

When I first began to participate in the morning recital, I had to really push myself to be on time, and I was constantly worried that someone might notice faults in my performance. I felt even more concerned that someone might disapprove of an ignorant lay person mingling among the ordained monks, so I tried my very best not to make any mistakes. Luckily, no one expressed any disapproval toward me, and day by day my self-confidence grew, until soon I felt thoroughly familiar with every aspect of the daily routine.

Morning and evening recitals were of course different in content, but both were similar in form, such as reciting mantras in Sanskrit and chanting sutras in Chinese. It took me a long time to memorize the entire liturgy, so at first I could only move my lips and pretend to recite.

From autumn until spring, the sun did not rise until after the morning recital was finished. After recital, the monks all went to the kitchen, where they stood by the door to gulp down two bowls of rice gruel and drink some tea, after which they returned to the meditation hall and quietly went inside to sit in silence. Master Wei Na came to supervise our meditation practice for two or three hours. When we dispersed from the hall, the monks all went to the classroom to study, while I went alone to receive teaching elsewhere. Most of the monks had little or no formal education, and only studied scriptures at the monastery. Their reading ability and comprehension therefore varied. Some were equivalent to or above high school level. There were also some who came from a background of hard labor, or were totally illiterate, or could read a bit of scripture but could not understand any of the meaning.

Just before noon, we heard the sound of tapping on an enormous wooden fish, which was the signal for us to go to the dining room for our midday meal. After lunch, those who lived in the meditation hall immediately returned there for the second period of meditation practice. Two or three hours later they dispersed again and went back to the shrine hall for the evening recital. After recital, we all had a bit of free time, before going to the dining room for the evening meal. After that, there was another period of meditation and at nine o'clock it was bedtime. Thus there were three periods of meditation practice every day, with each period lasting two to three hours. Each year there were also three periods of so-called seven-seven. Seven-seven referred to a set period of forty-nine days, during which we sat in meditation for eighteen hours each day.

The Hard and Bitter Practice of Spiritual Cultivation

Each month there were also some special days, including four days in which we had some leisure time, so that we could arrange our personal affairs. During those four days, morning and evening recitals and the three meditation sessions were all shortened. We used the free time to wash and mend our clothes, go to the monastery's bath hall for a hot bath, and so forth. In addition, we sometimes went for strolls in the forest, walked along the cliffside, enjoyed the scenery around the lake, each to his own preference.

Every month there were four "vegetarian days," on the first, eighth, fifteenth, and twenty-third days on the lunar calendar. The two meals on vegetarian days usually included some sesame oil, tofu, bean sprouts, mushrooms, and other tasty vegetarian dishes. On all other days, both for lunch and dinner, only white rice, one vegetable, and one soup were served. Actually, the white rice should have been called "black white rice"! At least one third of each bowl of rice consisted of weeds, dead bugs, grit, and other contaminants! The only vegetable served was pumpkin boiled in plain water. The so-called clear soup was merely the water remaining in the pot after boiling the pumpkin! Day after day it was just like this, without the slightest variation in food.

Although monks were not supposed to eat chili peppers, only the Yunnanese monks were not required to comply with this rule, and therefore they were able to enjoy what little nutritional value chilis provided. Due to this sort of sparse diet, nutrition was deficient, and at least half of the monks at the Hua Ting monastery suffered from smallpox, with ghastly ulcers festering on the skin of their arms and legs.

One day I took a monk into the city to see a doctor, and the doctor informed him that the only way to cure his condition was to improve his daily diet, but the abbot and teachers had no way of increasing the monastery's income in order to improve the quality of the food. I asked the monk why, in light of how well the monastery was managed, the more than one hundred monks living there were so poverty-stricken. He said, "Over ten years ago, when our monastery had almost become a wasteland, the venerable Master Hsu Yun came to Yunnan and decided to restore some temples and monasteries, including the Hua Ting monastery.

"He was the most famous and the greatest monk in China, and therefore many wealthy families jumped at the chance to earn merit by contributing money for these restorations. Within a few years, the Hua Ting monastery had completely recovered its former glory. Monks from throughout this province flocked to take residence here. But as soon as Master Hsu Yun returned to Guangdung, all those wealthy patrons no longer cared about us. After already spending so much money to reconstruct and repair the premises, no one was willing to contribute more money to support the livelihood of a few hundred monks. We had no assets of our own.

"Although the monastery owned some land that could be rented out to others, farmers today are also extremely poor. In times like this, landowners with a good conscience cannot raise rents for farmland. Other than that, the monks who do not reside in the meditation hall can still earn a little bit of money by chanting sutras for people in their homes. However, the farmers here are so poor that it remains beyond their means to spend money to have sutras recited for the sick or dying members of their families.

"Of course, even those in such dire straits that they don't know if they can survive from morning until night must still make some sort of arrangements for funerals, but they certainly cannot afford to spend much on it. Therefore, compared to the past, the income earned by monks from such outside activities has shrunk by at least 70 to 80 percent. If the sutra recital for a funeral is held within the monastery, monks living outside the meditation hall may also participate, but since so many monks are then involved, the share earned by each individual doesn't amount to more than ten or twenty cents. If monks go to a private home to recite sutras, each monk's share can be as much as several dollars. However, a monk who has his whole heart focused on striving for enlightenment would rather starve than spend his time and energy earning money."

Dissolving the Ego: The Wordless Teaching

I would like to describe the methods of Zen meditation, but it's difficult to elucidate "the wordless teaching." It's best to begin with a discussion of a few basic principles. One of the most fundamental principles is this: everything that has composite existence ("composite existence" has the same meaning as "phenomenal existence") is like a dream or fading shadow; it's all impermanent. All things and events are mutually dependent; absolutely nothing can exist independently by itself. Even the individual self or ego is like this; it's not an enduring and independently existing reality. Because sentient beings mistakenly believe that they each have a concrete "self," they are constantly confused and misled by this false concept and therefore cannot attain liberation, and all sorts of suffering arise from this. Only those who can dissolve the ego (self) can free themselves of all suffering and tribulation. In order to disintegrate the ego, one must extinguish all illusions and awaken to one's primordial nature. One's real primordial nature does not belong to any lord or master, but rather it belongs equally to all sentient beings. Still sitting meditation is an extremely effective way to rid oneself of illusions, and it can prevent one from ever again becoming mesmerized by the fallacy of ego, thereby allowing us to awaken to our true nature and attain liberation.

Regarding dissolution of the ego or "self," I would like to mention something that illustrates the way Zen masters teach. At the beginning of my residence at the Zen monastery, I could not immediately live in the meditation hall, so at first I lived by myself in a small room. One day a young monk came to visit me, and while the two of us were talking, someone suddenly knocked on the door. In a loud voice, I asked, "Who is it?" When asked this question, most Chinese would usually reply, "It's me." But this person remained silent and did not answer. At first, I thought perhaps I had misheard, and that in fact no one had knocked on the door. But a moment later I heard another loud knock on the door, which really startled me, so I quickly walked over and pulled open the door, expecting to see someone standing there, but I saw no one. I ran outside to look around, and still I saw no trace of anyone.

The next day, when I described this incident to others, they too were puzzled and unable to explain it. Fortuitously, an old monk overheard me and came over to say, "Why is it that you do not understand this? You've read Zen texts, so you should certainly understand it very clearly." I felt perplexed, and bowing my head with respect, I asked him to explain. He smiled and said, "When you asked who that person was, how did you expect him to answer?" I said, "I thought perhaps he would simply say, 'It's me.'"

The old monk gave me a strange look, as though he felt frustrated by my stupidity, and after a while he remarked, "You should never think that someone in a Zen monastery would ever reply 'It's me,' and then say his dharma name. Later you will learn that when we sit in Zen meditation, we constantly keep a single idea in mind, 'Who is chanting the Buddha's name?' If that person believes that the one chanting the Buddha's name is 'I,' he will have a very difficult time making any progress. 'Self' is definitely a status no one has. When the person who knocked on your door yesterday heard you ask 'Who is it,' it seems that he took the opportunity to make you understand that there could be no 'I' there, and therefore he did not say 'It is I,' and after knocking once again, without saying a word, he disappeared and made sure that you saw no one."

Using this incident as a concrete example, perhaps it would be easier to describe the method of training in Zen meditation. Each day during the first meditation period, Master Wei Na gave a short lecture, and he often chose "no I" (selflessness) as his topic. The main points were as follows:

"When meditating, you must eliminate the waves of idle thought that arise in the mind, and refrain from reliance on intellectual analysis. Instead, you should try your best to generate the spontaneous manifestation of innate wisdom. It's best to focus your attention on a single idea, such as 'Who is chanting the Buddha's name?' The ordinary response would be, 'The one chanting the Buddha's name is I.' But those who are familiar with Buddhist teachings naturally know that this response is incorrect, so who in fact is chanting the Buddha's name? The inner meaning of this question is: 'The so-called self is basically what?' In other words, if I were to eliminate all thoughts and feelings from my mind, what would remain? What remains is called 'primordial nature.' This is something ineffable and beyond thought, so how can it be described in words? Therefore, Zen teachings are called 'The Wordless Teaching.'

"Primordial nature is something that all sentient beings have in common. It does not belong to me; it does not belong to you; it is the essential nature of all sentient beings. The goal of meditation is to become aware of our primordial nature, and when we become aware of it, we know it but cannot explain it in words to others. Each individual can only arrive at this realization by direct experience. Someone who has reached this direct experiential vision may be referred to as an enlightened being, and is also known as someone who has attained the wisdom of Paramita.*

*Literally, "He who has reached the other shore," i.e., someone who has crossed the sea of worldly illusion and arrived at the state of transcendental wisdom, thereby gaining liberation from all suffering.

"After reaching enlightenment, although troubles still exist, they can never again disturb the peace and tranquility in one's heart. The idea that I have just taught you to keep in mind when practicing meditation can lead you directly to freedom from self-deceptive thoughts and feelings and help you realize the infinite, boundless, selfless, otherless, beginningless, endless state of your own primordial nature. I want you to clearly understand the meaning of 'All Buddhas of the three times [past, present, and future] and all sentient beings are all of one mind, and beyond this mind there is nothing else.'" (Note: this statement was orginally made by the Zen master Huang Po, in *The Zen Teachings of Huang Po.* The original text states "beyond this there is no other dharma," but Master Wei Na often changed it to "nothing else" to make it easier for beginners to understand the essential meaning. In Buddhist texts, the word "dharma" has the same meaning as "phenomenon.")

While meditating, it was up to each monk whether or not to use this idea as a point of focus. The most important thing was to eliminate idle thoughts and directly experience primordial nature (also known as "primordial awareness"). This is the goal of spiritual cultivation. Alas, I was not so gifted, and after practicing Zen meditation in the hall for ten months, I still had not realized my primordial nature. Consequently, I lost interest, but fortunately there are other ways to reach enlightenment. Zen practice may well be an excellent path to enlightenment, but not everyone is capable of reaping its fruits. When my interest flagged, the sea of desire once again began to churn in turmoil within me, arousing the base emotions. Tearfully I admitted defeat and had no choice but to take my leave and return to lay life. I asked the abbot to let me stay temporarily in a small bedroom in the guest dormitory, and since I no longer participated in the activities of a Zen adept, I made preparations for my return to Hong Kong. Having obtained his permission, I still had some spare time and spent it roaming in the mountains and around the lake for a few weeks, before packing up and going back to Hong Kong.

The Contented Old Monk

One day, I came upon a small hermitage facing Yunnan Lake, called the Pavilion of Triple Clarity, which I'd heard had long since been abandoned, but where now an old monk in tattered robes was living in the shrine hall.

Upon entering the shrine hall, I paid him formal respects, then sat down on a mat to speak with him. In a very friendly manner, he recounted his recent experiences there, saying, "Just now you addressed me as a master, but I dare not accept such an honor, for I have no education and can only recite a few sutras. When I became a monk at the age of eleven, I started out working in the kitchen, and later, as I transferred to other monasteries, I still continued doing the same work. The year before last, I discovered that a friend had been working secretly for the Japanese devils, and, suspecting that I might disclose his deceit, he accused me of being a communist infiltrator—even though there wasn't the slightest evidence to prove it—in order to prevent me from exposing him. At the time, communism was the most dreaded ideology, so without even investigating the facts, they found me guilty, although I don't really blame them for that. When there's a snake underfoot, one does not pause to check if it's poisonous or not, one kills it first and worries about the rest later. The presiding judge seemed to realize that I had not necessarily committed any crime, so he only sentenced me to one year of light confinement in prison.

"That prison was wonderful! They gave me a small room to live in all by myself, complete with bed and blankets. The guard told me that the foul stench in the blankets came from the many prisoners who'd used them before me. If I had tried to wash them, they would probably have disintegrated into shreds. I didn't really mind the smell, as long as they kept me warm. Another unexpected benefit was that once every month they took me out to have a hot bath, as though I were a wealthy magnate. I bet you never imagined that our provincial authorities could be so generous, treating me with the same impeccable hospitality that they might offer a bodhisattva."

I could see that this monk in his ragged robes was richly endowed with enlightened virtue, and while he may have been a bit too naive, he was overall a very lovable character. What he said aroused my curiosity, so I listened attentively. Recalling his memories, he continued, "While in prison, I was not required to do any hard labor, nor did anyone give me trouble, so I could spend the whole day sitting in meditation. Sometimes I sat with my legs crossed for more than ten hours before stopping. That was the happiest year of my entire life! How could any monk living in a monastery have so much free time?"

He told me a lot more about his situation in prison before falling silent again. I asked, "When did you come to this hermitage?" He opened his eyes wide, and staring straight at me, he mustered his spirit and said, "I came here a few days ago, and while this place is all right, it cannot compare with prison. When I arrived, it was extremely difficult to find anything to eat or drink. The hermits must have taken every scrap of food away with them when they abandoned this place."

The shabbily dressed old monk continued, "This place is totally dilapidated. No one has come by here for at least two or three days. I have no way of informing any of my friends that I'm here. For the first few days, I was so hungry that I could hardly bear it, but later I found a bunch of red candles in a cupboard. These are nutritious items. You've probably never tasted candle soup. Shall I boil some up for you?" I hastily declined, saying that I didn't feel hungry.

I didn't take my leave until nearly sunset, and thanking him for sharing his experiences with me, I started to offer my formal respects to him with a bow. But he quickly reached out his hand to stop me, and cried out, "Hold it, hold it, this humble monk dares not accept such a gesture of esteem! You need not be so polite, and please don't laugh at my lack of education and my coarse manner of speech!" I placed my palms together at my heart in a simple gesture of courtesy, and sincerely replied, "You, venerable master, have given this young adept many, many valuable lessons. Your words have made me understand that the foremost of all great virtues is knowing how to be content. If only we all knew how to simply be content, then no matter how turbulently tossed the waves in the bitter sea of life, they would have no power to disturb our peace of mind. There is no teaching of greater value than this. The model example you have shown me today shall surely enhance my peace of mind and bring me tranquility for the rest of my life. This is why I truly regard you as a master." When he heard these words, he couldn't help but smile, but he waved his hands at me to ward off any further praise.

Two weeks later, on the eve of my departure, as I said farewell to all the elders at the Hua Ting monastery, tears filled my eyes. Despite his extreme poverty, Master Wei Na gave me a silver ingot as a parting gift to help cover the cost of my journey. Two young monk friends accompanied me down the mountain to the boat, and when it came time to part, all three of us could not stop our tears from falling as we said good-bye.

Despicable Racial Prejudice

En route back to Hong Kong, I again passed through the two cities of Mengdze and Hanoi, but since the money I brought with me was just enough to cover my travel expenses, I could not stop over at these places, and after reaching Haiphong I spent the night at an inn there and boarded a ship bound for Hong Kong. The steamship belonged to a French company. While in Kunming, a friend had taken me to a small travel agency to purchase my bus and ship tickets, and the payment included the fee for a night at the inn. Except for my passport details, I filled out all of my travel documents in Chinese. The reason for this was that the small travel agency had never done business with a foreign traveler before, and they told me that it would be more convenient for them if I wrote in Chinese. Because I did not have much money, I purchased a second-class ticket for the ship, and when I boarded the ship, I discovered that there were no beds, only some comfortable lounge chairs.

Unexpectedly, not long after I sat down, a deck hand suddenly walked in and took me to see the captain. The captain very rudely asked me why I didn't know that Westerners were not permitted to occupy second-class seats. Before I could reply, he abruptly accused me of being a swindler. Speaking English with a strong French accent, he shouted, "Of course you knew! So you deliberately pretended to be an Asian in order to get a cheaper rate. How shameless of you!"

I couldn't suppress my anger from erupting, and felt like giving him a hard slap on the face, but realized that I must control myself. If this boor refused to take me to Hong Kong, what would I do then? I didn't have enough money left to stay even one more night at an inn, much less pay for meals. Finally he agreed to let me write him a check to cover the cost of first class passage, and pay him after arriving in Hong Kong.

Later, when I thought about this incident in my cabin, I decided that I should not be angry with him about it. His accusation that I was trying to cheat him was based on a misunderstanding. How could he have known that there were travel agencies in Kunming that could not process documents in foreign languages? My indignation arose mainly from the anger I felt at the arrogance of most Westerners in Asia. Why were white people not allowed to occupy second-class seats, and why were only "colored" people permitted to use them? This sort of racial prejudice was despicable and disgusted me! Even while I was still in high school, I already regarded this attitude to be one of the most repugnant flaws in Western people. Later in Hong Kong and China, after being a frequent recipient of kindness from Chinese people, and realizing how highly refined their character was, my simmering indignation toward the haughty arrogance of Westerners grew even more intense. While in China, I very seldom associated with Western people, so my awareness of this ignoble attitude in Westerners had somewhat faded. That day, upon boarding a

French ship, I once again encountered this abominable trait, and so I could not restrain my anger.

At dusk, a bell summoned passengers to go to the dining room for dinner. Upon entering, I saw three round tables, one of which had not been set for dinner. At the second table sat the captain along with seven or eight Westerners, having their dinner. At the third table were five or six Asians and the ship's second officer. It was the second officer's duty to act as host at that table, so he had no choice but to eat together with Chinese and Vietnamese passengers. Naturally I sat at the third table. There were Chinese sitting on both sides of me, and they had already heard about how I'd been insulted by the captain, so they invited me to drink many glasses of brandy as a gesture of sympathy, and asked me to describe the incident to them. Since I'd abstained from alcohol for nearly a year, I easily became intoxicated, and after getting tipsy I talked even more. The Chinese gentleman who invited me to drink spoke English, and since I wanted the second officer to hear what I had to say, hoping that he would pass it on to the captain, I deliberately spoke at great length about the disgraceful attitude of racists, and how angry they made me feel. The Chinese at the table smiled and cast knowing glances at one another, and I could see that they felt quite pleased. The second officer's face showed no expression whatsoever, and he pretended to look at the stars outside the window, but occasionally his eyes revealed a glint of sympathy, as though he quite agreed with what I was saying, although it was not convenient for him to say so.

Sitting across from me was a Vietnamese businessman who was studying abroad in France. He spoke fairly good English, and said, "This gentleman speaks the truth. I've read some essays written by Western scholars during the eighteenth century. They respected China as the most civilized nation on earth, particularly for the primacy of rational thought in Confucian philosophy, which does not regard worldly matters as being dictated by a deity in Heaven."

The Vietnamese businessman continued, "European writers at that time all expressed the highest praise for Chinese culture. But later, during the nineteenth century, as a result of developments in the Industrial Revolution, Western powers were able to defeat China repeatedly on the battlefield. China's highly sophisticated culture had not changed at all since ancient times; the only thing that had changed was the balance of military power. But from then on, Westerners never again regarded Eastern civilization with respect. How utterly ridiculous! If a sage were savagely bitten by a wild beast, we certainly would not use that as a reason to declare that the sage had lost his virtue. And if a man of wisdom is violently abducted by a gang of vicious bandits, how could those gangsters claim that because of his abduction that man had lost his wisdom? Of course they couldn't! In this tragic scenario, Westerners have played the role of the wild beast and taken the part of the vicious bandit, shamelessly claiming themselves to be superior to other races, and further declaring their firm belief that white people are destined by heavenly decree to rule the four corners of the earth! *Ai,* this sort of vainglorious arrogance really infuriates me!"

After hearing that, I felt like leading everyone in shouting out three cheers of support, and also adding a few similar remarks of my own to reconfirm what he'd said, in order to give the Westerners at the next table something to think about. Unfortunately, I found myself unable to utter a single word, nor even to stand up, for suddenly the brandy flew up to my head and rendered me totally drunk. My head dropped down to the table, and I lost consciousness.

Perhaps one might ask: "If you were so drunk, how could you recall so clearly what that man said?" I really don't know the reason, but I think it was because his words struck a chord in my heart. The feelings he expressed accorded exactly with the way I'd felt since my early youth. The next day, another Vietnamese passenger said to me, "Sir, I truly admire you. Because you were not permitted to occupy a second-class seat, you complained. It's common enough for people to declare their righteous indignation when being treated as inferiors. But I've never heard of anyone taking offense because he was treated by society as superior to others."

I'm Summoned Back to England to Continue My Education

Arriving in Hong Kong, the first thing I did was pay a visit to my pledged elder brother. The next day I crossed the bay and went to see the headmaster at the Min Sheng Academy in order to seek a teaching position there, and he received me with a warm welcome. I found myself quickly surrounded by a large flock of sixteen- to seventeen-year-old students, all beaming with joy, and they turned out to be the children I'd met there four to five years ago. Among them were two who were destined to become my lifelong friends and close confidantes. One was named Huang Shih-shing. He had always been very close to me, and often came to my room to pass the time. I had learned the game of Chinese chess while living in northern China, but very few Cantonese were familiar with the game, so there was no one to play chess with me at the Min Sheng Academy. Therefore, I had taught Shih-shing how to play. To my surprise, after playing only four or five boards with me, he began to win consistently. Thereafter, he had to give me the advantage of letting me first place nine chips on the board in order to make it possible for both of us to stand an even chance of winning.

Today, Huang Shih-shing and I are both old men, but our friendship remains the same as it was so long ago. When Hong Kong was invaded and occupied by the Japanese army, he escaped and took refuge in the rear zone of China and continued his education in Kunming. Sometimes I sent him some money to help cover the cost of his tuition. One time after the war, when I encountered some difficulties in my life, Shih-shing immediately offered me generous financial assistance as soon as he heard about it. That's how bighearted he was: it was not that he had abundant income to spare, but rather that without the slightest consideration for his own hardships, he always wholeheartedly fulfilled the needs of his friends first. Chinese people have always treated their friends with this sort of impeccable loyalty.

The second student at the Min Sheng Academy who had a predestined connection with me was the second son of headmaster Huang, and his name was Huang Li-sung. Later he and I had the good fortune to share a room together for a long period of time in Chungjing. While he was still in his youth, he had already distinguished himself in his studies, but at that time we had no idea that later he would have the honor of serving as president of three different universities, namely the University of Malaysia, Nan Yang University, and Hong Kong University. For the most part, we had very different interests, and his talents far exceeded my own. Despite this, our natural affinity remained very strong. The two of us always had the good fortune to reunite throughout our lives, and every time we met, regardless of the circumstances, we always felt at ease, like two old friends happy to see each other again.

Several months after resuming my work as a teacher at the Min Sheng Academy, I received a letter from my aunt urging me to return to England and reenter the university there for a year or two in order to obtain a degree. She was willing to pay for my tuition and all other expenses, without any conditions attached, and after graduation I would be free to come back to China. It was difficult to refuse such a generous gesture from my aunt, particularly since the situation in wartime China made it very hard for me to find suitable work there. Furthermore, if I didn't get my Bachelor's degree, I would probably have a difficult time earning a living for the rest of my life, and this is why my aunt encouraged me to return.

Only later did I learn that my father didn't really agree with this. Although he was happy to help me make my way in life, he felt that it was unnecessary for me to go back to the university. He said that seeing me abandon my studies once was enough, and why should he risk being disappointed again? He didn't want me to continue roaming around without roots, and hoped to see me take a job in some business enterprise. It was clear that although I had caused him deep disappointment, he still felt strong paternal love for me. If I sincerely

5
Travels in Szechuan on My Second Sojourn in China

Taking a Consular Post on My Return to China

Upon my return to England in 1939, I decided to enroll in the College of Asian and African Languages at London University in order to improve my Chinese. I had not anticipated that I would be required to select four curricula, and so I chose four Asian languages—Chinese, Japanese, Korean, and Malaysian—and found these subjects to be quite interesting. *Ai dzai!*

Just as I commenced my studies, World War II erupted. Even though I did not wish to volunteer for military service, it would have been very difficult to avoid conscription.

Fortunately, because I was relatively old for military service (twenty-nine years), I was allowed to complete one year of my education before entering the military. Those who voluntarily enlisted were permitted to choose their preferred branch of service, while those who were conscripted did not have this choice. Therefore, I enlisted for duty in the counterintelligence service. Luckily for me, I was already somewhat proficient in Chinese, and therefore in less than a month I was promoted from an ordinary private to the status of an officer, and assigned for service in the army, based in London.

In the middle of January 1941, something wonderful happened, something I would not have even imagined in my dreams.

One day my commanding officer summoned me in order to inform me that the British Embassy in Chungjing needed someone familiar with the Chinese language to immediately go there to take a post as cultural attaché. He told me that in order to accept this assignment, I would have to first forfeit my military status, so he asked me to think it over and let him know my decision that afternoon. Naturally, nothing could have pleased me more. Barely able to contain my joy, I accepted the assignment on the spot.

During the war, overseas transport became very dangerous. I had to take an airplane across Ireland, Portugal, Africa, and India, then transfer to another flight through Burma to Chungjing.

In Burma, our aircraft had to land in the town of Lashio in order to refuel. There we were confronted by a very frightening experience. While waiting there for our plane to be refueled, we saw Japanese troops emerge suddenly from a nearby jungle to attack the airport. The local crew responsible for refueling the aircraft all ran for their lives, leaving us there without a drop of fuel, and no way to escape, so all we could do was sit there and wait to be taken captive by the enemy. Just at that moment, we saw two British soldiers rushing toward us on motorcycles.

As the enemy troops approached, the two soldiers pumped gas into the aircraft's fuel tank, and the plane immediately took off. At the same time, several Japanese motor vehicles sped toward us. All of us on board the plane felt extremely concerned about those two brave soldiers. They had openly exposed their lives to grave danger in order to help us. Such great valor was very seldom to be seen anywhere. We saw them riding away at fast speed, but we had no way of knowing what happened to them. To this day, whenever I think about this incident, my heart throbs with unease.

The Community of Distinguished Literati in Wartime Chungjing

In the spring of 1942, after nearly being captured by Japanese troops when we passed through Burma, I finally arrived safely in Chungjing to take up my consular post. Though I'd like to describe the ambience in the provisional capital city of Chungjing in wartime China, I had very little interest in political affairs, and my job there was not connected with politics. Although I sometimes met important political figures (such as President Chiang Kai-shek and various military and government officials) at social events hosted by the diplomatic community, my memories regarding these figures are not worth recording.

After my arrival there, I was engaged in cultural and educational affairs. Most of the cultural institutes and universities were not located in Chungjing, but rather in neighboring counties or more distant locations, and therefore I was usually on the road. The good thing about this was that the rural villages and old-fashioned towns of Szechuan appealed to me much more than Chungjing. When I arrived in Chungjing, the city had already been bombed more often than one could tell, and most of the buildings there no longer retained their original appearance, but fortunately there had not been many casualties. Chungjing had countless natural caves that served as bomb shelters, and even the enemy finally realized that further bombardment would be pointless. Although Japanese aircraft still came to drop bombs, they did not appear as frequently as before.

Chungjing stood at the confluence of the Yangtze and Jialing rivers, with mountain cliffs everywhere in sight, beautiful fields and gardens all around, and abundant green landscapes that were a delight to the eye. The only drawback was that throughout the year the sky was seldom clear, and even on cloudless days the sky was so obscured with haze that rarely could one distinguish any contrast between light and shadow, and this had a very depressing effect on people. The old saying, "the dogs of Szechuan bark at the sun," meant that whenever the sun appeared in the sky in Szechuan, it was such an unusual event that the sun startled the dogs and made them bark at it.

Another remarkable thing about Chungjing was that the rats were bigger than cats. The rats could catch cats, but the cats had trouble catching any rats. Although I never measured the body size of these ferocious rodents, I daresay that this description is no exaggeration.

Ever since Chungjing had become the wartime capital of China, all the consulates there had been changed into embassies. The British Embassy was located at a very beautiful place called Guan Yin Cliff. The embassy was perched on top of the cliff, surrounded by big gardens. The original consulate had only two large houses, both with stately exterior design. After it became an embassy, these quarters were insufficient, and more buildings had to be constructed in order to accommodate the sudden increase in staff. Most of the employees still had to live outside the embassy compound, but I was lucky to get a small cottage located within the garden. It had two rooms and a separate bathhouse, and I felt very fortunate indeed. Originally the cottage had been used by an Englishman, but he disdained the two little rooms as exceedingly crude and complained to the ambassador that the cottage was "unfit for human habitation." I, however, loved its rustic simplicity and feeling of serenity. The walls were snow white and perfect for hanging a few beautiful scrolls. If I had a bit more literary talent, I'd recite poetic praise to the elegant beauty of that little cottage.

My work had three aspects: first, to maintain contact with various educational and cultural institutions throughout the province, and find ways to assist them in obtaining important English reference books and other research materials; second, to represent the British Cultural Association in helping China's Ministry of Education to select distinguished Chinese scholars to go to England to conduct advanced studies at various research institutes there; third, when necessary, to assist overseas Chinese students who held British passports and were enrolled in Chinese universities to continue their studies at suitable educational institutions in England. Performing these three duties required frequent travel to other provinces. This type of work had three benefits for me: it gave me the opportunity to make many new friends; it broadened my perspectives and helped me understand the unique features of many different regions of China; and it allowed me to establish close friendships with several highly distinguished persons.

Among the first notable characters I met were several famous painters, such as Hsu Pei-hung and Wu Tzo-jen. Although I don't recall in which county their residence was located, I remember that they both lived in an extraordinary dwelling that was round-shaped and looked like a pagoda, and to this day my memory of it remains very clear, and I can still savor the casual atmosphere of that "pagoda." Painters throughout the world all seem to have a proclivity for that sort of leisurely, eccentric lifestyle. Among the playwrights I met in Chungjing, my favorite was Tsao Yu. When we first met, he had just adapted Pa Chin's novel *Home* as a modern vernacular play. In China, vernacular plays were still a relatively new form of theater, and had not yet become a particularly memorable mode of expression. However, Tsao Yu's adaptation of *Home* deeply moved my heart, and instilled in me a fond taste for vernacular plays,* which I often went to see, although I never again saw another one that could compare with *Home*.

Regarding contemporary novelists at that time, I became very well acquainted with Lao Shih and greatly admired his talent. I feel that for the most part, the novelists of the late Ching and early Republic period were superior to those of the War of Resistance era. The pessimistic style of Pa Chin and other writers like him left the reader feeling depressed and unhappy, and they lacked a sense of humor. Their prose never expressed a positive point of view, but only made the reader feel disgusted with the faults of society at that time, and they never offered any constructive suggestions of any kind. Although Lao Shih

*Traditional Chinese theatre was performed in the ancient classical language, which only the most highly educated scholars understood. After the fall of the last dynasty in 1911, playwrights began to produce plays in the vernacular language, spoken on the street, which everyone, including the illiterate, could understand.

also depicted the suffering of the oppressed with deep sympathy, he nevertheless understood that the oppressed could also laugh at their own misfortunes, and his writing often left the reader laughing too. He never harped a tragic tune from beginning to end, and he didn't allow himself to be crushed by tragedy.

My Closest Confidant

During my leisure time, I cultivated friendships with Chinese men and women, and some of them became close friends for life. As an example, I would like to portray the character of my favorite male friend from that time, Mr. Hsieh Ching-yao. Not too modern-minded, nor excessively conservative, his viewpoint in discerning right from wrong favored neither Eastern nor Western culture, but was based instead on universal standards of human values, which he applied equally to old and young, modern and traditional.

The moment we met, Ching-yao and I had a strong connection. At the time, he was about twenty-three years old, quick and clever minded, with a lively spirit and handsome physique, meticulous taste in clothing, and the demeanor of a descendent from a noble family. He spoke the dialect of Peking in a tone that was sweet to the ear and delightful to hear. Although he was by nature a diligent and virtuous man, he easily gave others the impression of being rather flighty and frivolous. Perhaps that was because he always displayed such a casual attitude, and his eyes were always sparkling with humor, and so despite the fact that he was at heart a very sincere person, others might assume that he was not very serious at all. Only those who knew him very well could appreciate the depth of refinement in his character.

I often recall the way he savored an English-style breakfast. Arranged on the table were a pot of the finest Darjeeling tea, a bowl of Scottish-style oatmeal porridge, a plate of fried eggs with baked ham (or smoked salmon), with toast, butter, and orange marmalade on the side. Ah, such a sumptuous breakfast was a rarity in those days even in

England, but here was this hedonist in China, who wasn't even English, fully enjoying every morsel of it. He usually wore a long cotton-padded robe of blue satin, with a high collar and particularly long sleeves that he rolled up to reveal the spotless cuffs of a white silk shirt, and his hair, which was as black and shiny as varnish, was always cut very short and neatly combed. Although he presented the appearance of model Confucian elegance, he was thoroughly masculine in character, tall and sturdy, with a powerful physique.

As I recall the memory, Ching-yao never focused his full attention on his breakfast. On the table there stood a small wooden frame on which a book lay open. The book was likely to be a volume written by the English author Virginia Woolf. When at the table, if he wasn't reading a book, perhaps instead he'd be humming a favorite tune from Peking opera in a voice that was really quite good. The above observations suffice only to describe the external side of my dear friend and close confidante. That epicurean breakfast, the elegant attire, and the sophisticated taste in literature are a reflection of his highly refined finesse; but in his own mind, none of these things were at all important.

He was in no way an extravagant wastrel, nor did he overly indulge himself. As far as he was concerned, all luxuries and beautiful possessions were completely dispensable. In Chungjing, he held a minor government post, with a very small income, so obviously he could not often enjoy a luxurious lifestyle, and usually he ate only fried breadsticks for breakfast. He was a man endowed with great talent, and therefore he appreciated the most advanced thought of both Eastern and Western civilizations, as well as the choicest products, the finest art, the best literature, and other good things. He did not stubbornly chase after the Western and reject the Chinese, nor cleave only to the Chinese and disclaim the Western. This equanimity was one of the most important lessons he taught me. Previously, because I felt so deeply enamored of the great accomplishments of Chinese culture, I easily tended to spurn the West and reject the modern; but in fact, why should anyone be so biased? Chinese, Western, old, and new, all have their own strong points, and Ching-yao's tendency was to accept the positive and reject the negative in both, and beyond that he made no distinctions.

Even though at that time his salary was very meager, he never failed in his generosity. Every time he invited me out, the food and drink were bountiful, and the taste was always delicious. After knowing him for only a short time, I discovered that Ching-yao was a well-disciplined and thrifty young man who did not waste money and who restrained his eating and drinking habits, even though he had highly cultivated tastes in these things. The first time he came to my house to visit me, I followed the old embassy custom and offered him a small glass of sherry. This sort of liquor doesn't have much alcohol and is made from grape juice. He raised his glass and wished me good health, as though he was thoroughly familiar with the traditional Western custom. Then to my surprise, a few moments later, he turned paled and fainted. I was so shocked that my spirit almost flew out of my body, and I tried my best to revive him, then telephoned the embassy doctor to come over and have a look at him.

After checking him over, the doctor smiled and said there was nothing to worry about, my friend was simply intoxicated, and only later did I find out that up until that very day, Ching-yao had never tasted a single drop of liquor, and that's why he got so totally drunk on just one glass. Today Ching-yao is a prominent professor at a university in America, and our friendship still remains as strong as ever, just like brothers. Every time I go to America, I visit him and his family, and the moment I see him again always marks the highlight of my journey.

Strange Encounters

Not long after I took up my post at the embassy, I began to encounter all sorts of strange and inexplicable events. For example, there were several places, such as the town of Shapingta near Chungjing and the city of Chengdu, where three or four universities were all established at the same location, and this made it quite convenient for me whenever I went on inspection visits or to conduct interviews. The thing that really surprised me was that several of these neighboring universities seemed to be competing with each other to invite me as their distinguished guest. How very strange! I was definitely not an important or highly placed person. If I received invitations from two different schools for the same time, I naturally had no choice but to decline one, and this inevitably made the school officials at the other feel very unhappy.

Sometimes the school whose invitation I had refused would send someone to see me and ask me to reconsider my decision. One time, I playfully replied, "Let me first attain enlightenment and become a bodhisattva, and we'll discuss it again then. Bodhisattvas can emanate several etheric bodies, and thus it's easy for them to be at two places at the same time." The person I said this to quickly replied, "No, no, that's not necessary, all we ask is that you first go to the other school and quickly have a couple of glasses of wine there, eat a few dishes, then immediately come over to our place." As soon as I heard these conditions, I no longer refused their invitations, but I still did not know why they were so insistent that I come. The man only said that this was the old precedent, but he was not willing to explain it any further. The more I asked for clarification, the more uncomfortable he became. Only later did I understand that the real situation was this: at that time, all universities and cultural institutions in China realized that during wartime the British Cultural Association was unable to offer them much financial assistance, and they also clearly knew that I was only a minor functionary. Inviting me to banquets was a courtesy that reflected the traditional Chinese way of welcoming a guest from afar, but their real motive did not lie there.

During the war, many midlevel and lower officials, university teachers, and students came to Szechuan as refugees from regions occupied by the enemy. Under the prevailing circumstances at that time, it was very difficult to provide so many people with sufficient supplies of food. Refugees could not obtain adequate nutrition, and not only students, but even teachers and government officials often could not find enough to eat. Therefore, universities and government institutes habitually utilized the entertainment of foreign guests as a way to get a full meal by taking advantage of these occasions to spend some money from their official entertainment budgets to prepare three or four tables of good food. The staff from the host university or institute could eat their fill at the meal arranged to entertain the foreign guest. No wonder they didn't want me to decline their invitations!

Speaking of banquets reminds me of another strange event. One year, the British Cultural Association sent Professor Dodds from Oxford University's Royal Chair of Greek Language on an observation tour of several Chinese universities located in the rear region of China, in order to discuss ways of assisting them in their research work. One time, I accompanied him on a trip to Guiyang to have a look at Jejiang University, which had just recently relocated there. There were many teachers and students present, but textbooks and research facilities were almost totally absent. What was there for such a distinguished guest to see? The university came up with an unexpected solution to deal with the situation. Among the teaching staff was a gentleman surnamed Hwa, whose family was connected with the famous Mao Tai wine factory.* So they fetched some of their best vintage wine, and used it to entertain their visitors, resolving the problem in a most convenient manner.

When we two guests from afar arrived there, the president of the university had a happy smile on his face and said, "First, we'd like to invite our honored guests for a little meal." In fact, it was a very sumptuous banquet, with over twenty delectable dishes prepared for every table, and after each dish was served, our host proposed a bottoms-up toast with the finest quality Mao Tai. We continued to toast

*Mao Tai is one of China's most famous wines, made from fermented rice, then distilled to very high strength. It is produced near Guiyang.

after every dish straight through to the end of the banquet, after which everyone left the table feeling very happy indeed. Later, when we toured the school's facilities, we found nothing but empty book shelves in the library and empty work tables in the laboratories; all there was to see were some crude desks and chairs and lots of students. But since we were poured full of good wine, the coarse facilities were of absolutely no importance, and the two Westerners tottered on ahead, benumbed and befuddled, with toothy grins on their faces. The president of the university had achieved his goal.

Professor Dodds visited many other universities while in China, and he probably did not remember the situations at each and every one, but when he returned to England, he definitely would have not forgotten his visit to Jejiang University.

Before long, the British Cultural Association sent another famous professor to China, the renowned scientist Dr. Joseph Needham, with the purpose of investigating China's advanced scientific research facilities. This hugely talented scholar also had a hugely built body, and after less than a month in China, he had already collapsed three or four wooden beds and crashed through countless wooden chairs, so he soon became known by the nickname "Elephant Joe." He was very warmly welcomed by Chinese scientists. This extremely energetic and highly gifted colossus was totally captivated by the allure of Chinese culture, and he made great efforts to help Chinese scientists.

Over the years, Dr. Needham has devoted his heart and soul to the compilation of his great, multivolumed historical masterpiece, *Science and Civilization in China*. By the time this work is completed it might well be as voluminous as the Encyclopedia Brittanica.* Of course, Dr. Needham has many Chinese and Western scientists and historians assisting him with his research. But his greatest achievement in this massive scholarly project was the original vision for the work and the

*Dr. Needham died in 1995. According to the Needham Institute, the scholarly masterpiece is currently comprised of seven volumes and the project is still ongoing.

preliminary research, as well as long-term guidance of the project, all of which have been his sole responsibility. He personally conducted the research for many of the most important topics and also wrote the text for them. This monumental history therefore contains a huge amount of Dr. Needham's own original writing. I don't think China has ever had another Western friend and benefactor who could compare with Dr. Needham.

One of the greatest achievements in his work was the discovery of many important Chinese inventions that even the best Chinese scholars had never known about. Thanks to him we now know that even since the Han Dynasty (206 BCE–220 CE), and particularly during the Yuan Dynasty (1260–1368 CE), China did not lack highly developed industries. If it had not been for the fact that Confucian scholars and government bureaucrats looked down on science, China might well have undergone advanced scientific development and an industrial revolution long ago, and become the foremost power on earth. Dr. Needham's many contributions to Chinese science and civilization deserve the utmost respect and admiration from all friends of China.

Preordained Serendipity May Be Chanced Upon but Not Beckoned

Through my work as a cultural attaché, I once chanced upon some preordained serendipity in a very casual manner. I was sent on an assignment to Guangshi University in Guilin, and had to spend two or three nights there. During that time, I arranged a meeting with my good friend, Mr. Huang Li-sung. He's the one I mentioned earlier in this book, the second son of the president of the Min Sheng Academy (many years later he was appointed president of Hong Kong University). When Hong Kong fell to the Japanese, he took refuge in Guilin, where he taught chemistry as an assistant professor at Guangshi University. I couldn't help feeling that this was a case of big talent put to small use. When we met, we both felt elated to see each other again.

According to what he told me, he had attended Hong Kong University for nearly four years, but had not yet graduated due to the fall of Hong Kong, after which he had escaped to Guilin. Fortunately for him, his teacher thought that he was an exceptionally accomplished student, and therefore awarded him a special degree as a "Wartime Graduate." As we talked about his current plans, he told me that there was a relief organization set up to assist Hong Kong University located near Chungjing, and that if he could relocate himself to Chungjing, he would surely encounter much better opportunities.

When I was teaching him English in high school, Li-sung was very close to me, and his mother always spent a lot of time preparing good food for me to eat. His father hired me to teach at his academy many times and always paid me a very good salary. How could I not help their son? Moreover, he and I had always been very intimate friends, so I immediately invited him to come to Chungjing and stay at my house. After arriving in Chungjing, he contacted the organization mentioned above, and before long, he received an invitation from Oxford University.

Not only that, he was also selected as a candidate for a Rhodes Scholarship. This honor was not easy to obtain. Unforeseeably, the Chinese Ministry of Education seemed unwilling to allow a student from Hong Kong to win a scholarship that everyone in China drooled for. Consequently, Li-sung's application for an exit visa to leave China took a very long time to be approved. During this long waiting period, he spent the whole time living at my house. I should really be grateful to the Ministry of Education for making things so difficult for him, because it gave me the opportunity to become even closer to Li-sung, and to further develop an intimate friendship that would last a lifetime.

After Li-sung left Szechuan for the West, he first obtained a doctorate degree at Oxford University, then went on to America to continue his studies at the University of Chicago. After returning to Asia, he started out as a professor of chemistry, and later became the honorary president of the University of Malaysia, after which he was appointed president of Nan Yang University in Singapore, and finally he became president of his mother school, Hong Kong University, where he served for forty years before retiring. His so-called "retirement" was only a manner of speaking, for as of this writing he is still busy acting as consultant for the newly established Swatow University, while also participating in many activities of benefit to both Hong Kong and China.

Two Women Marry One Man

When I first went to China, I had very few Western friends, and I found that my Chinese friends were all that I needed. Most of the Westerners there had entirely different interests than I did, so it was difficult for me to become close friends with them. While serving at my post in the British Embassy, although I got along quite well with my colleagues there, most of my close friends were Chinese. However, there were a few exceptions, such as the sinologist Dr. Robert van Gulik,* whose Chinese name was Kao Lei-pei. At the time, he served as a high-ranking secretary at the Dutch Embassy. He had a very deep love for China and had cultivated a profound command of Chinese scholarship. His calligraphy was beautiful, he knew how to inscribe bronzes and stone tablets, he could play the ancient Chinese zither, and he was able to write books in Chinese. He truly reflected all of the finest qualities of the Western "Renaissance Man."

Old Kao wore a beard and mustache, exactly like the ancient Chinese literati, and his eyes and hair were the same color as the Chinese. Only his height and the slightly foreign accent in his Mandarin prevented him from being identified as a Chinese. The profound depth of his scholarship and brilliant literary talent were greatly admired by one and all.

---

*Author of *Sexual Life in Ancient China*, a landmark study of sexual relations in traditional Chinese society.

After we'd been acquainted for about a year, Old Kao told me that he had recently proposed marriage to a young lady from Peking. Delighted to hear this news, I asked him when I might look forward to receiving an invitation to his wedding party. Lowering his head and revealing a look of sadness, he said, "That's difficult to predict. She has not yet agreed." Feeling very sympathetic and rather anxious for him, I asked, "How can such a thing be possible? How could any woman not admire Old Kao?" He smiled and replied, "We're both very much in love with each other, so it's not that she's unwilling to marry me. The problem is this: she also wants me to marry her younger sister and take her as a second wife. Old Pu, you know perfectly well that it's impossible for a Western diplomat to take two wives in marriage. In my country, bigamy is a serious crime. Although I would feel most fortunate to marry two wives, don't you agree that being regarded as a criminal would be even more unfortunate than remaining a bachelor?" His bittersweet smile expressed a sadness that truly touched my heart.

I gave his situation some thought, and suddenly burst into laughter, for I had come up with a very good solution. "Old Kao, don't give up hope. I'm sure that your beloved is a gentle and warmhearted woman. She must love her sister very much, which is why she's unwilling to part with her. All you need to do is agree to let her sister live with you both for the rest of her life. Wouldn't that be nice?" Immediately his face lit up with joy, and chuckling to himself he kept repeating over and over, "What a wonderful plan, what a wonderful plan!"

A month later they announced their wedding. After the festivities, I asked him how he liked married life. Glancing first to the left and then to the right, Old Kao replied, "Not bad, not bad!" The blissful look on his face told me with absolute certainty that words could not suffice to express the true depth of his joy.

An Artist's Point of View

During the war, Chungjing was a dull city, and while there were some forms of entertainment, they were limited to social functions. Most of the streets ran steeply uphill, and some of them were constructed as stone step-ways. The shops were not attractive, the products they sold were very common, and walking the streets was not the least bit interesting. Furthermore, the sky was often cloudy for many days at a time, so it was easy for one's spirit to sink into a state of depression. One of Chungjing's few attractions was the excellent quality of its restaurants and the delectable taste of its Szechuanese cuisine, of which there was an abundant variety.

Szechuanese teahouses were particularly pleasant and extremely interesting places to go. Those who worked in the teahouses were not called "waiters" or "attendants," they were called "little masters," and their speech often came out in rhyme, as though they spent a lot of time communing with poets. Actually, members of secret societies* in Szechuan were fond of speaking in this manner, and since the "little masters" frequently overheard them talking this way in the teahouses, they learned to imitate them.

The little masters also had another specialty, which was their way of pouring tea. First they placed an empty tea bowl on the table in front of the customer, then they put some tea leaves in the bowl. The teahouses were always very crowded with customers, and when the little masters carried their huge kettles of boiling hot water to the customer's table, they were constantly jostled left and right, but it didn't bother them the

---

*China's secret societies were founded at the end of the Ming Dynasty, as secret patriotic associations to resist the Manchu conquest of China. By the end of the Manchu Dynasty they had become underworld gangster societies, although they always kept, and still keep today, their patriotic overtones. After the fall of the Manchus, these societies (popularly known as "triads" in English, although there is no such term in Chinese), restored their close connections with Chinese government circles, and they sometimes show their patriotism by performing "dirty jobs" that government intelligence agencies cannot get openly involved with.

least bit. While they were still some distance from the customer's table, and despite being crowded by people all around them, they were able to raise their steaming kettles high up and send a stream of steaming hot water shooting out from the spout and straight into the customer's cup, without a dram too much or too little, and without splashing a single drop on any bystander or onto the table. Utterly fantastic!

Occasionally our embassy staff received invitations from important provincial officials to attend banquets at their homes. Printed on the invitation was usually something like, "Please arrive as early as possible after noon." If the invited guest was not familiar with local custom, he would soon be in for a surprise. For if something happened to delay him so that he could not arrive until evening, he could consider himself very lucky indeed—the host would not be the least bit displeased, and the party would be in full swing. But if he really arrived "as early as possible after noon," he would find that the host was not even at home yet, and that there was nobody there to receive him. Although the invitations always stated "as soon as possible after noon," the intent really was to wait until dark before arriving. Why on earth was it done like this?

I still don't know the reason, but my conjecture is that the host was making it clear on the invitation that the meal was not to be a luncheon meal, but a dinner banquet, and given that, one was expected to arrive after dark and to stay as late as possible after arriving. Those familiar with the protocol would of course know immediately from the wording on the invitation what time to arrive. But strangers would have no idea how to interpret the meaning of these "code words."

Being able to speak Mandarin made it possible to understand most of the Szechuanese dialect. Our embassy never had any misunderstandings due to differences in language, but there were frequent misunderstandings that arose from differences in culture.

For example, our ambassador believed that during wartime everyone who lived in the rear zone should adopt a relatively frugal lifestyle. Whenever he hosted social functions at the embassy, regardless of how important the guests were he always served tasty but relatively coarse foods, and the tables were set with wooden and earthenware utensils. Chinese ministers of state did not necessarily understand his good intentions, and probably thought that he was rather miserly.

One year, the British government sent the famous war photographer Felix Topolski to the Far East in order to report the wartime situation in China. Sometimes I accompanied him on visits to various high-ranking officials. One time, he wanted to photograph the head of a government ministry out in a courtyard. Looking for something to use as a suitable background, he found an old straw mat that someone had discarded lying on the ground. Not only was the mat tattered, it was also weatherworn and faded due to long exposure to sun and rain. But in his mind's eye as an artist, the patterns on the mat were exquisitely beautiful, so he said, "Please ask this gentleman to wait a few minutes. I want to place this mat up against the wall, then ask the gentleman to stand in front of the mat while I take his photograph."

Appalled by his suggestion, I immediately expressed my objection and told him that the minister would surely take offense. Mr. Topolski got very angry and wanted me to explain his idea to the minister in Chinese, in order to convey his artistic vision. I had no choice but to comply with his wish. The minister refused, Topolski insisted, and both of them blew their tempers at me. Extremely upset, they argued with each other in two different languages, and needless to say, the photograph was never taken.

This very embarrassing situation put me in a difficult position, and I thought to myself how their different cultural backgrounds made it impossible for them to understand one another, creating a situation that could not be resolved. The most unfortunate of all was me—for from that day onward, every time I encountered that minister, he pretended that he'd never met me.

She's Not the New Bride After All

Because Chinese and foreigners express themselves in different languages, all sorts of funny things can happen. In the new office building built at the British Embassy, there were several rooms lent to the consular representative of India. One time, a gentleman from India named Mr. Tai informed me that he had found a Chinese woman to become his wife through an advertisement in a newspaper, and that she was a woman of very good character, reserved and well behaved, but unfortunately, due to language differences, it was very difficult for him to train her properly as a suitable wife for an Indian citizen returning to his country.

When an Indian wife hears her husband calling her, she's supposed to reply with the honorific response, "Ji Han" (a very polite term of address used in northern India). However, his fiancée always replied by uttering, "Uh huh!" Such vulgarity would simply not do. So he brought this woman to see me, and asked me to teach her how to say, "Ji Han." Unforeseeably, the Chinese woman got very angry and irately replied, "This man of mine is really far too fussy and full of useless twaddle. Only because my father thinks he's all right for me did I accept his proposal, and my way of replying has always been 'Uh huh.' There's no way I'm going to change my way of replying to 'Shi-han, Shi-han!" After hearing this, I figured there was nothing more I could do to help, so I said this frankly to Mr. Tai. But I thought to myself that the old man in the moon* must have made a big mistake.

At the time, Mr. Tai had already announced their engagement, but they had not yet gotten married. As the wedding date approached, the display of betrothal gifts from the groom's family remained the same, the groom was still Mr. Tai, but the bride turned out to be a different woman, not the original one who stubbornly refursed to address Mr. Tai the way he wished.

Yue lao, literally "the old man in the moon," was the mythical matchmaker who brought prospective brides and grooms together.

The wedding ceremony was set for ten o'clock in the morning on the designated day, and held in the formal reception room at the British Embassy. On the appointed day, over sixty invited guests were waiting there, but there was no sign of the new couple. Time ticked by without cease. By eleven o'clock, the groom was still nowhere to be seen, but the bride arrived by herself. The guests were already growing impatient and were just about to leave, when suddenly the groom rushed in.

The two of them knitted their brows, as though they'd just had an argument. The groom then begged forgiveness from his guests and said, "This morning my betrothed converted to Islam, and had to be fully immersed in water as part of the initiation ceremony. When she emerged from the water, she discovered that her newly coiffured hair had been spoiled. I told her that our guests had probably all arrived already, and begged her not to worry about her hairstyle. Doesn't a woman's hair look even better when it's a bit mussed? But she refused to listen to me, and insisted on going back to the hair salon to have her hair done again, before proceeding with the wedding. I hope you will all forgive us." Naturally we sympathized with the bride, and seeing how angry and flustered she was, we felt quite certain that her wrath would still not be pacified by the time they reached the wedding chamber!

Thereafter, every time Mr. Tai wanted to reprimand his wife, he asked me to translate for him. Fortunately, in every calamity there's also a blessing, and regardless of whether that woman obeyed her husband or not, at least she had no objection to addressing him as "Ji Han."

The Starving Saint

One day I heard that a great monk from Inner Mongolia was living in seclusion in Chungjing, and that he was none other than the "living Buddha"* known as Diloja. Before the war, he was the highest-

---

**Huo fuo,* "living Buddha," is a Chinese term of honor, equivalent to the term "saint" in Western religious tradition, applied to a Buddhist monk who is considered to have attained the state of enlightenment.

ranking lama in Inner Mongolia, where he exercised even more power than the king. Ever since the Japanese had established control over northern China, they wanted to use this living Buddha as a puppet to rule Inner Mongolia.

This saint repeatedly refused to cooperate with the Japanese, who continued to pressure and threaten him, until he finally had no alternative but to escape to a region still under Chinese control. He came south and placed himself under the protection of the central government of China, for he did not wish to become a traitor to the Chinese nation. At that time, the government was still based in Wuhan, and due to the chaotic political situation, they were not inclined to give much consideration to the welfare of a living Buddha, so they only offered him a very small monthly stipend, as though this loyal and righteous Mongolian leader was not worthy of serious respect. When the government retreated further south to Szechuan, this Buddhist saint had no choice but to follow. But as inflation continued to swell and the cost of living soared, his monthly stipend no longer sufficed to support his lifestyle, and he sank into a desperate state of poverty.

I felt deep sympathy for this saintly old man's dire situation, and he also aroused my curiosity, so I arranged to meet him through a friend. Early one morning, he came to my friend's house to meet me, wearing a long blue robe tied at the waist with a silk sash. A pair of sparkling bright eyes shone from his pock-marked face, and his warm smile conveyed an immediate sense of intimacy. His clothing was old and frayed, and it was obvious from his physique that he was very undernourished.

After a lengthy conversation, I said, "It's almost noon, and there's a nice little Shantung restaurant just down the street, so if you don't mind its rustic simplicity, would you care to join me for a bite to eat there?" The old monk's face brightened in agreement, and he stood up to go with me. I knew that most lamas were not vegetarian, and I also knew that Mongolians were very fond of lamb, so I ordered a platter of roasted lamb, three or four side dishes, a large plate of steamed buns, and two bowls of stuffed dumplings. The dumplings were very large, with twenty-five of them in each bowl, but it took the two of us only a few minutes to completely finish eating all fifty dumplings, four or five big buns, and most of the lamb and side dishes. Even the Shantungese proprietor seemed astonished by our appetite.

Good Lord, this virtuous old monk should never have been so badly neglected that he reached such a state of near starvation! Although he was not an ethnic Chinese, he was nevertheless loyal to China and unwilling to let the enemy bribe him into betrayal. When he escaped, he had to disguise himself as the servant of an American teacher in order to avoid being detected and detained by Japanese intelligence agents. Although I knew that the central government was in the midst of fighting for its survival, I still felt that it was their responsibility to provide for this loyal and saintly man, and that they should not neglect him to the point that he had to endure such extreme privation. Fortunately, the following year the American ambassador arranged for this Buddhist saint to go to America, where he became the abbot of a large Lamaist monastery.

Mount Omei: A Visit to the Sacred Abode of Samantabhadra Bodhisattva

On a cliffside along the Jialing River was a place called Bei Pei, where literati liked to gather, and nearby were numerous bubbling hot springs. Among the wartime cultural institutes located there was a government-sponsored editorial and translation bureau, a secretariat for the national palace museum, and other offices. Either on business or just for relaxation, I often went out to Bei Pei on weekends to spend a few days there. It was a very pleasant place to visit, and sometimes I went there for the hot springs baths, or to visit writers living there, or to see exhibits at the museum. Whenever rare national treasures from the imperial palace were put on display, I stayed overnight at the house of some friends in order to have more time to study them.

The friends were Mr. and Mrs. Yang Hui-yi. At that time the two of them worked together at the editorial and translation bureau, and today they are renowned translators at China's foreign language publication institute. They both graduated from Oxford University, and the wife was a thoroughly sinified Englishwoman. At Bei Pei she always wore long blue robes, cooked Chinese food, and was very adept in running a traditional Chinese household. They were very warm and friendly people who loved laughter, had very sensitive minds, conversed at length on unusual topics, and were in no way frivolous. They had the carefree attitude of literati who loved the romantic life, but they approached literary matters with the utmost respect and careful attention to detail. To enjoy the river scenery, savor fine tea, drink wine, and talk about life with this kind of friend at Bei Pei was an endless source of pleasure for me.

Hui-yi, Ching-yao, Li-sung, and other friends like them were all very charming and talented people. At that time, China abounded with such worthy and highly accomplished young men and women, capable and dignified, of virtuous character, patriotic and resolute, and dedicated to helping their country overcome the current crisis. How unfortunate that at the time such great talent was not taken seriously and allowed to express its full potential, and that instead it was dismissed and wasted. After the war, many of these gifted young scholars had no option but to go to distant lands abroad in order to earn a living, and thus they scattered to the four corners of the earth.

While in Szechuan, I fell in love with a young woman and became completely lovesick over her, and when I realized it was hopeless, I just couldn't get over it. Only Ching-yao, Li-sung, Hui-yi, and three or four other dear friends were able to pull me back from the abyss of despair into which I had tumbled. In my view, becoming close friends with talented men of learning prevents one from losing direction in life.

One summer, I had the opportunity of traveling to Mount Omei,*

*One of China's most sacred mountains, located in Szechuan, famous for its many Buddhist temples and hermitages and its magnificent misty mountain landscapes.

but regrettably, due to pressing official business, I had only three days to climb to the top and return, so I was unable to fully savor its beauty, much less do it justice in words. Mount Omei was revered as the sacred ground of the bodhisattva Samantabhadra, the bodhisattva most revered by my pledged brother Tsai Yuan-ruo. At that time elder brother Tsai still lived in Hong Kong, but Hong Kong was then under the despotic control of the Japanese military. On the evening of my second day on the mountain, I arrived at a small monastery at the peak and immediately asked some monks there to conduct a special ceremony for the safety of my elder brother, and to say prayers for him. I also participated in the ceremony in order to fulfill my responsibility as a younger brother. The next day I went back down the mountain.

After my return to Chungjing, the ambassador summoned me to let me know that an English priest stationed in Chungjing had accused a certain member of the embassy staff of bringing shame to all English people, and that his heathen behavior might lead Chinese Christian converts to "fall again into evil beliefs." The ambassador was an unbiased English aristocrat, so he did not blame me, but he did advise me to beware of the prejudice of others and to avoid provoking any more malicious criticism from them. I thanked the ambassador for his good intentions, but could not prevent my heart from complaining. This was the second time that I'd suffered both insult and injury from recalcitrant Westerners in China.

This incident resulted in another disgraceful consequence. As described previously, seven or eight years earlier I had taken formal vows as a lay Buddhist initiate with the famous monk Neng Hai and acknowledged him as my spiritual master. Thereafter I had not seen him again. Shortly after receiving the ambassador's stern advice, a colleague and I went together to visit a Buddhist monastery in Chengdu, and as we passed by the main shrine hall, we heard the sonorous sound of sutras being recited. While we were examining an ancient artifact out in the courtyard, the sound of the sutra recital suddenly stopped. The monks who'd been chanting inside left the shrine hall and walked toward their private monastic quarters, passing right by us on the pathway. As they approached, I recognized one of the old monks as none other than Master Neng Hai. Although I was only his lay disciple, I nevertheless should have immediately performed the ceremonial ritual of respect before him. Because I had not seen him for such a long time, a simple bow would definitely not suffice to express my respect.

Ai dzai! Had I knelt down and touched my head to the ground before him, especially there in broad daylight, the ambassador would hear about it and would definitely have seriously disapproved; but if I refrained from properly offering my respect, then how could I dare address him? I'm ashamed to say that as the master walked by, his eyes stared straight at my face, as though to ask, "Is this not my disciple named Pu?" But when he saw the blank expression on my face, the master obviously thought he'd been mistaken, and continued walking on ahead. I wanted very much to follow and catch up with him, and to pay him formal respect inside his room in order to compensate for my rudeness. Just as I was in the throes of indecision, my colleague said, "We'd better get going, our friends are probably waiting for us to have lunch." The next morning, I went back to the monastery by myself in order to beg the master's forgiveness, but alas, one of his disciples informed me that he'd already departed. From then until the master's death, I never again had the good fortune to meet with him, and the very thought of it always arouses feelings of shame and guilt in my heart.

Treading Across Water by Raft to Visit a Remote Hermitage at Ching Cheng

After the war was won, before leaving Szechuan and returning to England, I went to Chengdu one more time in order to visit the famous Mount Ching Cheng. Starting in Chengdu there was a road that ran by the foot of the mountain, but it did not connect directly with the trail onto the mountain. From the road it was necessary to take a raft across a river before reaching the mountain trail. On the raft were several small benches, about three inches high. When fully loaded with passengers, the raft was pressed down below the surface of the water, so that the bottom of the passengers' rumps, feet, and luggage all got soaking wet. There are all sorts of strange transportation facilities in the world, but I'd never heard of such an odd thing as treading across water by raft.

The mountain trail was rough, and the slope was very steep. Dense groves of trees carpeted the hillsides, and there were very few signs of human habitation. Caves dimpled the face of the mountain, silent and secluded, and the only sound to be heard was the trill of birds. The two or three temples on the mountain were not very imposing, and they looked antiquated and dignified. When I reached the summit of the mountain, I took lodging at an old Taoist hermitage, and though I don't remember its name, I'll never forget its atmosphere of remote tranquility. The loose flowing robes worn by the Taoist hermits, their long hair combed up and tied in topknots, and their thick beards, all made me envy their ancient way of life, and I admired their relaxed and genteel attitude. These dedicated Taoist adepts cultivated a very disciplined way of life and made contentment their primary practice. Although there were no restrictions in their diets, they never over-indulged. Their food was sufficient yet frugal. Exercise, meditation, reading, recreation, bathing, and sleeping all had their own natural order and balance, never too much of one or too little of another.

Meals at the hermitage were served by young Taoist novices. They looked and acted just like the older hermits, except without beards, with their hair tied up in topknots and wearing exactly the same robes, dignified in appearance and refined in attitude. When serving food and pouring wine, these lads bowed to the guests with friendly smiles to express their respect. Even in those days, the only place one still encountered the restrained and graceful manners of traditional times was in Taoist hermitages. But today, I doubt that there is anywhere on earth where one could ever see this again.

I could only stay for three days, so I did not have a chance to receive any teachings, but I thoroughly enjoyed that old-world ambience. What I did not realize at the time was that I would never again have the opportunity to savor the grace and refinement of such a highly civilized way of life. Today, regardless of whether in China, Taiwan, or Southeast Asia, Chinese youth has no idea how precious and praiseworthy were the spirit and manner of their illustrious ancestors.

6

Exotic Encounters in Southern China

What I've written above concludes my account of events that happened in Chungjing while I was working at the British Embassy there. Now I want to recount some of my experiences when I was sent on assignments to other provinces during that period. The events described here occurred during 1944. In the spring of that year, I had to make a trip to Changding in Fujien province and to Shaoguan in Guangdung. The former was a place of refuge for Shia Men (Amoy) University, and the latter was near the wartime campus of Jung Shan (Sun Yat-sen) University. This long journey took me through seven provinces, so naturally I felt very happy about it.

Every time I went to other provinces, my main purpose was to establish contact with various Chinese universities on behalf of the British Cultural Association in order to determine the sort of assistance they required to support their teaching and research programs. This was very interesting work, and my travels provided me with many pleasant experiences, such as enjoying good regional cuisines, hearing unusual music, visiting close friends, observing colorful local customs, and so forth.

Western and southern China abounded with unique regional customs that drew the attention of the visitor. The only annoying drawback was that transportation was extremely inconvenient. Though the railroads were not bad, there were very few route lines. Traveling by water was more comfortable, but extremely slow. The many defects of the public road system were enough to drive one mad. The surfaces of the roads were never graded flat or rolled with tar, so they were all deeply rutted and uneven, strewn with pebbles, and shrouded with dense clouds of dust that painfully stung the eyes. When vehicles bumped along these roads, the passengers inside were tossed around insufferably. Not only that, the public buses were often so overloaded and driven beyond their capacity that they were constantly breaking down and had to make frequent stops en route for repairs, causing passengers endless irritation.

A Mountain Tribe Born with Tails

The day I departed for Fujien and Guangdung, I was full of anticipation that I would encounter all sorts of exotic experiences, and this in fact turned out to be the case. That day, I entered Guijou province, and by dusk I arrived in the city of Guiyang, where I lodged at a large inn. I decided to have a bath and a short rest before going out to look for a local teahouse where I could sample some Guijou cuisine. After returning to my room from the bath chamber and lying down on the bed, I suddenly heard a loud knock on the door, and someone burst into my room, startling me to sit straight up in the bed. Without waiting for me to indicate whether he was welcome or not, the intruder said in an excited tone of voice, "Your worthy surname, sir, is Pu, and my own humble surname is also Pu, so I have come here specially to say hello and pay you a visit." Only after he'd finished speaking, did he focus his attention on my Western features, and his face froze in astonishment. Standing there befuddled, he stammered, "Mr. Pu, I daresay you look like a foreign . . . like a Westerner. If it were not for the fact that we share the same surname, I might easily be led to believe that you are . . ." He didn't say any more, but just stood staring at me, as though waiting for me to explain myself.

Trying to suppress my laughter, I said in a serious tone, "My humble homeland is England, and my unworthy personal name is Le-dao. May I inquire where you come from?" Hearing me speak in such a civilized manner, he seemed to relax a bit, and said, "My petty personal name is Ge-lang." By then his attitude had become quite polite, as though he realized that his behavior just a moment ago had been rather rude. He apologetically explained that he had noticed on the registration ledger that a guest with the surname Pu had checked into this inn, and because Pu was a relatively rare surname in China, he was accustomed to greeting any visitors to Guiyang who were surnamed Pu and showing them around town. He further informed me that the Pu clan had migrated to China from Persia during the Tang Dynasty, and that later their descendents had split into two branches, one in Szechuan and the other in Guangdung. Although there were also a few Pu's scattered around in other places, there were not many. When he finished his explanation, a look of doubt appeared in his eyes. He seemed to be wondering how on earth a foreigner could get the surname "Pu."

I told him that during my youth in England, I had asked a Chinese classmate from Wenjou, Mr. Li Shao-ying, to select a Chinese name for me. People from Wenjou pronounce the letter *p* as *b*. Therefore, he chose the surname "Pu" to represent the *b* in my English surname Blofeld, with "Le" for the *lo* and "dao" for the final *d,* omitting the three letters *fel* in between.

Upon hearing my explanation, Ge-lang loudly exclaimed, "Fantastic! Your worthy friend Mr. Li was obviously a highly accomplished scholar. Not only do the noble surname and distinguished personal name he selected for you sound good in Chinese, they also have significant meaning." Standing up to bow at me, he then said, "Please allow me, on behalf of everyone in China who carries the surname Pu, to welcome you, Mr. Pu Le-dao, as an honorary member of our noble clan. This is a great honor for us." I quickly climbed off the bed, stood up straight, and bowing in gratitude I said, "I'm most unworthy, most unworthy, of such a great honor." Thereupon, we went out together for dinner.

While we were drinking wine in the restaurant, I casually asked him about the native hill tribes in Guijou. To my surprise, he expressed a very strong interest in the Miao tribe. After dinner, he took me to a local teahouse, and before long four or five Miao people came in and greeted Mr. Pu as though he were an old friend, then sat down at our table. They all wore skullcaps on their heads and were dressed in short black jackets and pants, with red cloth buttons and broad red belts. The strange thing was that their pants were extremely baggy and bulged down behind their rumps, as though they had long tails tucked away inside. This of course was impossible, but the strange shape of their pants really made me wonder. In Hunnan province, people say that in the mountains there does indeed live a tribe of people who are born with tails, and while naturally I knew that this was just a legend, at the time I nevertheless could not help but have my doubts.

The Miao tribesmen sitting at our table were very simple and sincere people, and whatever was said to them or asked of them was always fine with them. They realized that I was not making fun of them, and that, on the contrary, I was deeply interested in their ways. They did not know why their pants were designed with such a strange shape, and said, "How would we know? Our ancestors liked them like this, and that's all there is to it. If we were to change it, the souls of our ancestors would get very angry. They would blame us for not preserving our ancient traditions. They are always watching over us from the astral realms. We don't dare alter any of the old customs, and altering our traditional costume is even more out of the question. We want people to know that we are not Chinese, and also that we are not Muslim. We are the descendants of the original inhabitants of this region since ancient times; we are the royal clan. Long, long ago, the 'Great Dog' far across the eastern sea took a Chinese princess as his wife, and their children were the ancestors of the Miao tribe. Later, the descendants of their children divided into nine families, and came west in nine wooden boats. When they reached China, they went further west and came to this region, where they established the great Kingdom of

Miao. Because the Chinese people were so numerous, they were able to defeat the Kingdom of Miao, but they shall never be able to suppress the Miao tribe into extinction. This is not just a fable, it's the true history of the Miao!"

They also told me that what the Miao people fear most of all is violating the rules set by their ancestors, that they dare not tell lies, and that their greatest taboo is theft.

The Miao Tribe's Effective Preventive against Misconduct in Marriage

The Miao people believe that disease is a calamity cast upon them by their ancestors as a form of punishment for misconduct, so the moment they get sick, they slaughter a chicken and butcher a pig as offerings and beg their ancestors for mercy. The Miao very seldom commit any unvirtuous deeds. In their villages, crimes such as theft and rape are extremely rare. Greed, lust, and other wicked impulses do not motivate Miao people to commit evil acts.

Every three or four years, they dismantle their houses, move to another place, and build a new village, so that they can cultivate new land that no one else has ever cultivated before, and in this way they continuously colonize previously unsettled areas. Large families occupy relatively large tracts of land, while small families take smaller plots. If there are not enough members in a family to cultivate a large parcel of land, then what's the point of taking more land?

Men marry and establish their own families in their early twenties. Before marriage, whenever weather permits, young men and women leave the village at night and sleep together in the mountain forests. Partners change frequently, and both men and women like to switch lovers. This way, they satisfy their lustful desires prior to marriage, so that after marriage they are not led astray by unfulfilled sexual fantasies. If an unmarried girl gives birth to several children, that's regarded as the best thing of all. Most men far prefer women who already have children as marriage partners. Whoever has the good fortune to marry such a woman will have the advantage of a larger family with many helping hands, and this means that the family can occupy a larger piece of land. On the off chance that a man has an illicit liaison with another man's wife, the elders will compel him to pay the injured party a certain sum in silver, or else to perform labor for him for a number of months. This system is very simple and very easy to enforce.

When anyone in the group of Miao people at our table spoke, all the others would continuously chime in, "Isn't that so? That's correct! He's absolutely right!" They wanted to invite us two Pu's to go out to their village to smoke a few pipes of opium with them. Citing my early departure by bus the next morning as an excuse, I politely declined and thanked them for the invitation.

The next morning at dawn, I boarded a bus bound for Guilin. Guijou province is mostly steep mountains and cliffs, and in every direction all there is to see are rugged crags. The land is barren and unproductive, the roads are twisted and uneven, and on both sides precipitous peaks and green mountains attract the eye's attention. In the shimmering light of early morning, the towering pinnacles looked like gigantic city battlements. Soon this vision faded away, then recurred briefly again in the coral glow of sunset. When the sun was shining high in the sky, the glare overwhelmed the eyes with bright light. At that time of day, the roads were empty and desolate, and vehicles were very scarce.

When ascending the steep hills, the bus belched and groaned, as though it were stuttering a curse at Heaven and bemoaning its fate. At one of the mountain passes, the slope was so sheer and difficult to climb that the bus slowed down below the pace of a pedestrian. Just then I saw a large group of Miao people walk by, the men dressed in black and red clothing as described above, and the women wearing costumes embroidered in bright rainbow colors, with their hair combed up in high buns tightly tied with colorful ribbons, multicolored scarves wrapped around the collars of their jackets, and heavy silver jewelry hanging from their necks. Most attractive of all were their thickly pleated blue skirts, the hems of which were ornately embroidered in exquisite designs and beautiful colors. A passenger sitting beside me on the bus said that if the pleats of their skirts were opened up and flattened out, the cloth would stretch more than twenty-six feet across. This meant that the surface area of the embroidered material along the hem was really very long. My fellow passenger also told me that when he came to live in Guijou many years ago, he wanted to buy one of those Miao skirts as a gift for someone and asked a Miao woman how much it would cost to buy one. The woman got very upset and replied, "You want me to sell you my life? It takes at least seven years to embroider one skirt. How could we ever part with one?"

The Mortal Danger of Insulting a Fox Spirit

I arrived in Guilin in the evening and stayed at the university there for a few days, then boarded a train to Hengyang. Upon arrival there, I took lodging at a very elegant traditional inn with charming old-world ambience. That night I went out by myself to look for a good restaurant. When I got there, a waiter led me into a small room with a table just large enough to seat two persons. The furniture in the room was exquisite, made from intricately carved rosewood, and all the other fixtures were equally beautiful. I thought to myself: this restaurant must be extremely expensive; and to be served dinner in this private room must make it even more costly. But if I refuse now, it would certainly be a breach of etiquette. Never mind, what harm is there in enjoying being treated like a wealthy tycoon just this one time?

Contrary to my expectations, the person who came in to serve me wine was not that young waiter, but rather a charming young prostitute. Although she wasn't particularly beautiful, she was youthful and slender, dressed in a short jacket of white satin and black silk pants, with a high collar and a few sprigs of fresh jasmine blossoms tucked into her well-coiffed hair. The strange thing about it was that she said to me, "Third Master Chen, so you have arrived. Sister Shan isn't feeling well today, so she cannot be here to accompany you this evening. My name is Little Jyun, and Sister Shan asked me to take her place."

Now I realized why I'd been taken to a private room: they had mistaken me for another Westerner who'd reserved this room. Since things had already developed to this point, I decided to let events take their course. I said, "My name is Pu, not Chen." I smiled, opened my eyes wide, and looked at her with interest, as though to say, "Ha-ha, now what's your response to this little misunderstanding?"

Not the least bit flustered, she smiled prettily and replied, "If Second Master Pu does not object to retaining Little Jyun to pour his wine, that really would be very nice. None of my regular customers has come in for fun tonight, so Little Jyun feels bored to death." Pouting her little lips, she pretended to feel hurt. My feelings have always been easily aroused, and I simply could not resist this sort of charm, so I said happily, "That's fine with me. Will Little Jyun sing a song for me?" She couldn't sing, and wasn't very well spoken either, but her demeanor was quite enchanting. She used a pair of chopsticks to put delicious morsels of food into my mouth, in the traditional manner of entertaining a guest.

After a while, I began to tire of her little doll behavior. As soon as she noticed my displeasure, she said with great excitement in her voice, "Second Master Pu, Little Jyun can recite stories, but I didn't bring along my storybook, so all I can do is tell you a tale. Would you like to hear it?" I wasn't very hopeful, but didn't wish to hurt her feelings, so I said, "All right. Since we're not far from the Southern Peak,* how about telling me a tale about strange spirits and ghostly mysteries?" Her theatrical talent was excellent, and the story she proceeded to tell me made my hair stand on end. My skill cannot match hers, so the best I can do is recount the main points as follows:

*A sacred peak of Mount Heng in Guijou, said to be inhabited by many strange spirits.

In a certain hermitage on Mount Heng, there lived a young Taoist adept whose name was Purple Pine. He diligently cultivated his energy and gradually mastered the mysterious arts. From time to time, he had to descend the mountain to purchase provisions for his master. One day, while passing by the pagoda of a fox fairy,* he suddenly felt the urge to urinate, so he stopped near the pagoda to relieve his bladder and inadvertently let some urine seep into the base of the pagoda. This provoked the fox fairy who inhabited the pagoda to complain furiously. The young Taoist felt offended by the scolding the fox fairy had howled at him, and so he said with a laugh, "Your own rank odor, old fox, is so foul that I can hardly even breathe, and compared to that smell, my urine could be regarded as quite fragrant!" The fox spirit residing in the pagoda grew enraged and vowed, "Insulting a fox fairy is an unforgivable mortal offense. Only by drinking your blood shall my anger be pacified! Mark my words: within three months, I shall have my revenge on you!" Purple Pine could not suppress a shudder of fear and left in silence, feeling greatly distressed.

That evening, while the young Taoist was returning to the hermitage from the city, just as he reached the foot of the mountain a dense fog suddenly descended, completely enshrouding the entire area. Losing his way, he took the wrong fork in the trail, and after a long while, he finally saw a ray of light shining near the side of the path, so he quickly walked toward it. At last he came upon an ancient temple so densely veiled in mist that even the large characters inscribed on the tablet over the gate were too obscured to read. All he could

*Mythical beings who are said to have attained spiritual immortality while human, then transformed themselves into fox spirits. From time to time, they returned to human form as irresistibly beautiful women in order to mate with virile young men and steal their energy by draining them of their sexual fluids, as a means of boosting their own power.

see was that the front gate stood ajar, and feeling calmer now, he heaved a sigh of relief and went inside. There he saw a young boy waving at him, so Purple Pine followed him inside and across a courtyard, stopping before the door of a small cottage. The little lantern hanging over the door cast a few dim rays of light into the night. But the light flowing from the window seemed to beckon him with a warm welcome.

The Taoist had an intuitive feeling that this place was rather strange, and that it might hold some sort of danger for him, but he had no other choice, so he went inside. At this moment, the young boy suddenly disappeared, and he heard the soothing sound of a harp, which so entranced him that he lost all sense of fear. Knocking on the door as he stepped inside, he saw two people sitting there completely enraptured by the music from the harp, and they both ignored him. The harp player was a stunningly beautiful girl with a face like a peach blossom, blooming with the ripe spirit of youth. Sitting to her side was an old man wearing a short vest over a long gown, very well groomed and dignified, with a long beard; but his demeanor was cold and reserved, and though he seemed to be intently listening to the music, he definitely noticed the Taoist standing there.

Purple Pine paid no further attention to the old man, nor did he pause to consider that he might be stepping into a trap. He just stood there dumbfounded, as though he'd lost his soul, and stared fixedly at that beautiful girl's jade-like face, just like a little bird mesmerized by the eyes of a snake. Soon the harp music gradually faded away, and the young beauty stood up with a sweet smile and bowed, saying to the old man, "Father, we have a guest." The old man glanced at the Taoist and said coldly, "Please have a seat. Perhaps you have already guessed that our surname is Hu."* The old man was no doubt the fox fairy who lived in that pagoda.

*The surname "Hu" is a homonym for the word "fox."

A moment later, the old man said, "You came at just the right time. We were just about to have dinner when the family next door sent someone over to report that their old grandfather is critically ill, so I must go over there and visit them. Please stay and accompany my daughter for a cup of wine and a few bites of our simple food." When he finished speaking, he stood up and abruptly left without the courtesy of saying farewell, as though he didn't feel the slightest regard for his guest.

As they ate, Miss Hu served him with the utmost attention, and conversed with him without the slightest inhibition, and soon the two of them were as close as though they'd known each other forever. After a servant came to clear away the dishes and left them alone, the young girl flashed him a bewitching smile that silently revealed her intentions, and in this manner she extended him the invitation that could not be spoken aloud. The two of them immediately fell into a passionate embrace and went to bed together, and they didn't part until dawn.

After returning to his hermitage on the mountain, the young Taoist lived in seclusion as before and did not again descend the mountain and enter the city, nor did he ever again go out for strolls to enjoy the scenery. Why did Purple Pine cut himself off from the world and live like this? Was it because he wished to avoid another encounter with the fox fairy? Not at all! Regardless of who the man might be, all it took was one illicit coupling with a fox fairy, and his fate was thereby sealed. Thenceforth it was impossible to escape from the net, and even though he clearly knew from the start that this witch would suck his spirit dry, he would nevertheless have preferred to die in her arms than to forfeit the opportunity to enjoy the incomparable pleasure of copulating with her.

According to others who lived at the hermitage, a female fox was often seen darting back and forth around the walls of the hermitage, and this fox's fur grew shinier and more resplendent day by day, while Purple Pine's vital life force gradually withered away, and he became ever weaker and more exhausted. His master must have known the cause of his disciple's ailment, and he must certainly have had a magic spell he could cast to help rid him of this calamity, but in order for the spell to work, Purple Pine would have to resolve himself to killing his beloved fox fairy—otherwise the spell would have no effect. The old Taoist master took "noninterference"* as his guiding principle, for how could he possibly force another person to make such a choice?

Three months after copulating with that fox fairy, Purple Pine suddenly disappeared. Soon thereafter, someone came up the mountain to report to the master of the hermitage. He said that on that day at a dilapidated old temple at the foot of the mountain, he saw a corpse sprawled out in the courtyard and recognized it as the Taoist Purple Pine, his skin pale as a ghost, his entire body drained of blood. All around him were paw prints of a fox, as though left there by a large pack of foxes. From this it was clear that the old fox fairy in the pagoda had fulfilled his vow of revenge.

The tale Little Jyun told represented a phenomenon firmly believed by people in those days, a folk tale handed down from generation to generation ever since the Tang Dynasty, but people today may not be familiar with it. Therefore, I decided to record it in this book in order to introduce readers to an old Chinese folk tradition. By the time Little Jyun had finished telling me her story, it was already quite late, so I returned to the inn and went to sleep. The next day I boarded a bus to Gansien, and a day later I arrived in Changding.

**Wu wei,* "noninterference," is a fundamental guiding principle by which Taoists live, always letting nature take its course without interfering.

The Native Fujienese Art of Drinking Tea

The refugee enclave where Amoy University was located had a very rural flavor, with a relaxed atmosphere and a simple, easygoing lifestyle, but the quality of material facilities there could not compare with the rear zone in Szechuan. Most of the teachers were southerners from Fujien province, so they were all familiar with the native Fujienese art of drinking tea and cherished the pure spring water and fragrant tea from Wuyi Mountain as precious treasures. I don't recall the official business that brought me there, but I very clearly remember how the people at the university performed the traditional art of drinking tea for me. They used small, unglazed terra-cotta teapots and tiny white porcelain teacups as their tea utensils, and the best grade oolong tea leaves, to prepare tea with a delicacy that could be described as sweet dew. Preparing this tea properly required the long experience of many years of practice, and that is why it is known as "Gung Fu Tea."*

The way to prepare Gung Fu Tea is as follows: First, boiling hot water is poured into the pot and cups in order to preheat them. Tea leaves are then put into the warm pot and very briefly soaked with some hot water, which is quickly poured off. This step is called "washing the tea." More boiling water is then poured onto the presoaked leaves in the pot. The tea is allowed to steep for about twenty seconds, during which time the teacups are again preheated with hot water. The tea is then poured out into the warm cups and given to the guests to taste. The steeped tea leaves expand inside to completely fill the pot, which means that the pot holds more leaves than water, therefore the tea is not allowed to steep too long, in order to prevent it from becoming bitter. Each batch of new tea leaves placed in the pot may thus be infused with boiling water several times. According to tea connoisseurs, the second infusion produces the best-tasting tea.

*"Gung Fu" means "skill" and "work," as well as "time," hence gung fu refers to any skill that requires a long time and much practice to develop.

When the teachers at Amoy University saw that I, a Westerner, also enjoyed drinking Gung Fu Tea, they were very pleased and treated me like a good friend. Most connoisseurs of this tea are like that, regarding fellow aficionados as close confidantes, and so they invited me to take part in their tea service again and again. Frankly, my own skill in preparing this tea was not very well developed, but they nevertheless praised my performance, which I took as quite an honor!

With regard to my liaison work in China, although the British Cultural Association's objectives were highly commendable, they were very difficult to fulfill in wartime conditions. Fortunately, Chinese universities understood the practical difficulties of the situation, so they did not harbor unrealistic hopes. Despite these circumstances, they always accorded me the most courteous hospitality, as though I were some sort of "Santa Claus" with thousands of precious gifts stuffed into my sack. I only hoped that after each meeting with them, they would not feel too disappointed. Only once, in the midst of a meeting, did I have to endure a relatively cold reception. That was at Sun Yat-sen University, and the situation developed as follows:

From Changding I traveled through Gansien to Jaoguan, and from Jaoguan I took a boat to Pinghsi and arrived at Sun Yat-sen University, where I was welcomed as usual by university staff. Later, during a meeting there, I had to contend with a thorny situation. After I had finished giving my presentation, I invited everyone to express their opinions or to raise any questions they might have. In a very serious tone of voice, an elderly gentleman accused England of having oppressed China for many years, and said, "Mr. Pu has of course come to visit us with the best intentions, but I'm afraid the results of his visit will prove to be paltry. Today England faces a grave danger, and therefore it fosters good relations with its allied countries. But after victory has been achieved England's attitude toward its wartime allies may not necessarily be so friendly. If England's friendship with China were truly sincere, then why does it not relinquish imperialism? Why not announce that after the war it will give up all of its colonies, including Hong Kong?"

As I listened to this, I felt an urge to clap my hands in applause! What he had said was absolutely true. Ever since my early youth I had always advocated that England surrender all its territories in China, and return Hong Kong to China as well! Therefore, I felt a natural impulse to express my heartfelt agreement with that professor in front of the entire audience. However, as a representative of the British ambassador, there was no way I could voice any opinion that did not agree with the policies of the British government. So all I could do was remain silent, as though I implicitly supported Britain's imperialistic policies, and this made me feel extremely uncomfortable.

Some of the teachers there noticed the look of unease on my face, so they warmly praised the British Cultural Association and its cultural attachés for their great efforts on behalf of China. Obviously they were just being polite, but their intentions were kind. The man who had spoken his mind so directly and without restraint saw the way things stood and kept his silence.

(Three or four years later when I bumped into him again in Hong Kong, he mentioned the incident at that meeting, and said that at the time he completely understood how much I loved China and thus sympathized with my situation and decided not to reproach me any further. This shows how broad-minded Chinese scholars can be.)

Taoist Hermits on Mount Heng Refining Themselves in Seclusion

On my way back to Szechuan, I had to pass again through southern Hunnan, so I took this opportunity to visit Mount Heng. Arriving in Hengyang one evening, I set out toward the foot of the mountain the next morning, and after a breakfast of some local tea and fried breadsticks at a roadside eatery, I slowly hiked up the mountain. The scenery on Mount Heng doesn't compare with Mount Hua and Mount Tai, but it still pleases the eye and inspires the heart. That day the mountain trail was crowded with all sorts of people—tourists, pilgrims, bearded

Taoists in robes, soldiers, all were there. Taoist robes hadn't changed at all since the Han Dynasty, whereas Chinese military uniforms reflected the influence of the West, and placed side by side these two contrasting styles of clothing, with the famous mountain as a background, served as a suitable symbol for China at that time—on one side stood an ancient cultural tradition with a very long history, and on the other side stood startling social change.

I often noticed that among the Taoist adepts one encountered in the big cities of China, there were very few who actually cultivated their practice to a high degree of refinement. Some were just charlatans in robes who made a living cheating gullible men and women. But the Taoists one met in the mountain forests were mostly pure and diligent practitioners of the Way. That their hair tied up in topknots, their long beards, their ancient style robes, and their extremely courteous manners were matters of external appearance all goes without saying. But as genuine adepts who cultivated the deepest practices, their bright eyes sparkling with laughter, their spirit of self-presence and immutable sense of calm, their healthy and supple bodies, and their exemplary behavior, all provided ample proof of the efficacy of their "internal arts."

The goals of cultivating the internal arts were to prolong life, promote health, preserve youth, nurture vitality, and enhance awareness. Attaining all of these goals is not easy, but diligent practitioners are able to achieve most of them. Cultivating the internal arts has nothing to do with superstition, but rather involves yoga, meditation, and inner focus. Whenever I visited the famous mountains, I didn't like to stay at the well-known monasteries, but preferred instead to lodge at the most remotely isolated places. That's because Taoist adepts and Buddhist monks who are truly devoted to self-cultivation always avoid places frequented by crowds of visitors.

The day I climbed up to the Southern Peak of the mountain, I found a small hermitage located far from the mountain trail to spend the night. Among the three or four hermits living there, only one came out to greet me. The others were secluded in retreat for a few days, sitting in silent meditation from morning till night. The one who greeted me was a friendly middle-aged adept, and the two of us stayed up talking till dawn for two nights in a row. I asked him to explain the basic foundation of Taoist teachings, and he wrote down for me a few lines from the Tao Teh Ching: "'Nonexistence' is the origin of Heaven and Earth. 'Existence' is the mother of all phenomena. These two have the same source but different names." After writing this down, he explained the meaning with great clarity. To this day I still recall the joyful expression on his face as he spoke, and the gaze of deep compassion in his eyes.

As I recall it, this is the basic meaning of what he said: 'Nonexistence' refers to the intrinsically formless essence of the nature of Tao. 'Existence' refers to the form of the myriad phenomena in the manifest universe. Heaven and Earth arise from the formless essence of Tao nature, which has no beginning and no end. Although all forms are impermanent, their basic essence is nevertheless indestructible. Superficially, these two aspects seem to be opposites, but fundamentally there is not the slightest difference between them. Therefore, all forms are essentially inseparable from the formless nature of Tao, human beings are inseparable from Tao, and Tao is inseparable from human beings. The great Tao is infinite, and nothing obstructs or limits it. All living things share the essential nature of Tao, so how could they have any limitations? Adepts who have realized the Tao understand this truth and have no fear when death approaches. Taoist adepts clearly know that the essential nature of Self is identical with the essential nature of Tao, that they are one and the same, and that the real Self is thus immortal. The only thing that dies is the physical form of this body. In reality, the physical body is just like a little ripple rising on the surface of a lake, appearing for a brief moment then disappearing again. Why should anyone wish to cling to such an ephemeral phenomenon? While we are still alive in this world, we should spend our time and energy cultivating Self-Presence. As death approaches, we should maintain our Self-Presence, and remain fully conscious of the fact that the physical body is not worth clinging to and that we should therefore let it go.

Our Self nature is inseparable from Tao nature and can therefore never be destroyed. All men and women who have attained this realization may be regarded as enlightened sages. Whenever they encounter pleasurable things, although they clearly understand that they are only ephemeral illusions, they may still enjoy them fully in the moment, then let them pass. Similarly, when they encounter calamities, they recognize them as no different from dreams, and therefore face them without concern. The ability to maintain stable peace of mind on the basis of this viewpoint may be regarded as the attainment of the first stage of Taoist self-cultivation.

Many years ago, when I was together with elder brother Yuan-ruo, I heard him explain the Buddhist teaching that "all sentient beings are of a single Mind" (or "one basic nature"), and the meaning of this idea is exactly the same as the Taoist precept.

7
Souls from Distant Lands Fulfill Their Distant Destinies

In 1942, I was already twenty-nine years old, my spirit was strong, and my appearance fairly attractive, except for a slight paunch in my belly. I held a position at the British Embassy, and in those days the social status of a diplomatic officer was quite good. So my friends all wondered why I did not find a wife. In fact, I too was beginning to feel rather concerned about this issue, and since I could be considered as an eligible man for marriage and would soon be approaching middle age, I felt that I should not delay the matter of marriage for too much longer. However, I also knew that finding a suitable partner would not be easy, particularly since I wanted to marry a Chinese woman, because most Chinese families of good social standing would definitely not welcome a Westerner as a close relative in marriage to one of their daughters.

Besides this, there was also another big obstacle: if I were to take a Chinese wife, it would surely cause my father great grief, and that was something I absolutely wished to avoid. Abandoning my studies to come to China had already caused my father deep disappointment, and my decision to stay in China also went against his wishes, so I really did not want to cause him any more sadness. (The reason I felt such filial piety toward him was no doubt due to my long residence in China, where I was influenced in this way by my close Chinese friends.)

Another aspect of the situation was that I felt pressured by time and worried that my advancing age, in the eyes of the Chinese mind, would even further disqualify me as a suitable partner in marriage.

There was yet another issue that I had to consider, and that was the fact that I did not really wish to forfeit the personal freedom of bachelorhood. I often felt that being single was more interesting than being married—sleeping when tired, eating when hungry, opening a book or picking up a pen whenever I wished to read or write, or simply doing nothing at all when I felt lazy or lost in thought. After marriage, it would be difficult to enjoy this sort of freedom and self-determination. The only drawback to bachelorhood was loneliness. Even though there was always the seductive charm and beauty of the girls at houses of pleasure, complete with their literary refinement and clever conversation and their consummate skill at feigning true affection, in the end it was difficult to kindle feelings of deep love with them, and besides that, I couldn't very well keep one or two pretty young girls constantly by my side.

Furthermore, ever since leaving Peking and coming down to the rear regions in the south, I seldom encountered intelligent and talented prostitutes, and consequently I began to prefer the company of "modern" girls. Almost all of the so-called modern young women in China came from good families, and while they were willing to make friends with single men, they never went too far and always maintained an attitude of cautious reserve. During the war, there were many young women from the coastal provinces living in the relative safety of the rear zones. They usually lived alone in dormitories or apartments reserved exclusively for unmarried women. Some worked for the government, some were employed by private companies, some were students, and some were self-employed. Because they were not living together with their families, they did not have to observe all the old-fashioned family rules. When spending their leisure time with male friends, with or without a chaperone, they were always open-minded and friendly, but if a man wanted to have carnal relations with them, it was extremely difficult to accomplish.

If one pursued them with passion, they would usually accuse the man of being licentious and lacking gentility, but if one treated them with an attitude of courtly respect, they would spurn him for being cold and heartless. With such contradictory signals, it was difficult for both sides to avoid misunderstandings.

For example, there was a particular young woman who was quite intimate toward me, and I mistook her warmth as a willingness to marry me, and whenever I treated her with a bit more ardent feeling, she in turn misunderstood my behavior as an implicit proposal of marriage, although in actual fact neither was the case. This sort of situation could easily give rise to anguish and disappointment.

After much consideration regarding these matters, I came to the following conclusion: neither cultivating friendships with girls from good families nor indulging my passions with girls at houses of pleasure could compare with the benefits of finding a companion with character and literary taste. Although I still felt very unwilling to cause my father any further heartbreak, I decided that a suitable way to deal with that problem would present itself after I'd found my ideal soul mate.

Passion Thrice Thwarted

Having prepared the reader with this basic background, I now wish to describe three experiences that strongly aroused my passions:

> One was an intriguing affair in which my heart was not hurt, and the one who proposed marriage was not me.
>
> One was a tragic affair in which my heart was broken, and the one whose hopes were dashed was me.
>
> One was a disgraceful affair in which the offense was unforgivable, and the offender was me.

A Woman I Still Remember after Forty Years

Once I was sent on an official assignment that took me to the three provinces of Guijou, Guangdung, and Fujien. After completing my business at Changding in Fujien, I departed for Shaoguan in Guangdung. My route would take me first through Gansien, then by boat to Dayu, and finally by bus to Guangdung. Early one morning I went to the bus station in Changding to purchase my ticket. At that time, public buses were converted cargo trucks, in which the only two or three relatively comfortable seats were those beside the driver in the front cabin. Therefore, it was necessary to go to the bus station very early and pay some extra money in order to get a seat in front.

When I boarded the bus, I saw that there were already two women sitting in the front. Sitting next to the driver was an old woman, and to her left sat a much younger woman who might have been her daughter. The cabin was very narrow, so I had to squeeze myself in between the young woman and the door, and when the bus started moving, the three of us were constantly bumping shoulders. Smiling to myself I thought, "How wonderful! I'd rather be squeezed to death by this young woman, than have the life pressed out of me by that old crone!" Soon the old hen fell asleep, and the young woman asked me in a soft voice, "Do you feel uncomfortably cramped, sir?" I told her that I was already accustomed to it from my frequent travels.

Perhaps there was an air of frivolity in my attitude, for she smiled and cast me a sidelong glance that revealed a streak of humor. The look in her eyes seemed to say, "Does the foreign gentleman regard being squeezed beside a young woman as a small hardship, medium hardship, great hardship, or no hardship at all?" Her attitude reflected absolutely no sexual overtones, but was instead rather innocent and playful. Thereafter, neither of us indulged in any artificial affectations and conversed very happily together, like two old friends. Young Westerners were always like this, especially travelers, but until then I had always assumed that young Chinese of the opposite sex were averse to this sort of casual pleasantry. Later, when I recollected the situation that day, it was difficult to guess whether or not she felt repulsed by my rather casual attitude.

Because the seats were very cramped, it wasn't convenient for me to look closely at her face; all I could do was glance at her from time to time. She seemed to be about eighteen or nineteen years of age, with a rather attractive face, but not especially beautiful (later, when we disembarked from the bus, I saw that this was indeed the case). She told me that her name was Crystal, that both of her parents were already deceased, and that the old woman was a relative, and they were going to Guilin to live with her eldest brother.

During the trip, she spoke with me a lot, but she chose her words very carefully, and there were many things she did not tell me. To this day I still don't know her surname, or where she grew up. Her tone of voice was very soft and tender, with a southern accent, and she spoke Mandarin very proficiently. Every time my conversation touched upon her background, she pretended not to hear me and quickly changed the subject, talking instead about the passing scenery outside the bus window.

By the time we reached Gansien, it was already dark and raining heavily. The driver informed us that due to the recent influx of refugees there, it was very difficult to find rooms at the inns, and this made the old woman feel very agitated. I asked the two of them to wait there, while I went out alone in the rain to look for some rooms, after which I would hire a car to come pick them up. It was not an easy task, but after forty-five minutes of searching, I finally succeeded. The two rooms I found at an inn were very crude, but we had no other choice.

I went to fetch my fellow travelers and told them, "You'll have to squeeze together and sleep on one small bed, as all the rooms with double and twin beds have already been taken, and dinner has already been sold out, so please join me to go out and get something to eat." The old crone was too exhausted to go and declined my invitation, but I managed to persuade the young woman to go out for dinner with me. On the one hand, I felt very pleased, but on the other, I was also quite surprised, because in those days it was very rare for a Chinese woman to go out at night with a man she didn't know, especially a foreigner. Although Crystal was not a bashful girl, at first she was not willing to go with me, and only after much dillydallying did she agree.

When we arrived at the restaurant, she set her mind at ease, and her conversation grew more and more lively and cheerful. She did not drink wine, but she ate to her heart's content. After the meal, while we were having tea and dessert, I said, "Tomorrow morning at 4:00 a.m., I have to get up and go to the wharf to board a boat for Dayu, then in the afternoon . . ." Before I could finish speaking, Crystal turned pale, and a look of shock appeared on her face, then suddenly tears poured from her eyes! Not knowing what to make of this, I quickly hired a car to take us back to the inn. Before entering her room, she modestly thanked me for everything, then bowed politely and went inside. She had expressed great reluctance to part with me, and this was something that came completely unanticipated, although I felt very moved by it. When I went to bed, I could hear her sobbing softly through the wall panel, and it filled my heart with sadness. I had originally regarded her as no more than an amiable traveling companion, and only when we parted did I realize that she was actually a very warm and appealing girl.

Very early the next morning, while the sky was still dark, I was startled by a sound that awoke me. Someone had entered the room and brought in a pan of hot water with which to wash my face, but whoever it was did not switch on the light until I said, "Turn on the light!" The light went on, *ai ya,* it was none other than Crystal! She lowered her eyes and said, "I don't know why, but I couldn't sleep, so I went to the kitchen to heat some water for you. First wash your face, then I'll take you to the wharf to see you off. Would that be all right?" A howling wind and torrential rain were blowing up a storm outside the window, so of course I tried to dissuade her from accompanying me out, but she insisted on going. Out on the street we didn't see any taxis, and soon both of us were completely drenched from head to foot.

When we reached the wharf, a boatman shouted for me to board the boat immediately. He said the boat was fully packed with passengers, and that they had to quickly arrange the seating, or else they would not be able to fit everyone on board. Crystal urged me not to delay. Feeling very flustered, I hurriedly expressed my thanks and told her to quickly go back to change into dry clothes, then without even pausing to bow farewell, I turned and ran up the gangplank, and without looking back again I went into the cabin. After the seating had been arranged, I chatted with the person beside me for a long time, then suddenly heard a boatman shout to me, "Sir, the young woman who came to see you off at the boat is really distressed. She's not willing to come on board, and she's not willing to leave. Please go quickly and do something about it." Struck with surprise, I ran to the bow of the boat, and in the pouring rain I saw her standing there all alone on the riverbank, eyes cast down and completely still, like a soldier at attention, with the rain streaming down in torrents, as though the wrath of Heaven had been unleashed. Just at that moment, a boatman released the mooring line, and the boat slowly drifted away from the shore . . . only then did Crystal raise her eyes and gaze at me, until we were out of sight.

Forty years later, whenever I recall this event, and see Crystal standing immobile and silent in the pouring rain, then suddenly raising her head and fixing her eyes on me, it always makes me sigh and feel a deep ache in my heart. I ask myself why such a lively, charming, good-natured girl like her would act like this. From beginning to end I remained strictly polite and proper with her, and did not say or do the slightest thing to flirt with her feelings. If, in a similar situation, a bewitching woman used explicit sexual behavior to try to seduce me, I doubt that I would be able to control myself.

Crystal had a very sweet personality, her behavior was exemplary, her demeanor was restrained, and I treasured her friendship, regarding her as an excellent traveling companion; but I harbored absolutely no ulterior motives toward her, nor did I try to arouse her feelings. Why?

Even I find it difficult to understand. Who was she? What was her position in the world? Was she still a virgin, or had she already been married? I had no way of knowing any of this.

At first, the thought crossed my mind that maybe she was a prostitute from the southern coast seeking refuge from the war, and that the old crone was a professional procuress. But I don't believe this was the case. Crystal was not the least bit frivolous nor the least bit flirtatious in her attitude, nor was she in any way greedy. With the sole exception of inviting her out for one small meal, I did not spend any money on her, nor did I give any impression of being a wealthy young spendthrift. The clothing and luggage I carried when traveling were very plain and simple. Although she knew that I held a post at the embassy, she also knew that it was only a temporary position. After carefully considering the situation further, I finally told myself, "Absolutely not! When I lived in Peking, I became quite familiar with the floating world of prostitution, and I daresay that Crystal is definitely not that sort of girl."

It also occurred to me that perhaps she had been married, and that her husband had been killed in battle. The status of pretty young widows from good families was pathetic in China, and even worse for a widow whose parents were both deceased. Fortunately for her she had an older brother waiting for her in Guilin. However, her brother had also gone there as a refugee and probably did not have much money, so it would be difficult for him to provide support for her. If this were the case, she might have seen me as a suitable partner whom luck had sent her way.

Regardless of how it really was then, forty years later I still remember her clearly in my mind, still feel sympathy for her in my heart, and still like her very much. If forty years ago the time we had to spend together while traveling had not been limited to just one day, but had instead been extended by a few more days, perhaps something would have developed from it, but that is very difficult to guess.

Mistaken Feelings Lead to a Rash Proposal of Marriage

During the War of Resistance, both at the front lines as well as in the rear regions, society was subjected to constant upheaval and change. When I first arrived in Chungjing, China had already been at war for five years, and chaos convulsed the whole nation. Before the war, Chinese families still upheld the ancient Confucian precept that "men and women should associate without physical contact."* After moving to Chungjing, I very rarely encountered this sort of strict social prohibition, and therefore my own ethical restrictions gradually began to change. When I lived in Peking, I looked down on female university students and reproached them for their failure to uphold the rules of traditional etiquette, and for their undisciplined behavior. But in Chungjing, not only did I begin to feel respect for most university girls, I actually fell madly in love with a particular young student. In order to describe this affair, I shall refer to her by the pseudonym "Pearl."

Pearl was born into a prominent family in Jiangsu province, and at the time I met her she was about twenty-one years of age. Pearl had a face as pretty and lustrous as jade, outstanding academic aptitude, and a pleasant, easygoing personality. Although she was acclaimed as a true beauty by everyone who knew her, she was not the least bit conceited, always maintained a modest demeanor, and never behaved pompously. If she had any faults, they weren't sufficiently noticeable to draw anyone's attention. An old proverb states, "In the eyes of the lover, the beloved always appears as a beauty." This saying is very true. Perhaps it sounds like I've exaggerated Pearl's virtues, but in fact I have not.

When the two of us first met, she had been invited to participate in an English language discussion group. That evening my role was to serve as the leader of the opposition debate team, and I tried my

---

**Nan nyu shou shou by chin*, literally "men and women should pass objects from hand to hand without touching." This was a strict social injunction formulated by Confucius to regulate social contact between men and women who were not married to each other.

best to show off my verbal skills. Pearl seemed to think that my performance was outstanding, and so she accepted me into her circle of close friends. Thereafter we often had the opportunity to meet face-to-face, and sometimes the two of us went out together by ourselves. That was certainly not something to be regarded as unusual or improper. I'm sure that when she was attending the university in Shanghai, she must certainly have grown accustomed to going out for fun in the company of male friends. Even in Chungjing, it was relatively common for male and female couples to go out together for recreation. Moreover, her character and chastity were beyond any shadow of doubt, and she was a very poised and completely self-confident young woman, talented and dignified, and not easily given to bashfulness.

And as for me? I was not at all accustomed to keeping company with modern young Chinese women. Ever since my arrival in China, I had spent most of my time associating with old-fashioned people, so how could I ever have had a chance to go out alone with young women? Perhaps it was because of my inexperience that I misunderstood Pearl's intentions, and that within a very short period of time I fell passionately in love with her, and also assumed that this love was mutually felt.

Pearl was a woman with a very sensitive mind. She must surely have sensed my ardent feelings for her, but must have also assumed that I knew perfectly well that, even though she felt no personal bias against marrying a Westerner, our relationship could not possibly lead to marriage. None of her elders, relatives, or friends would ever approve, and her own sense of self-respect, as well as her highly rational personality, would never allow it. Making friends was making friends, seeking a spouse was seeking a spouse, and the two pursuits were not necessarily one and the same. The wartime situation made circumstances unique, and permitted Chinese women to associate as friends with Western men. If our friendship held an element of fantasy for either of us, that was not a problem, but it had to be kept hidden within our hearts and could not be spoken. We had to bear in mind that after the war it was inevitable that we must part and each would go our own way.

I'm certain that Pearl felt this way from the very beginning. At the time, I too vaguely understood this, but because I was so overwhelmed by my emotions, I could not stop myself from acting like a lunatic. Pearl worked in a government office that was located in a relatively remote hillside area, and outside the gate to the office building there was a broad patch of lawn. Today, in my mind's eye, I can still see that pagoda-shaped building surrounded by a vast expanse of greenery.

One day, when the weather was quite cold, I put on a black wool coat and went to see Pearl. I don't recall exactly what precipitous thoughts prompted me that day to immediately go there and propose marriage to her, but in any case I mustered up my courage, walked all the way over there, and said to the female receptionist, "Please ask the young lady to come out for a few minutes. I'll wait for her outside the gate." Having spoken those words, I went out the gate to wait for her on the lawn. I'm sure that the moment the receptionist saw the expression on my face, she knew instantly that I had an urgent and unusual purpose in wanting to see Pearl, otherwise she would not have gone in to inform Pearl without even asking my name. Within a minute or two, Pearl came out, walked quickly over to me, and stared at me with a steady gaze. I didn't know why, but she had a very surprised look on her face, and seemed quite agitated.

As we stood there face to face, I quickly spoke up without any sort of preliminary explanation, and without taking care to choose my words, I just said, "Pearl, I want to marry you. Do you agree?" An astonished expression appeared in her eyes, and her face fell in dismay, as though her heart felt sorry for me. Even now at this very moment, I can still understand clearly how she must have felt at the time. She had never loved me, but she had treasured our friendship, enjoyed my conversation, and welcomed this totally sinified friend from the West. But that was all. And now what? Openly proposing marriage on the basis of a misunderstanding was a serious breach of Chinese etiquette. After this, it would be extremely difficult for us to restore our old relationship, difficult to recover the easygoing, carefree, self-sufficient friendship of the past. Regarding my proposal of marriage, she did not utter a word, but she made me understand her response very clearly with her eyes. Besides that, she did of course say a few things to me, but I cannot remember a single word of what she said. After all, besides "No way!" what else was there to say?

Alas! Just like Adam and Eve, I had been banished from the Garden of Eden. Thereafter, whenever we met, although we still approached one another with a friendly attitude, it was already impossible to retrieve the natural sense of intimacy that we had once shared so easily. My heart was knotted with sorrow and frustration, and the pain I felt could not be eased by day or night.

A year ago, we met once again. Pearl's hair already looked like frosted grass, but the youthful sparkle in her eyes had not changed a bit. As for me, my hair was white as snow, my face was covered with wrinkles, and I was already in the autumn of my life. The moment I saw her, my heart jumped for joy, and I was surprised to find that she could still make my soul turn somersaults, which is really rather amazing. I've always had very passionate feelings, but they've never lasted very long, and I never imagined that there was any woman in this world who could, without the slightest effort, rekindle the flame in this burnt-out heart of mine.

Sharing a First Look

In the very beginning of my life in China, I used to fantasize that the virtuous young virgins of old-world China were some sort of fairy maidens, but there was no way that I could get close to them. Modern girls, on the other hand, easily aroused my scorn. I'd heard that the girls from Ching Hwa and Yen Jing universities liked to have fun by smashing the little clay statues of the Buddha and various folk deities that came from little temples in the countryside. Although I myself did not worship those local folk deities, I nevertheless respected the religious beliefs of others, and thus I felt disgusted by the crude and biased behavior of these students. I also disliked their excessive degree of westernization. However, since I had no direct contact with them, I had no way of knowing what they were really like.

After arriving in Chungjing, I began to meet some young women who had graduated from university. Among them were a few who showed little regard for traditional etiquette, and their behavior justified my disdain. However, after leaving the coastal cities, most of the westernized women readily cast off Western influences, and so they no longer made me associate them with the Chinese lackeys who used to work with Western merchants and missionaries during the nineteenth century, and most of these girls were quite likable and worthy of respect.

After being rejected by Pearl, I felt rather lonely, so I asked my friends to introduce me to a suitable girlfriend and possible marriage partner. They asked me what sort of female friend I preferred. I said that my first criterion was that she had some traditional Chinese literary sensibilities, and that she was not overly Europeanized. One friend replied, "That shouldn't be too difficult. But the problem is, that type of semi-old-fashioned girl would probably not be willing to marry a Westerner!" Another friend asked with a laugh, "Is the type you're looking for someone like Lin Dai-yu?"* I said, "That certainly won't do! Better to find me a Hsieh Bao-chai."† He approved of my taste and said, "Please explain your wishes in a bit more detail."

I thought it over for a while and said, "Find me a talented girl, like Yun in *Six Chapters of a Floating Life,*‡ how's that? According to the scholar Lin Yu-tang, she's the most charming female character in the entire history of Chinese literature." To my surprise, that friend had

*The main female character in the famous Chinese novel *Dream of the Red Chamber,* written during the Ching Dynasty. She was a very fragile, poetically inclined, and highly traditional daughter of a prominent Chinese family.

†The unusually talented, well-cultured personal maid of the main male character in *Dream of the Red Chamber,* Chia Bao-yu, who lost his virginity to her.

‡A famous personal memoir written by a young Chinese scholar during the Ching Dynasty. Yun was his highly talented, extremely devoted wife.

never read *Six Chapters in a Floating Life*. I explained to him, "In the book, the character Yun is not particularly beautiful, but she is full of charm and extremely talented, and she can compose poetry, discuss classical literature, cultivate bonsai, arrange flowers and rocks, design gardens, burn incense, cook fine food, plant trees, and so forth. Her conversation is highly refined and full of good humor. Her . . ."

My friend yelled, "Enough, enough! Who can remember all that, and who could possibly find you such an ideal person? Even if by chance someone found her, who would ever let you marry her? For example, I myself would rather die than let such an exquisitely talented girl marry you!"

But beyond all expectation, within a few weeks, they actually did introduce me to a girl, and her appearance did in fact seem to resemble Yun's elegant style. I'll use "Chen Yue-gu" as a substitute for her real name.

At the time, Yue-gu worked in a government institute. The friend who introduced us had already known her for quite a long time, so he explained matters to her frankly. My "middle man" friend said that it would be best for me to first get to know Yue-gu for a while, and slowly think it over, before deciding whether to advance or retreat. He told me that she'd been a bit taken aback by the idea, and had hesitated for quite some time before agreeing to meet me.

Even before we met, something made me feel that perhaps I had a preordained connection with her. Precisely on the very day that I first heard her name, I received a telegram informing me that my father had suffered a heart attack, lost his balance, fallen down, and died. Upon receiving this telegram telling me of his death, I felt deeply grieved and wept bitterly, but later I thought, "My father lived to the ripe old age of over seventy years before his life was over. He always said that what he feared most was to suffer through a long terminal illness, causing others the trouble of taking care of him, nursing him, and trying to cure his illness. Leaving the world suddenly was his biggest hope, and now this hope has been realized. That, at least, is a good thing."

The next day, my friend brought Chen Yue-gu to visit me. What I didn't expect was that as soon as he'd introduced us, he immediately said goodbye and left us alone. This made Miss Chen feel very uneasy, and she stood up in preparation to follow him out. I too felt nervous, but tried my best to calm her down, and said, "Since you've already come, please stay for a while and have a cup of tea before leaving." She bashfully glanced at my face and seemed to relax a bit, and though she wasn't really very willing, still she sat down again and replied in a subdued tone of voice, "All right . . . Mr. Pu." She was a young girl, with a bright and pretty demeanor, and though she was not a ravishing beauty, she was really quite attractive, and she dressed in a simple unpretentious style that I found very pleasing. She forced herself to smile at me, as though imploring me not to make her feel any more uneasy than she already was. As we began to talk, she gradually recovered her self-composure and relaxed.

She said that she'd been born and raised in a small town in Hubei province, that her father was still living there and her mother had died early, and that her older sister was a high school teacher. She also told me that she lived in a dormitory for single women and worked as an office clerk. She had a very pleasant sounding voice that carried a Hubei accent. She didn't ask me anything about myself, so I'm sure that my friend had already told her about my situation. But she kept staring at my face with those bright eyes of hers, as though she were trying to fathom what sort of man I was. When I looked at her, I also felt some doubts arise in my mind, such as, why was she not yet married? And why would such a poised and desirable young woman be willing to take a Westerner as a partner in marriage? I dared not ask, but I guessed that in times of war there were all sorts of exceptions to the rules. Many of the young women who came to take refuge in the rear zone had no relatives with them, and therefore no one to help them with marriage arrangements.

For a young girl to come over and let a man inspect her features, her physique, and her manner of speech must certainly cause her to feel embarrassed. It was obvious that Yue-gu did not find it easy to overcome her discomfort, and also that her intellect and learning were not particularly well developed, although they certainly sufficed to satisfy my requirements. Fortunately, Yue-gu's knowledge of literature was quite strong. I had no way of knowing what sort of impression she had of me, because she did not reveal how she felt, but at least I knew that she was not completely disinterested. In any case, she agreed to come see me again.

A Brief Engagement

After I started seeing her, I began to feel that she might indeed become a suitable marriage partner for me, and this made me feel uneasy because I worried that if I fell in love with her but failed to win her heart, I might once again get hurt. What I did not anticipate, however, was that she turned out to be the vulnerable one.

The next time we met, she was no longer nervous and revealed her sense of humor. With a laugh she said, "I hear that Mr. Pu admires the character Yun in *Six Chapters of a Floating Life,* so that probably means you're not very fond of us modern girls. Take me, for example: I don't cook very well, I don't know how to arrange flowers, and I definitely cannot compose poetry. Although I do have a taste for relatively refined works of literature, no one could take me for a poet or writer. How about letting me look around and find you a girlfriend who's totally infatuated with literature?"

The third time she came to see me, while we were walking side by side as I took her home, I raised my arm and gently wrapped it around her shoulder. To my surprise, the moment I touched her I felt a hot surge of desire rise up within me! While this was certainly nothing abnormal, from that day on I began to love her. We'd known each other for less than two months when we became engaged to marry. Two prominent government officials served as witnesses at our engagement ceremony.

Awhile after that, I fell seriously ill and decided to stay at an old monastery in the mountains to recover my health. Occasionally Yue-gu came there to visit me. My sick room was located at the very back of the monastery, and to get there visitors had to pass through the darkness of the main shrine hall, then walk down an even darker corridor. The first time she came to visit, an old monk accompanied her to my room. When she came by herself the second time, her face had completely blanched and her whole body was trembling, as though she'd received a terrible fright. She was so scared that it seemed her soul had taken leave of her body. Feeling very worried about her condition, I quickly took hold of her hand and asked her what was the matter. As it turned out, she'd been frightened out of her wits by all the huge, somber statues of Buddhas and gods hovering in the darkness of the shrine hall as she passed through it.

Ai ya, such little courage, this really made me feel a bit disappointed. I had always respected her, but seeing her this time behaving like a little child made me lower my opinion of her. My most basic expectation in a partner was that she would be someone I could admire, and regardless of how lovable she might be, if I lost my admiration for her, my love for her would also naturally diminish. This psychological inclination of mine was totally irrational, but there was nothing I could do to change it, for it was an innate psychological response that had nothing whatsoever to do with reason, and therefore it could not be controlled. As a result, on that day, my newly born love suffered a major setback.

I explained to Yue-gu that the reason the shrine hall was dark was that, except for when they were conducting formal ceremonies in there, the monks always kept the windows and door closed. As for the huge statues of deities, no matter how foreboding they might look, they were, after all, nothing more than carved wooden images, so what on earth was there to fear? Feeling chagrined, she blushed till her ears were red and said weakly, "I was afraid of ghosts!" *Ai,* this displeased me even more and sounded even less like what an adult would say. I asked her, "Were you afraid that a long tongue would dart out and lick your face?" The moment she heard these words of sarcasm, she yelped out in fright. I furrowed my brow and said, "You once told me that you don't believe in Buddha, you don't believe in deities, and you don't believe that any sort of supernatural phenomena exist in the world. Although I don't agree, I still respect your beliefs. And yet you say that you believe in ghosts, but not in Buddhas or bodhisattvas. Isn't that rather strange? If there is nothing good in the world, then how can there only be evil? If indeed it were possible that the universe manifests nothing good, then it's also impossible that it manifests only bad and that there are no supernatural manifestations of good to offset the bad. Your way of thinking can only be regarded as totally superstitious."

I had never reprimanded her before, and it really startled her, leaving her wide-eyed and dumbfounded. I could see that in her heart she felt hurt, and I realized that I'd spoken too harshly, and that I should not have treated my beloved with such hostility, so I quickly apologized. She lay down on the bed, leaned her head against me, and wept for a long time, feeling utterly dejected, as our tears mingled together. That was the first time she expressed her boundless love for me.

I basked in that feeling of warmth, and though it made me feel happy, I still retained a feeling of disappointment in my mind. I have a tendency (perhaps it's a mental flaw) to worship the woman I love, and to regard her as a goddess. When I discover that my "goddess" has a weakness, then regardless of how much I love her, as soon as I see that she is not worthy of worship as a goddess, I cannot help but to begin looking down on her.

At the time, this aspect had not yet occurred to me. Many months later, after I had betrayed and abandoned Yue-gu, I finally realized in the depths of introspection that the deterioration of my admiration for her began that very day at the monastery on the mountain, when I became disappointed in her behavior. I admit that this is most unreasonable and very heartless, but this is a proclivity of mind over which I have no control and that cannot be dissuaded by moral considerations, for it's an inclination that goes back to my early childhood, and may even be predestined from previous lives.

After I'd recovered from my illness and returned to Chungjing, Yue-gu came to see me every day, and she no longer felt the least bit bashful or inhibited in expressing her love for me. I should have felt more grateful for her kindness, but it seems that when it comes to matters of love, all sorts of inexplicable things can happen. Innocent girls like her don't have much experience with the hard realities of life, while women who are deeply familiar with the ways of the world, such as prostitutes, know very well that most men love to chase after the target they can never obtain. Therefore, a woman should make a man believe that even if he has possessed her body, he does not yet possess her heart, and the more difficult it is to win her heart, the more the man will love her. Therefore, I believe that after engagement and marriage, a woman should refrain from being too warm and tender to her man. A woman who does not keep her feelings hidden will probably have trouble controlling her husband's heart.

After our engagement, Yue-gu suddenly became a very considerate and tender young woman toward me, agreeing with everything I said and did. Originally I had thought that she was a highly independent individual with her own point of view, but later all I heard from her was, "Yes, yes, you're absolutely right." This soon became rather tiresome. Before long, I began to regret the loss of my bachelor status.

Just as I was hovering indecisively between "hurry up and get married" and "don't rush into marriage," I heard the sudden good tidings that China had won the war, so I had to hurry back to England in order to take care of some family matters. And Yue-gu was eager to go back to the east coast to find her father. Consequently, for better or for worse, we had no choice but to postpone the wedding. In order to preserve her self-respect and reduce her heartache, I did not ask to annul our engagement, and I used all sorts of false assurances to make her believe that everything was fine, and that it was only due to circumstances beyond our control that we must part for a while. However, she was firmly set against allowing us to part on this basis, and wanted us to first get married before beginning a brief separation.

Seeing her feel so hurt and in tears, I also felt very sad, and I hated myself for being so heartless, to the point that I almost decided to go ahead with the marriage. But after further consideration, I came to the following conclusions: if I abandoned her, I would injure her heart, harm her reputation, forfeit my honesty, and turn my back on moral virtue; but if I went through with this marriage, I would inevitably grow distant from my wife, become disloyal to her, and ruin her happiness for the rest of her life.

Yue-gu was adamant in her wish for us to go ahead and get married, but in order to avoid the great trouble that lay ahead if we did, and to refrain from destroying her future happiness, I resisted proceeding with the marriage. Moreover, as we were both on the verge of leaving Chungjing, her reputation was not in jeopardy. Very few people outside of Chungjing knew anything about our situation, so our imminent departure was very fortuitous. One should always choose the lesser of two harms. But now I admit that all of the reasons given above may perhaps be nothing more than convenient excuses. Some people may say that Old Pu doesn't have much reason to stand upon. He simply wanted to part with her, but here he is coming up with all sorts of empty words of explanation. Alas! Perhaps that's true. I myself find it very difficult to understand the motives hidden in my heart.

I admit my guilt, and I'm definitely not trying to disown my responsibility for it. My purpose here is simply to recount the actual situation at the time, and that's all there is to it.

In any case, my fate made me pay a price in punishment for this. Three or four years later, I married Miss Chang. In less than a week, I discovered to my dismay that my partner was absolutely not the considerate, tolerant type. Instead of the words, "Yes, yes, you're absolutely right," that had annoyed me so much in the past, now all I heard was, "No, no, you're totally wrong." Truly it is said, "Heaven punishes the guilty."

Heaven Punishes the Guilty

After the war, Chungjing quickly lost its bustling ambience of wartime excitement. All of the foreign embassies followed the central government when it relocated the capital to Nanjing. I took this opportunity to resign my post and return to Peking. Concurrently, I was fortunate to receive a cash grant from the Chinese government to conduct research on the development of Buddhism in China during the Tang Dynasty. After submitting my resignation, I first went back to England for a while, where I resumed my studies at Cambridge University. This time my primary purpose for resuming my studies was to compensate for the interruption in my education caused by my enlistment in the military and my subsequent assignment overseas by the government. Due to the foundation I already had in the study of philosophy and literature, I was able to complete all requirements for graduation in only six months and receive my master's degree in literature.

In 1946, I flew from England back to Hopei province in China. At the time, inflation was rampant, and the cost of living rose steeply, so that the grant I'd received was not sufficient to live on. Fortunately, I had the good luck to be appointed as an English instructor at Shi Fan University, and in addition to this income my father had left me a small inheritance when he passed away, so I had enough money to cover my needs. Returning again to my beloved second homeland filled my heart with joy.

Better yet was the opportunity I had to rent a spacious villa that had once belonged to an aristocratic family during the early Ching Dynasty. Each wing of this villa had three large rooms, and they all looked onto an elegant inner courtyard. In addition, there was a kitchen located off a smaller courtyard in front, as well as a storeroom, separate quarters for the servants, and other facilities. The main parlor was particularly graceful, with its entire interior finished in lacquer. The courtyard was planted with bamboo, pine, brushwood, and other beautiful trees and bushes. There were two servants, who were actually a married couple surnamed Dzan, both of impeccable character and outstanding ability. The only thing missing in this charming scenario was a wife to organize the household. Alas! What a pity!

That year I turned thirty-four years old. In China, a person who has reached middle age without getting married was regarded as an oddball. Personally, I did not mind living alone, but all of my friends urged me to take a wife. Although I wanted to marry, I did not want to risk again the bitter suffering of a lost love. Proposing marriage only to be refused, besides the pain it caused, also made one feel humiliated. Because I had been reckless, I had encountered this sort of calamity. Even worse, I had hurt an innocent and virtuous girl, and henceforth I wished to avoid repeating this mistake as well. I thought to myself that marrying a girl who was a complete stranger to me was also sure to be fraught with danger!

If I were to wait until after marriage to find out whether or not I could love and cherish my wife, and then discovered that I could not, what then? And if I did love her, but she did not reciprocate with the same feelings, would this not also end in tragedy?

In this state of uncertainty and indecision, I discussed my situation with some friends. They said that after marriage love blossomed quite easily, and if not, it was difficult only for the woman, because a man still had many ways to find happiness. In this sort of situation, a man should treat the woman kindly in order to avoid causing her too much suffering. Ever since ancient times until the present, this had always been a woman's lot. And why worry about a hardship that had not yet occurred? They also said, "These matters are decreed by Heaven, not decided by man." And so I asked them to introduce me to a partner. At the same time, I also decided not to have a long engagement. Whenever I thought back to the time that I had been engaged to Yue-gu, I realized that if we had not delayed our marriage for so long, perhaps we would not have parted ways and would now be living quite happily together!

My friends asked me what sort of wife I wanted. I replied, "Young and attractive would be fine, but I'd prefer someone who is not too fond of modern fashion." My friends exchanged knowing glances, and said, "Old Pu, you'd best not expect to get one of the most select girls. That sort of ideal woman is getting rarer every day, and since everyone wants them, they have many suitors. Do you really think such a woman would be willing to marry a Westerner?"

At last, I finally married a young woman whose surname was Chang. She was half Manchu and half Chinese, and her name was Mei-fang. She was a woman of excellent character, intelligent and capable, but she was extremely argumentative! This goes to show that the old saying, "Heaven punishes the guilty," is not just an empty slogan. My past offense had its present retribution. Yue-gu had lost my affection only because she was so gentle and yielding. By contrast, after marrying Chang Mei-fang, I seldom heard words of agreement from her, and often heard words of objection and protest. At first I couldn't stand it, and bemoaned my fate to Heaven and Earth, but later I finally acknowledged the truth of the adage, "The punishment suits the offense," and so I learned to endure my fate and accept my punishment willingly. In any case, we always plant the seeds of our own karma, and we cannot avoid the consequences, so what's the point of complaining?

When I reflect upon myself, I feel that it is very difficult for me to be a good husband. My feelings are easily aroused and become very passionate. But I always have excessively high and unrealistic expectations of the woman who wins my heart. A man as stupid as me is of course easily disappointed. A reasonable man would understand that because women are human, they naturally have imperfections, and that a husband should be tolerant of certain flaws in his wife. But as for me, as soon as I see that my beloved does not meet my expectations, my passion suddenly cools, like cold water splashed onto a fire. After that, even though I can still sympathize with her, and even find it quite easy to be tolerant, my passionate feelings can never be revived. I think that a man with such major flaws would be much better off remaining a solitary hermit for his entire life. But I'm afraid that path is also not so easy to tread.

Another Dear Friend

My experience in marriage isn't worth discussing any further. But during the last few years that I lived in China, there was something else that drew me beyond the ordinary bounds of a "half-baked foreigner," and gave me a chance to come into contact with the highly refined ideals and literary milieu of the nearly extinct species of old-fashioned Chinese literati. What I mean is that I once again had the good luck to acquire the allegiance of a very worthy pledge brother, the venerable Mr. Jin Pei-shan.

At that time, he was already over sixty years old, not very tall, with short hair and a beard, and he liked to wear a long blue robe and black cloth shoes with white soles. Sometimes he also wore a riding vest, but no skullcap or any other sort of headgear. His attire could be described as quite ordinary, but his dignified bearing commanded attention. Elder brother Pei-shan was a descendent of Manchu royalty and belonged to the same imperial clan as the empress dowager Tze Hsi, so it was no wonder that he had such a refined air and austere demeanor.

This honorable gentleman was born and raised in Peking and spent his entire life there, and he spoke Mandarin with the distinctive accent of the ancient capital, sprinkling his speech liberally with the typical "er" suffix,* such as "mer," "jier," "har," "jer," and so forth.

In his youth, his family lived in the opulence of the imperial compound, and during the latter years of the Ching Dynasty, he obtained a position as an official in the imperial bureaucracy. After the 1911 revolution, he remained loyal to the Ching Dynasty and refused to participate in revolutionary activities. Except for his official duties, he had absolutely no experience with the practical affairs of daily life, and finally ended up taking a position as a secretary in the British Embassy. (While the British Embassy had a few English secretaries

*People from Peking are readily recognized by the way they speak Mandarin, adding a soft rolling "er" suffix to most nouns and many verbs. In Peking, the "er" is put after many words as a softener, giving the entire dialect a nice round whirring sound.

who understood Chinese, their writing style and calligraphy were not sufficiently developed to meet the high standards required for officials documents prepared for submission to the Chinese Foreign Ministry, and therefore the embassy required the services of a well-educated Chinese scholar as a recording secretary. English staff would first write up a rough draft in Chinese, stating the ambassador's meaning, then give it to elder brother Jin for revisions and corrections.)

During the War of Resistance, the Japanese military authorities mistook my honorable brother's character and assumed that because he remained loyal to the Ching Dynasty, he would not mind betraying the Republic of China. They invited the venerable Mr. Jin to take part in the puppet government they had established to govern China, but they did not anticipate that he would rather die than submit to their threats and enticements, and as a result he fell into extremely difficult circumstances. Because he lost his vocation, he soon used up all of his money, and in order to prevent his family from starving, he gradually sold off all of his family heirlooms, and finally all of his precious antiques, exquisite furniture, and other possessions were gone.

After World War II the foreign embassies did not return to their original locations in Peking, but moved instead from Szechuan to Nanjing.* My venerable brother was already in his late years and did not wish to move his family to the south. Fortunately, however, the old British Embassy in Peking became a British Consulate, and they continued to retain Mr. Jin Pei-shan's services as a recording secretary. Regrettably, all the way into his old age, this worthy gentleman never received a promotion to a higher position in the embassy.

From the moment we met, we were like two old friends and felt a strong mutual attraction to each other, and we quickly became intimate confidantes. This venerable elder brother, just like my brother

*In 1944, the central government of China reestablished the national capital in Nanjing, south of the Yangtze River, where they had located it after the Japanese occupied northern China in the 1930s.

Yuan-ruo, maintained the old traditions of China. Both of these brothers conducted themselves in a most congenial manner, but Pei-shan's temperament was more restless. He revered only Confucian philosophy, and did not believe in any other religion. Even before I avowed him as an elder brother, I acknowledged him as a teacher. He taught me to write Chinese in the classical style, and also taught me to perform a few traditional Chinese formalities, such as bowing with hands clasped together in front. Regarding the ceremonial knocking of the head to the floor, he trained me in various different ways to do this. He often cited the precepts transmitted by the great sages Confucius and Mencius. This sort of teaching benefited me in many ways. I had previously studied Buddhist doctrine and Taoist mysticism, and now I learned the fundamental principles of Confucian philosophy.

Mr. Jin Pei-shan's influence on me became etched in my bones and ingrained in my heart. To this day, my manner of speech still carries many phrases and inflections I learned from him. For example, he had the habit of saying, "Go die,"* to express his displeasure, and, "That's not human speech," to mean, "That's completely wrong." To this day, whenever I witness deceit and treachery that arouse my wrath, I always say, "Go die!"

Yesterday evening I overheard a niece visiting from Shanghai refer to a steamed bun as a breadroll, and I couldn't stop myself from shouting out loud, "That's not human speech!" Afterwards I felt that this was rather rude, but there was nothing I could do about it.

Whenever a guest came to visit the Jin residence, the master of the house would loudly shout inside, "Someone has arrived," as though there were many servants within the household to heed his summons. In fact, there was nary a single butler or maid, only his own wife responded. She was my "second elder sister-in-law." Elder brother Jin's Manchu wife had passed away early, and his second wife was of Chinese descent. The moment she heard him shout, "Someone has

Chyu-seh is a common Chinese expletive to express displeasure with someone.

arrived," she immediately replied, "Ya, I'll be right there!" and there followed the pitter-patter sound of her "Golden Lilies" tapping along the floorboards. When Mrs. Jin came in to serve tea, she treated every guest as though she were serving an important high-ranking official. Unfamiliar visitors might surmise that Mr. Jin was excessively strict with his wife, but friends knew that the two of them had not forgotten the opulence they'd enjoyed in former times, and that this theatrical display was their way of making jest of their present meager circumstances. They used laughter to prevent their tears from falling.

On the day that we pledged our brotherhood, the two of us went together to the Temple of Martial Valor. The deity who witnessed our oath was Kuan Kung,* along with the old man who took care of the temple. When the old man saw how I performed the ritual formality of knocking my head to the floor with absolutely flawless traditional precision, a look of great surprise appeared on his face. Modern Chinese people no longer observe the old formalities, and they are utterly incapable of properly performing this ancient propriety with dignity and ease, much less believing that a Westerner could do so.

After completing the formal pledge ceremony, Mr. Jin Pei-shan and I first went to his home to pay our respects to the spirits of his ancestors, and then we went to my humble home.

My household did not have a family shrine with ancestral tablets or a chart listing my family genealogy, so all we could do was use photographs of my father and grandfather as substitutes. Just as I was lighting the incense, it suddenly occurred to me that my father had not known any Chinese people in his lifetime, and that perhaps he might not be so happy to become a sworn relative of a Chinese stranger. Then again, even though he was not very fond of most foreign races, he had the utmost respect for aristocracy, regardless of their nationality. With this thought in mind, I informed the spirit of my father that this venerable

*A red-faced, black-bearded general, one of China's most beloved deities, regarded as the paragon of loyalty and valor.

elder brother was the direct descendant of an emperor, and therefore for his son to be accepted by Mr. Jin Pei-shan as a pledged younger brother brought great honor and glory to all of our ancestors. Although his spirit remained silent, I felt certain that my father would approve of this rationale.

The Clairvoyant Immortal

During those two years that I returned to live in Peking, my life was so replete with peace and happiness that I rarely thought about the political situation in China. At that time, Peking had not yet recovered its prewar grandeur, and the vestiges of the Japanese military occupation still remained. The furnishings in most residential houses and government buildings were dilapidated, and all items of value had been stolen by the enemy and their Chinese collaborators, or else sold off by their owners. The restaurants, shops, teahouses, and other structures were all old and ramshackle. Nevertheless, Peking still had infinite charm and beauty, and in my mind no place else on earth could compare with it. Despite the adverse conditions, the city's ancient flavor still delighted my heart.

At that time I never dreamed that soon I would be compelled to leave the adopted homeland that I loved so deeply; on the contrary, I was very eager to find a long-term residence there. Oh, alas! Before long I began to hear frequent reports of relentless attacks on central government forces by the Red Army. Although the newspapers usually reported Red Army victories as "defeats," everyone knew that the power of the Communist Party was growing, and that the situation was becoming more critical by the day. Even I, as a foreigner, could no longer close my eyes to this predicament, for it was clear that the crisis was pressing close.

In those years, my own life in Peking was very interesting. My work as a teacher at the university was pleasant and satisfying. At the same time, my research work also provided me with deep fulfillment, and was beginning to show success. My translations of two important volumes of Buddhist teachings by Tang Dynasty Zen masters were in the midst of being printed by a publisher in England. One was *The Zen Teaching of Huang Po* and the other was the Zen master Hui Hai's *The Zen Teaching of Hui Hai: On Sudden Illumination.* In addition, in my spare time, I also translated Lao She's novel *Memoirs of Cat City* into English. (I don't know why, but those two Tang Dynasty works proved to have broad popular appeal and were continuously reprinted, and they still remain in print to this day. But that short novel by Lao She, with all its heartrending sarcasm, was turned down by several English publishers.)

In 1948, on the night before the Lantern Festival,* I unexpectedly encountered a very peculiar event. That day I had heard about a "living immortal" who was staying in the western quarter of the city, and this came as strange news to me. Although I was not certain that there existed such a thing, I really wanted to go meet this so-called immortal. Because I'd heard that this living immortal would soon be going to the south, and I might therefore miss my opportunity, I decided then and there to immediately pay him a visit. My servant Old Dzan called a motor car, and as the weather was extremely cold, the open car had a quilt inside to block the wind. The passenger rode as though tucked inside of a Mongolian tent, but the stench was really hard to bear.

It took over an hour to reach the immortal's residence. A note on the gate informed visitors that the immortal was in the midst of meditation, and no one was permitted to enter. I was freezing to death, and needed to warm myself by a fire. Using this as an excuse, I mustered my courage and went resolutely inside. The gatekeeper told me that it was forbidden to enter, but he didn't dare raise his arm to block me and just stood there agitated, so he did not stop me from walking up to the front door and knocking. A servant opened the door and led me

*The fifteenth day of the first month in the traditional Chinese New Year, based on the old lunar calendar. It celebrates the first full moon of the New Year and usually falls in late February or early March.

into the parlor to warm myself by the fire. And there before my eyes sat the immortal. He was sitting cross-legged on a mat, meditating. He sat with his back to the door and did not notice that someone had entered the room, and for a long time he just sat there like a lifeless statue.

When he finally stood up, turned around, and noticed me, he did not seem the least bit surprised, and said casually, "Good, good! Mr. Pu, you have arrived." Struck with wonder and curiosity by his prescience, I asked myself how he could possibly know that my name was Pu. Until the moment that I told my servant to find me a cab, even I did not know that today I would be going to visit this complete stranger. After arriving at his residence, I hadn't mentioned my name to anyone there. So the moment I heard him address me as "Mr. Pu," I stood there wide-eyed and slack-jawed with wonder, and felt very astonished.

He called for tea, and invited me to sit down. We sat facing one another, with a small tea table between us. I bowed to pay my respects, then said politely, "It's a great honor to meet you, esteemed immortal, and please forgive me for disturbing you. Do you have a few minutes to spare? Otherwise, I could . . ."

It was obvious that he was not pleased to hear me address him as "immortal," and so he riposted with the question, "Is it possible that there exists such a thing as an immortal in this world? And if indeed there really are such strange creatures, by no means should you mistake me as one of them. In my humble opinion, immortals are characters fabricated by human beings. Regrettably, my humble self is sometimes praised by others as being an immortal. How on earth could there possibly be such a thing? Please, sir, address me as Taoist Dzeng." This white-haired Taoist wasn't wearing Taoist robes. He wore a long padded tunic of blue satin and felt boots. His hair was cut short, like most elderly men in contemporary China. It was clear that he felt great disdain for charlatans posing as immortals. I said, "Although the venerable Mr. Dzeng is not an immortal, you certainly are endowed with great spiritual power. Otherwise, how could you foretell that my name is Pu?" He poured me a cup of tea before replying, "My humble self may perhaps have a small measure of obscure clairvoyant ability. That's a very common result of practicing meditation."

"May I inquire, sir, what business brings you here, that you would risk the cold to come to my residence?" At this moment, Taoist Dzeng's expression seemed to carry a tinge of sarcasm. With a straight face I replied, "My humble self has for a long time wished to meet a Taoist adept who is highly accomplished in the mystical arts, and to ask him for guidance regarding which type of practices are most effective for restoring youth and prolonging life." The venerable old Dzeng smiled and said, "'If you don't believe in the teaching, you cannot obtain its benefits.' How can I possibly explain this in words? Ha-ha, Mr. Pu has climbed famous mountains, and has received teachings from many great Buddhist monks and Taoist adepts, so why would you find it worthwhile to ask for guidance from my humble self? I daresay, sir, that you must be familiar with some words of advice from the Tao Teh Ching. The general meaning of this advice is that visiting famous mountains and traveling afar to seek teachings about the Tao is not nearly as useful as staying home, shutting the door, and examining your own mind." When he finished speaking, he gazed steadily into my eyes, as though concentrating the full power of his attention on making me understand.

At that moment, a very peculiar sensation suddenly arose within me. All of a sudden, he, I, and everything in the space between us, while still retaining their external appearance, seemed to condense into an inseparable singularity, as though we had suddenly dissolved into one amorphous entity. This dimension of existence gave me a feeling a great joy. For a short while, my mind was mesmerized and my spirit was lost, but at the same time, I knew that this condition was definitely not a distorted fantasy. The strange thing was that although I felt very happy and at ease in that state, I also felt that I could not withstand this man's spiritual power much longer, and that if I did not soon break free of his gaze, I might never return to the normal world, and so I quickly lowered my eyes and terminated that mysterious sensation.

Just then, a group of visitors arrived to see him. They seemed to have come by previous appointment. Therefore, I did not wish to disturb him any longer, bade him farewell, and took my leave. A few days later I heard that the venerable Dzeng had already departed by train for the south. I had missed the opportunity to inquire in detail about several strange matters. For example, how had he known my surname? How had he known that I visited many famous mountains, and that I'd sought teachings about Buddhist doctrine and Taoist mysteries from numerous renowned masters? Relatively speaking, these few matters were not very important. Before we'd met, it was possible that the old man had casually heard that there was a Westerner named Pu living in Peking who had a strong interest in Taoism, and possibly he'd heard people discussing my appearance and other things about me. Although this was only a slight possibility, it was also not impossible. But Old Dzeng had definitely caused me to experience the phenomenon known as "myriad objects uniting into one whole," and for a very short time I had entered into this mysterious dimension.

I'd like to discuss in more detail the meaning of this so-called "uniting as one whole" phenomenon, both from the perspective of Taoist teaching as well as modern science. When Old Dzeng fixed his penetrating gaze on me, I definitely and very clearly perceived the inseparable and boundless nature of all phenomena. That is to say, my perception at the time was that even though all objects had their own separate relative identity, at the same time they were also all completely unified as one primordial entity. That of course defies logic, and is a principle that lies beyond rational debate. I had long ago learned from my Buddhist and Taoist studies about the relative nature of reality, and that only through a higher level of wisdom could one really understand the true nature of phenomena. And yet, in only a few fleeting moments, Old Dzeng had given me a direct experiential perception of the fundamental nature of reality.

Regarding this matter, there is a passage in the Tao Teh Ching that states:

We look but we don't see it
and call it indistinct
We listen but don't hear it
and call it faint
We reach but don't grasp it
and call it ethereal
Three failed means of knowledge
I weave into one
with no light above
with no shade below
too fine to be named
returning to nothing . . .
and discover the ancient maiden
*This is the thread of the Way**

The words "weave into one" in this passage refer to the essential, indivisible unity of all phenomena. The last sentence states that we must clearly understand that all phenomena arise from the same formless, invisible source, the infinite ocean of primordial energy, which Lao-tze refers to here as "the ancient maiden," the "mother of all things."

Modern science can now provide evidence for this idea of the primordial unity of all manifest form throughout the universe. It has been demonstrated by science that matter (form) and energy (formless) are interchangeable and that they both share the same essential vibrational nature. Einstein's famous equation $E = mc^2$ defined the dynamic commutability between these two dimensions of existence. Furthermore the advanced science of quantum physics now agrees with the fundamental hypothesis of ancient Eastern cosmology that the entire manifest universe is formed and shaped by consciousness, and that nothing whatsoever exists beyond the infinite luminous field of primordial

*Translation by Red Pine (Bill Porter) in *Lao Tze's Taoteching* (San Francisco: Mercury House, 1996).

awareness. After my meeting with the old Taoist Dzeng, I never again had the opportunity to communicate with another genuine Taoist master in China. That was the last time I received the benefit of direct personal guidance from a traditional Chinese master regarding the ancient teachings of the Great Tao.

Quick-witted Servants

When I returned home that day, although I knocked on the door for a long time, I only heard the clamor of voices inside, but no one came to open the door for me. I could tell that someone was in the midst of a bitter argument, perhaps even coming to blows, and I thought that it must be Old Dzan squabbling with his wife. I banged hard and urgently on the door. Finally Old Dzan, panting breathlessly and dripping with sweat, his whole face streaked with scratch marks, came and opened up the door for me. Pretending that I hadn't noticed, I walked into the house without a word.

Although those two servants usually got along quite well, sometimes they became embroiled in vicious quarrels that grew quite frightful. Old Dzan's physique was short and thin, while his wife was stout and strong, and so the two of them were closely matched in strength, with neither having the advantage. Old Dzan didn't want to be seen as a weakling, so when he brawled with his wife, he wasn't willing to retreat a step. I felt that the old couple's disputes were none of my business, and acted as though I didn't notice, neither listening nor asking. Old Dzan and Mama Dzan really appreciated my personal attitude toward them, and they did their best to please me in order to express their gratitude. Old Dzan's skills were remarkable. I'll illustrate this with an example.

Before I got married, I was usually rather careless regarding matters of entertaining at home. One day, I invited seven or eight Westerners to my home for dinner, but I forgot to tell Old Dzan about it. On the appointed day, when it was already nearly dark, I suddenly remembered, but by then it was too late to make preparations, and it just so happened that at the time I did not have any money in hand, so I could not change plans and invite my guests out to a restaurant for dinner.

Extremely agitated, I ran into the kitchen to see what could be done. Old Dzan calmly listened to my lament about the impending predicament, and after serenely considering the situation for a few moments, he said, "You need not worry, sir. Your humble servant has a way to handle this."

My guests were students from the Peking Language Institute, Westerners who had recently entered the British diplomatic and consular services, and they had been sent to Peking to study Chinese. At eight o'clock in the evening, they all arrived together. One of them said, "We've heard that Mr. Blofeld is a great connoisseur of gourmet Chinese food, so we're delighted to have this opportunity to come to your house for dinner this evening. We all know that the food and wine will be excellent, and therefore we all deliberately skipped lunch today. Ha-ha!" *Ai ya,* when I heard this, I didn't think it was the least bit funny. I felt very distressed inside, and the sound of his laughter echoed ominously in my mind.

Soon Old Dzan came to announce that dinner was ready to be served. As soon as my guests entered the dining room, they exclaimed, "Fantastic!" I came in behind them, and saw that the big table that was normally there was gone, and instead there were two round tables that I'd never seen before. In the middle of each table stood a huge steaming fire pot, with the best fresh foods arranged around it: beef, lamb, and pork, chicken and duck, sliced fish, crab, and prawns, green vegetables, tofu, rice noodles, and many other things, with nothing missing. And since it happened to be very cold that day, it was the perfect occasion to enjoy a fire pot meal.

Thanks to Old Dzan's practical wits, not only were the food and wine excellent, even the tableware and settings were skillfully arranged. I was greatly astonished, and just stood there staring dumbly. After we were all seated, I finally said, "Please forgive me, everyone, for serving such coarse and simple fare tonight. I'm afraid it may not be very tasty." They knew, of course, than my manner of speaking imitated the courteous speech of old Chinese custom, and the whole room erupted with laughter. The banquet was a big success, and the guests gave it endless praise.

Later on I asked Old Dzan how he managed to do such an amazing thing. He said, "What good fortune that you came to live in this particular neighborhood, sir. The house next door used to be a prince's residence." Old Dzan continued, "The family who lives there now is also quite wealthy. Their cook and I became friends while shopping for food at the market in the mornings, and I also keep myself in the good graces of their housekeeper by doing my best to help them with small chores from time to time, so they're both on very good terms with me. This evening, when I heard you ask me to think of a way to fix the situation, I immediately went next door to see their housekeeper. He felt that this would be a lot of fun, and so he personally telephoned a few of his friends to ask them to help. In this way, we found some meat here, some fish there, and were able to put together most of the ingredients for two tables of fire pot with no problem. All I needed to do to top it all off was to go to the Dung An Market to buy some tofu and rice noodles. The tables came from the Fan household. Mr. Fan went to Tienjin yesterday, and Mrs. Fan immediately agreed to lend us the tables."

This little story very well illustrates how delightful and endearing most servants and human nature in general were in Peking. Unforeseeably, Old Dzan's fate was unlucky, and three or four years later, before reaching the age of thirty, he suddenly fell ill and died. That was after the communists took control of China, and I had already moved to Hong Kong. Unfortunately, I had no way of finding out what became of his wife and children, and no way of sending them some financial assistance. Alas!

A Gloomy Departure

1948 was a fateful year. At the beginning, my own personal life was still very interesting, my living conditions were very comfortable, and all my needs were fulfilled, but whenever I thought about the state of national affairs, I felt a deep sense of foreboding. The strategies of the revolutionary elements who were assaulting the central government were beginning to succeed, and their power grew day by day, like a gathering storm. Throughout the country, Red Army attacks intensified in number and ferocity. The newspapers deliberately falsified reports of their victories as "defeats," and most readers no longer believed the news that appeared in the press. Despite all this, most of the city's inhabitants did not realize how critical the crisis had become.

During this period, I became friends with the British Consul stationed in Peking. The strange thing was that he refused to acknowledge the colossal change looming before his eyes, and he consistently underestimated the Red Army's troop strength. My elder brother Peishan agreed with the consul's opinion, to the point that he criticized my point of view as "excessively pessimistic and alarming." Possibly he was only feigning optimism out of loyalty to his senior officer, or perhaps he just found it too difficult to accept the severity of the impending turn of the tide.

Occasionally I asked close friends what they thought about China's chances, and about the possibility that the Communist Party might soon come into power. Regarding the nation's fate, they all seemed to share the somber certainty that regardless of how good or bad the Communist Party might be, sooner or later they were bound to win "The Mandate of Heaven."* As for whether or not communism was

*An ancient Chinese idea that whoever is destined to govern China does so by virtue of receiving "The Mandate of Heaven" to rule, meaning that victory in a civil war is in itself manifest evidence of Heaven's favor and proof that the victor had been preordained to rule. This rationale was used for thousands of years to justify dynastic change in China, and to explain why dynasties sometimes fell from grace and lost power.

desirable, some weren't willing to take a firm stand one way or another, while others stated conclusively that if a communist government were established in China, it would be an enormous disaster for the nation.

But the majority of the city's residents—men and women, old and young alike—had no way of judging whether a communist system would be good or bad for them. Ever since childhood, they had grown accustomed to civil strife and foreign aggression, and consequently they did not take any government to heart, but were concerned only with the welfare and survival of themselves and their families. Under the military occupation of the Japanese invaders, they had suffered all sorts of hardships. After China's victory, the situation improved a bit, but it couldn't be called good. Postwar inflation was dreadful and had reached alarming levels, and income was never sufficient to cover the cost of living. It was difficult for the central government to satisfy the people's expectations, but the people didn't harbor much hope for better from the communists either. Due to the unpredictable forces of circumstance, they held a sort of fatalistic attitude—like a sailor thrown from a ship and tossed upon turbulent waves in a raging sea during a typhoon, his life or death uncertain, resigning himself to fate and letting nature take its course.

We foreign expatriates living in China could not feel at ease. The question was not what sort of attitude we held toward the Communist Party, but whether the communists would permit us to continue living in China after their victory. My entire life's interest was focused on China, and even in my wildest dreams I had never imagined that one day I would not be able to continue living in China. In the event of major change, the future situation for us Westerners was difficult to predict.

One summer day that year, we suddenly heard that the Eighth Route Army had been bombarding the new airport. The reports which had been appearing in the newspapers had not led us to imagine that the Eighth Route Army had this sort of military power. If they could bomb the airport, then obviously they also had the capacity to invade the city ramparts! Events that I had never dared imagine were suddenly erupting before my eyes. All of my lifelong hopes were fading away like dissolving bubbles, and my heart was overwhelmed with grief.

At first I had decided that I'd rather die than abandon Peking. Peking was my adopted homeland. I was not a political player, and I had never offended any party, so what did I have to fear? But after many reconsiderations, I finally faced reality and thought, "Under communist jurisdiction, regardless of whether Chinese culture advances or retreats, it will be a far cry from the traditional Chinese culture that I love so well. Even if I were not expelled by the communists, to stand by and witness my Garden of Eden trampled by others would be more than I could bear. As the ancient adage states, 'It's not the height of the mountain that counts, it's the presence of immortals that makes it famous; it's not the depth of the lake that counts, it's the presence of dragons that gives it spirit.' I think that in this adage the so-called 'immortals' and 'dragons' are the equivalent of the exquisite settings seen only by the poetic eyes of literati. Would mountains with cable cars still have immortals? Would lakes with steamboats spewing black smoke still have dragons? Of course they wouldn't! This is no joke."

I would like to express the deepest feelings in my heart about all this, but my literary talent is insufficient, and words fail me.

If someone were to accuse me of being a wishful thinker, I would readily admit that it's true. In my mind's eye, even the Republic of China's government was far too new-fashioned, and the Communist far more so! Therefore I thought that in order to avoid inviting trouble upon myself, my only option at this time was to voluntarily depart. Moreover, my wife was pregnant, and when the Red Army attacked the city, even if the government troops were able to hold the city moat, residents within the city would surely suffer great hardship, and I could not bear to make my wife endure such suffering while she was pregnant.

Finally one day, bereft and heartbroken, my spirit shattered, I bade a tearful farewell to my pledged elder brother. I asked myself, where on earth could I possibly go after leaving my beloved China, and what point was there in continuing to live in this world? Turning my head to gaze once more at the Western Hills, I saw billowy white clouds being scattered across the horizon by the wind, just like the hopes and dreams I'd cherished in my heart ever since my early youth.

The Painful Loss of Dear Friends

Luckily in Hong Kong, I was able to stay temporarily at the home of my elder brother Yuan-ruo. When I arrived there, I was feeling extremely sad, but as soon as I saw my dear brother's smiling face, I couldn't help but feel happy and much consoled. I thought to myself, "Even in the depths of darkness there is always a ray of light." Parting with my elder brother Pei-shan was very painful for me, but that in turn was also the cause of my reunion with my other pledge brother Yuan-ruo. I no longer felt that life was so desolate and futile.

I firmly believe that Chinese surpasses any other language on earth as a means of literary expression, but it's not easy for an outsider to master—unless one starts learning it while still very young, and continues practicing for the rest of one's life. Fortunately, I can still appreciate its beauty, and moreover I had two profoundly learned scholars as my friends and teachers. Not only did they write brilliantly well, they both strived to emulate the highest standards of wisdom and excellence, and thus they are the most valuable kind of friends. Whenever I think back upon the past, I always feel that gaining their true and sincere friendship has been the greatest good fortune of my entire life, and my most precious blessing.

The year that I moved to Hong Kong, my wife gave birth to a son, whom we named Ming Deh ["Bright Virtue"], and whose childhood nickname was Siao Feng ["Little Wind"]. Shortly thereafter, a school hired me as an English instructor, and we moved to Kowloon. About a year later, our daughter was born, and we named her Shueh Chan ["Snow Beauty"], and gave her the childhood nickname Siao Yun ["Little Cloud"]. During this time, we lived well, and our circumstances were quite comfortable, but my spirit could not rest at ease. Because I constantly felt nostalgic for China, I became very homesick. Sometimes I would suddenly awaken from a dream late in the night, with tears streaming down my cheeks.

What I mourned was not the beautiful landscapes and colorful scenery of China, but rather the final collapse of China's ancient, highly refined culture.

The traditional wisdom handed down from generation to generation by China's sages was peerless, and that's why for over two thousand years it stood preeminent in the world, and had a formative influence on the civilizations of all countries throughout the Far East. Prior to the Tang, Sung, and Ming dynasties, although China was influenced for more than a hundred years by various foreign cultures, in the end it always restored the glory of its own indigenous heritage. But within my own lifetime, these ancient winds stopped blowing and would never again fan my face, and it seemed certain that the former glory of Chinese civilization could never be revived.

The demonic souls who invented the atom bomb, poison gas, and germ warfare cannot be controlled by the wisdom of sages. Sages rely on the human conscience in order to influence and improve the human condition, but demons have no conscience. Within the generation to which my two pledged brothers belonged, there were still gentlemen of high cultivation, but today such gentlemen have became a rarity.

I'd been living in Hong Kong for about a year, when suddenly I received a letter informing me that my elder brother Jin Pei-shan had fallen ill and died. As I read this message I burst out weeping, and for a long while I could not continue reading it. The letter was written by my brother's only son Heng Ti, and it said, "In 1949 after the Communist Party established power, the situation at the British Consulate became untenable, and our family fell into difficult circumstances. In his state of anxiety regarding these developments, my father's longstanding illness grew worse and soon thereafter he died."

Alas! Over the years my brother endured the extreme hardships of anti-Manchu revolution as well as Japanese aggression, and he withstood all sorts of frightful conditions without ever losing his courage. But in his old age, as he witnessed the earthshaking changes that befell his country, his spirit was unable to once again rally to the challenge. He was a man of royal lineage, and when he realized that his life was near its end, he probably felt happy to leave this world. Regrettably, after his death his family went through more than twenty years of torment before the situation improved and their prestige was restored.

In 1951, I was appointed a professor of English literature at Chulalongkorn University in Bangkok, Thailand. At the time, I had originally planned to move to Taiwan in order to again immerse myself in Chinese culture. Bur friends advised me, "The future of Taiwan is uncertain, so why take the risk of encountering such troubles a second time?" This advice made sense. At that time, no one could predict whether Taiwan would be able to resist occupation by communist forces. If a foreigner were living in Taiwan when that happened, he would inevitably be forced by the situation to leave. After further consideration, I finally decided to accept the appointment in Thailand. In the middle of April I departed.

I'd been living in Thailand for about six months when I heard the news that my elder brother Yuan-ruo had died after a long illness. He was not yet fifty-three years of age. *Ai, ai,* such woe! Within a short period of time my two beloved brothers had both left this world, and the sorrow I felt was hard to bear, leaving me in tears for many days. To this day I still miss them, and I still feel deep regret that such dear friends have left this world before me.

From Brilliant Splendor Back to Common Mediocrity

My later circumstances are irrelevant to this book and need not be told in detail, so I will just summarize the most important points.

I taught at Chulalongkorn University for ten years, after which I served as chief editor for a United Nations East Asian economic institute based in Thailand for twelve years, until my retirement, when I devoted the rest of my time to writing books about Asian culture, over a dozen of which have been published in England and America.

Before my retirement, I felt an insurmountable sorrow in my heart, and tried hard to overcome my longing for China, like a forsaken lover who strives to forget his beloved in order to prevent his heart from shattering. Therefore, for over twenty years I seldom spoke Chinese, and even less did I read or write Chinese. Consequently, I forgot a large part of the Chinese language.

Since participating in a recent tour of Guilin, I have once again made an effort to learn how to express myself in written Chinese. Six or seven years ago, I was fortunate to meet an excellent teacher—Professor Ma Li-chi, a lady from Peking who excels in editing essays and has a great command of Chinese literature. Her way of teaching has been very effective. Regrettably, old age has dulled my wits, so I lack the literary talent required to make my teacher take pride in me.

Over the past five years, I have made several visits to both mainland China and Taiwan, and have also gone to America three times to present lectures on Confucian philosophy, Taoist mysticism, and Buddhist doctrine, the so-called Three Great Teachings of China. During my travels, I visited some old friends, such as Li-sung, Shih-shing, and others in Hong Kong, Ching-yao in Washington D.C., and Shian-yi in Peking, which made me very happy. Except for my visits to old friends there, traveling in China felt as though I had arrived some place I had never been before.

Particularly in Peking, the ancient grandeur and majestic beauty of the city have been almost totally destroyed, and the great city ramparts and soaring gate towers that once commanded attention have all been torn down. Not only have many ancient artifacts from the Ming and Ching dynasties completely disappeared, the legacies of even more ancient times have also suffered the same fate. Except for the imperial palace and a few large temples, the Peking of today and the old capital of former times seem like two entirely different cities. This new metropolis doesn't have the slightest trace of poetic feeling and artistic sense, and its banal features, so utterly devoid of the distinctive style of traditional Chinese culture, protrude everywhere to prick the eye. Actually, regardless of whether one goes to mainland China or Taiwan, except in museums visitors very rarely get a real glimpse of the unique merits of Chinese culture, and everything from architecture, furniture, and clothing to the customs and daily habits of life have all become westernized. Alas! The Chinese culture that I loved so passionately can now be found only in my dreams.

What a pity! Such a pity! This exquisitely refined culture is teetering on the brink of extinction and can never be revived. Exactly as the scriptures state, "Everything follows the Law of Dharma, like the fleeting shadow of a dream, like a drop of dew, like a flash of lightning." Yet though my body declines daily with age, my older years have still been a very happy time for me. No one can turn back the tides of history, so people today will never have the good fortune to behold the rare treasures of ancient Chinese culture. But fortunately for me, when I was young, my love for China ran very deeply, and I immersed my whole heart and soul in her, so that even today, whenever I wish, I can still roam and enjoy her charms in my dreams. What happiness could compare with this?